Grade 5

Scott Foresman

Reader's and Writer's Notebook

 PEARSON

Glenview, Illinois • Boston, Massachusetts • Chandler, Arizona •
Upper Saddle River, New Jersey

ISBN-13: 978-0-328-47675-6
ISBN-10:   0-328-47675-7

22   18

CC1

Unit 1: Meeting Challenges

Unit 2: Doing the Right Thing

Unit 3: Inventors and Artists

Unit 4: Adapting

Unit 5: Adventurers

Unit 6: The Unexpected

Name _____

Unit 1 Independent Reading Log

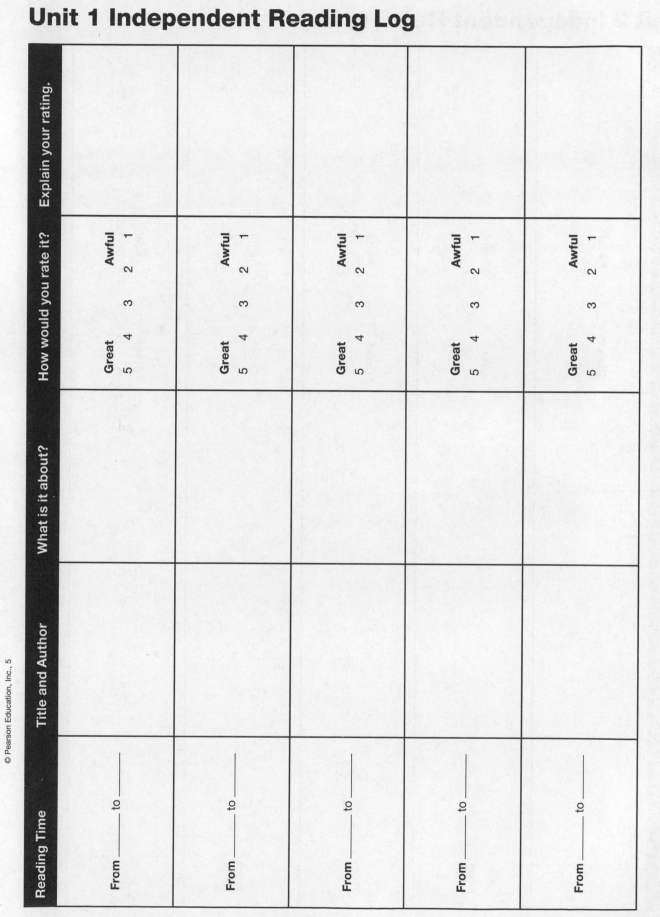

Reading Time	Title and Author	What is it about?	How would you rate it?	Explain your rating.
From _____ to _____			Great 5 4 3 2 1 Awful	
From _____ to _____			Great 5 4 3 2 1 Awful	
From _____ to _____			Great 5 4 3 2 1 Awful	
From _____ to _____			Great 5 4 3 2 1 Awful	
From _____ to _____			Great 5 4 3 2 1 Awful	

Name _____

Unit 2 Independent Reading Log

Reading Time	Title and Author	What is it about?	How would you rate it?	Explain your rating.
From ——— to ———			Great 5 4 3 2 1 Awful	
From ——— to ———			Great 5 4 3 2 1 Awful	
From ——— to ———			Great 5 4 3 2 1 Awful	
From ——— to ———			Great 5 4 3 2 1 Awful	
From ——— to ———			Great 5 4 3 2 1 Awful	

Name _____

Unit 3 Independent Reading Log

Reading Time	Title and Author	What is it about?	How would you rate it?	Explain your rating.
From ____ to ____			Great 5 4 3 2 1 Awful	
From ____ to ____			Great 5 4 3 2 1 Awful	
From ____ to ____			Great 5 4 3 2 1 Awful	
From ____ to ____			Great 5 4 3 2 1 Awful	
From ____ to ____			Great 5 4 3 2 1 Awful	

Name _____

Unit 4 Independent Reading Log

Reading Time	Title and Author	What is it about?	How would you rate it?	Explain your rating.
From ____ to ____			**Great** 5 4 3 2 1 **Awful**	
From ____ to ____			**Great** 5 4 3 2 1 **Awful**	
From ____ to ____			**Great** 5 4 3 2 1 **Awful**	
From ____ to ____			**Great** 5 4 3 2 1 **Awful**	
From ____ to ____			**Great** 5 4 3 2 1 **Awful**	

Name _____

Unit 5 Independent Reading Log

Reading Time	Title and Author	What is it about?	How would you rate it?	Explain your rating.
From ____ to ____			Great 5 4 3 2 1 Awful	
From ____ to ____			Great 5 4 3 2 1 Awful	
From ____ to ____			Great 5 4 3 2 1 Awful	
From ____ to ____			Great 5 4 3 2 1 Awful	
From ____ to ____			Great 5 4 3 2 1 Awful	

Name _____

Unit 6 Independent Reading Log

Reading Time	Title and Author	What is it about?	How would you rate it?	Explain your rating.
From ___ to ___			Great 5 4 3 2 1 Awful	
From ___ to ___			Great 5 4 3 2 1 Awful	
From ___ to ___			Great 5 4 3 2 1 Awful	
From ___ to ___			Great 5 4 3 2 1 Awful	
From ___ to ___			Great 5 4 3 2 1 Awful	

Selection Title _____ Author _____

Realistic Fiction means that a story is possible or seems real. It consists of the same elements as other story genres, including setting, character, plot, and theme. Characteristics of realistic fiction include the following.

• Characters generally behave like real people.

• Settings may or may not be real.

• The plot, or events that happen in the story, may or may not seem real.

Directions As you read *Red Kayak,* look for examples of character, setting, and plot that make this story seem real. Write those examples below.

Character _____

_____

_____

Setting _____

_____

_____

Plot _____

_____

_____

Explore the Genre

Think about another story you've read that is realistic fiction. What similarities and differences do you find between the characters in that story and *Red Kayak*? Write a summary of the similarites. Use a separate sheet of paper if you need more space.

_____

_____

Selection Title _____ Author _____

A **tall tale** is a humorous story that uses realistic details to tell a story about characters and events that are impossible. Characteristics of a tall tale include the following.

- Many details are from everyday life.
- Characters are greatly exaggerated.
- The events described could not really happen.

Directions As you read *Thunder Rose,* look for examples of realistic details, exaggerated characters, and impossible events that make the story a tall tale. Write those examples below.

Realistic Details _____

_____

_____

Exaggerated Characters _____

_____

_____

Impossible Events _____

_____

_____

Explore the Genre

Think about another story you've read that's a tall tale. What similarities do you find between that story and *Thunder Rose*? Briefly paraphrase, or tell in your own words, the plot of both tall tales. Keep events in the order in which they happened. Use a separate sheet of paper if you need more space.

_____

_____

Name _____

Selection Title _____ Author _____

When we **infer,** we use our background knowledge with information from the text to come up with our own ideas about what we're reading. To infer, or make inferences, try the following steps.

- Think about what you already know about the topics.
- Combine what you know with information from the text to make inferences.
- Based on your inferences, think about ideas, morals, lessons, or themes in the text.

Directions As you read the selection, use your background knowledge and clues from the text to make inferences. Use the chart below to show how you made your inferences. Then write a statement that summarizes the theme, moral, or lesson from the selection.

What I Know	Information from the Text	What I Infer

Statement that summarizes the theme, moral, or lesson _____

_____

_____

_____

Selection Title _____ Author _____

A **biography** tells the story of all or part of a real person's life. Events in the person's life are generally told in the order that they happen. Characteristics of a biography include the following.

- The subject is part or all of the life of a real person.
- The events in the person's life are told in the order that they happen.
- Events are told in a third-person narration using *he, she, him,* or *her* when referring to the person.

Directions As you read *Satchel Paige,* look for examples of who the subject is, events in order, and third-person narration that make this selection a biography. Write those examples below.

Subject _____

_____

_____

Events _____

_____

_____

Third-person Narration _____

_____

_____

Explore the Genre

Think about another selection you've read that is a biography. Briefly paraphrase, or tell in your own words, two important events from each biography. Keep events in the order in which they happened. Use a separate sheet of paper if you need more space.

_____

Name _____

Selection Title _____ Author _____

Text structure refers to the way an author organizes a text. Cause and effect and compare and contrast are two types of text structure. Knowing how a text is structured can improve our comprehension. Here are ways to identify text structure.

- Before you read, preview the text. Make predictions, ask questions, and use titles, headings, and illustrations to try to identify the structure.
- As you read, look for language that gives clues to the organization.
- After reading, recall the organization and summarize the text.

Directions As you preview and read the selection, write down features of the text that help you identify the text structure. Remember to ask questions, use text features, and look for language clues to identify the text structure. After reading, write the name of the text structure and a brief summary of the selection.

Before Reading _____

_____

_____

_____

During Reading _____

_____

_____

_____

Text Structure/Summary _____

_____

_____

_____

© Pearson Education, Inc., 5

Selection Title _____ **Author** _____

We **visualize** to create pictures in our minds as we read. Creating pictures can help us better understand what we're reading. To visualize, try the following.

- Combine what you already know with details from the text to make a mental image.
- Think about the events of the story or selection. Use your five senses to create pictures and to try to put yourself in the story or selection.

Directions As you read the selection, use your senses to help you visualize what's happening or the information the author provides. Write down what you can see, hear, taste, smell, and touch.

See _____

_____

_____

Hear _____

_____

_____

Taste _____

_____

_____

Smell _____

_____

_____

Touch _____

_____

_____

© Pearson Education, Inc., 5

Selection Title _____ Author _____

> **Literary nonfiction** tells the story of a true event or events. Elements that are found in fiction may be used in literary nonfiction as well. Characteristics of literary nonfiction include the following.
> - The plot centers around true events.
> - Characters may include people who really existed at the time that the events took place.
> - The story may include fiction elements such as dialogue, descriptions, and illustrations.

Directions As you read *Hold the Flag High,* look for examples of true events, real people, and dialogue, descriptions, and illustrations that make this selection literary nonfiction. Write those examples below.

True Events _____

_____

_____

Real People _____

_____

_____

Dialogue, Descriptions, and Illustrations _____

_____

_____

Explore the Genre

Think about another selection you've read that is literary nonfiction. What differences do you find between the events in that selection and *Hold the Flag High*? Write a summary of the similarities between the events in both selections. Keep the events in the order in which they happen. Use a separate sheet of paper if you need more space.

_____

Selection Title _____ Author _____

Folk tales are stories that were created by an unknown storyteller and handed down orally from generation to generation until someone wrote them down. Characteristics of folk tales include the following.

- The subject matter is often the customs or beliefs of a particular culture.
- Human and animal characters usually represent some human trait or aspect of human nature.
- Themes about human nature are expressed.

Directions As you read *The Ch'i-lin Purse,* look for examples of subject matter, characters, and theme that make this story a folk tale. Write those examples below.

Subject Matter _____

_____

_____

Characters _____

_____

_____

Theme _____

_____

_____

Explore the Genre

Think about another story you've read that is a folk tale. What similarities and differences do you find between that story and *The Ch'i-lin Purse*? Write about it. Use a separate sheet of paper if you need more space.

_____

_____

© Pearson Education, Inc., 5

Selection Title _____ **Author** _____

Strategic readers **monitor** their understanding of what they've read and use fix-up strategies to **clarify** understanding. Ways to monitor and clarify include the following.

- Ask questions during and after reading and summarize to check your understanding.
- Adjust your reading rate, read on, or reread the section that caused confusion.
- Visualize what you are reading.
- Use text features and illustrations to help clarify the text.

Directions As you read, write down the page numbers of places that you had trouble understanding. Then describe the fix-up strategy you used to clarify the meaning.

Where in the text I had trouble: _____ _____ _____

_____

Fix-up Strategies I Used

_____

_____

_____

_____

_____

Selection Summary

Write a two- or three-sentence summary of the selection. Use a separate sheet of paper if you need more space.

_____

_____

_____

_____

Name _____

Selection Title _____ Author _____

Poetry is the careful selection and arrangement of words in lines that express a writer's thoughts and feelings. While many poems use a rhyming pattern, some poems do not. Characteristics of poetry include the following.

- Lines of poetry may rhyme in a pattern with rhymes occurring within or at the ends of lines.
- Some poems have a rhythmic pattern.
- Poets often use words that appeal to the senses to help the reader experience the poem.

Directions As you read *The Midnight Ride of Paul Revere,* look for examples of patterns of rhyme and rhythm and words that appeal to the senses that make this selection a poem. Write those examples below.

Rhyme _____

_____

_____

Rhythm _____

_____

_____

Words That Appeal to Senses _____

_____

_____

Explore the Genre

Think about another selection you've read that is a poem. What similarities and differences do you find between that poem and *The Midnight Ride of Paul Revere*? Write about it. Use a separate sheet of paper if you need more space.

_____

© Pearson Education, Inc., 5

Selection Title _____ Author _____

Dramas, or plays, are stories that are to be acted out for an audience. Dramas are divided into numbered acts and scenes consisting mainly of dialogue and stage directions for the actors. Characteristics of dramas include the following.

• Characters and setting

• Dialogue

• Scenes

Directions As you read *The Fabulous Perpetual Motion Machine,* look for examples of characters and setting, dialogue, and scenes. Write those examples below.

Characters and Setting _____

_____

_____

Dialogue _____

_____

_____

Scenes _____

_____

_____

Explore the Genre

Think about characters and setting, dialogue, and scenes in another drama that you've read. What similarities and differences do you find between that drama and *The Fabulous Perpetual Motion Machine*? Write about it. Use a separate sheet of paper if you need more space.

_____

_____

Name _____

Selection Title _____ Author _____

We **visualize** to create pictures in our minds as we read. Creating pictures can help us better understand what we're reading. To visualize, try the following.

- Combine what you already know with details from the text to make a mental image.
- Think about the events of the story or selection. Use your five senses to create pictures and to try to put yourself in the story or selection.

Directions As you read the selection, use your senses to help you visualize what's happening or the information the author provides. Write down what you can see, hear, taste, smell, and touch.

See _____

_____

_____

Hear _____

_____

_____

Taste _____

_____

_____

Smell _____

_____

_____

Touch _____

_____

_____

Selection Title _____ **Author** _____

When we **predict,** we tell what we think might happen in a selection. Predictions are based on our preview or what we've already read. We **set a purpose** to guide our reading. We can do the following to predict and set a purpose.

- Read the title and the author's name. Look at the illustrations and other text features.
- Think about why you're reading and set a purpose.
- Use your prior knowledge—what you already know—to make a prediction.
- As you read, check and change your prediction based on new information.

Directions Preview the selection. Make a prediction and set a purpose for reading the selection. As you read, check your predictions and set a new purpose as necessary. When you finish reading, write a summary of the selection.

Before Reading
Make a Prediction _____

_____

Purpose for Reading _____

_____

During Reading
Check and Change Prediction _____

_____

Set a New Purpose _____

_____

After Reading
Write a Summary _____

_____

_____

_____

Selection Title _____ **Author** _____

Text structure refers to the way an author organizes a text. Cause and effect and compare and contrast are two types of text structure. Sequential order and logical order are two more types of text structure. Knowing how a text is structured can improve our comprehension. Here are ways to identify text structure.

- Before you read, preview the text. Make predictions, ask questions, and use titles, headings, and illustrations to try to identify the structure.
- As you read, look for language that gives clues to the organization.
- After reading, recall the organization and summarize the text.

Directions As you preview and read the selection, write down features of the text that help you identify the text structure. Remember to ask questions, use text features, and look for language clues to identify the text structure. After reading, write the name of the text structure and a brief summary of the selection.

Before Reading _____

_____

_____

_____

During Reading _____

_____

_____

_____

Text Structure/Summary _____

_____

_____

_____

© Pearson Education, Inc., 5

Selection Title _____ Author _____

Expository text tells about real people and events. Expository text is a type of expository nonfiction. Characteristics of expository text include the following.

- The topic provides information about the real world and people.
- The information in the text is factual.
- Selections often include text features such as diagrams, maps, charts, and graphs.

Directions As you read *Special Effects in Film and Television,* look for examples of expository text. Write those examples below.

Selection Topic _____

_____

_____

Facts _____

_____

_____

Text Features _____

_____

_____

Explore the Genre

Think about another selection you've read that is expository text. What similarities and differences do you find between that selection and *Special Effects in Film and Television*? Write about it. Use a separate sheet of paper if you need more space.

_____

_____

_____

Name _____

Selection Title _____ Author _____

Good readers ask questions as they read. **Questioning** helps us monitor our comprehension and clarify anything that's confusing. Questioning also helps to make inferences, interpret the texts we read, and promote discussion. As you read, use the following questioning strategy.

- Preview the selection and think about any questions you have about the topic.

- Establish a purpose for reading by asking yourself what your teacher might expect you to learn by reading this text.

- Read with a question in mind and make notes when you find information that addresses the question.

- Write down other questions that come up as you read and look for answers in the text.

- Remember that not all questions are answered in the text. Sometimes we have to make inferences or interpretations based on the information the author provides.

Directions As you read the selection, use the chart below to write down any questions that you have about the text in the column on the left. Write down any answers you find or inferences you make in the right hand column.

Questions	Answers, Inferences, Interpretations

Selection Title _____ Author _____

Realistic fiction tells the story of imaginary people and events. Characteristics of realistic fiction include the following.

• The characters seem like real people that you might know.

• The setting is realistic, such as a city or town, a school, or other places you might know.

• The plot is possible and could happen in real life.

Directions As you read *Tripping Over the Lunch Lady,* look for examples of character, setting, and plot that make this story realistic fiction. Write those examples below.

Character _____

_____

_____

Setting _____

_____

_____

Plot _____

_____

_____

Explore the Genre

Think about the plot in another story you've read that's realistic fiction. What similarities do you find between that story and *Tripping Over the Lunch Lady*? Write a summary of the similarities between both plots. Arrange your ideas in a logical order. Use a separate sheet of paper if you need more space.

_____

_____

_____

Selection Title _____ **Author** _____

Important ideas in nonfiction texts are the main ideas and details about a topic that the author wants the reader to understand. You can do the following to help identify important ideas and details as you read.

- Preview the selection and read the title, headings, and captions.
- Look for words in special type such as italics, boldface, and bulleted lists.
- Watch for signal words and phrases such as *for example* and *most important*.
- Use text features including photographs and illustrations, diagrams, charts, and maps.

Directions As you read the selection, use the chart below to write down any important ideas and details that you find. List any text features or signal words you used to locate these ideas. Then choose one important idea and paraphrase, or tell in your own words, that idea using details that you listed in the chart. Be sure to maintain a logical order.

Important Ideas	Details

Paraphrase one important idea _____

_____

_____

Name _____

Selection Title _____ Author _____

Story structure is the important parts of the story that happen at the beginning, middle, and end of a story. To identify story structure, strategic readers do the following.

• Look for the conflict, or problem, at the beginning of the story.

• Track the events of the plot in the order in which they happen as conflict builds.

• Recognize the climax when the characters face conflict.

• Identify how the conflict gets resolved.

Directions As you read the story, chart the story structure using the plot map below. When you are finished, briefly paraphrase the story, or retell it in your own words, on a separate sheet of paper. Make sure you keep the events in the order in which they happened.

Characters

Setting

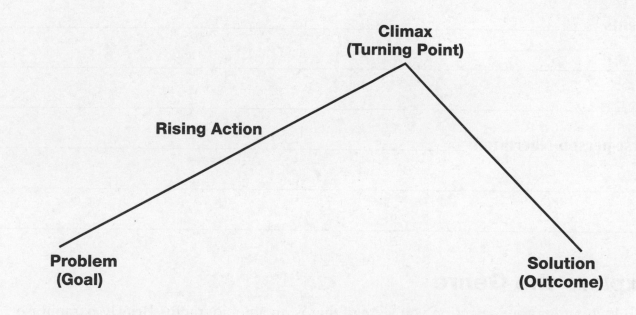

Climax
(Turning Point)

Rising Action

Problem
(Goal)

Solution
(Outcome)

Name _____

Selection Title _____ Author _____

An **autobiography** is a form of literary nonfiction. Like a biography, it tells the story of all or part of a real person's life. But with an autobiography, a person tells his or her own story. Characteristics of an autobiography include the following.

- The subject is part or all of the life of a real person.
- The events in the person's life are usually told in the order that they happen.
- Events are told as a first-person narration.

Directions As you read *The Gymnast,* look for examples of the subject, events in order, and first-person narration that make this selection a biography. Write those examples below.

Subject _____

_____

_____

Events _____

_____

_____

First-person Narration _____

_____

_____

Explore the Genre

Think about another selection you've read that is an autobiography. Briefly paraphrase, or tell in your own words, two events from each autobiography. Write about the events in the order in which they happened. Use a separate sheet of paper if you need more space.

_____

_____

Selection Title _____ Author _____

Fiction is a made-up story, either serious or humorous, of imaginary people who generally behave as we expect people to behave. Fiction might include real places and events, but the story is created from the author's imagination. Characteristics of fiction include the following.

- Characters generally behave like real people.
- Settings may or may not be real.
- The plot, or events that happen in the story, may or may not seem real.

Directions As you read *The Skunk Ladder*, look for examples of character, setting, and plot that make this story fiction. Write those examples below.

Character _____

_____

_____

Setting _____

_____

_____

Plot _____

_____

_____

Explore the Genre

Think about the setting in another story you've read that is fiction. What differences do you find between that story and *The Skunk Ladder*? Write a summary of the differences between both settings. Arrange your ideas in a logical order. Use a separate sheet of paper if you need more space.

_____

_____

Name _____

Selection Title _____ Author _____

When we **infer,** we use our background knowledge with information from the text to come up with our own ideas about what we're reading. To infer, or make inferences, try the following steps.

- Think about what you already know about the topics.
- Combine what you know with information from the text to make inferences.
- Based on your inferences, think about ideas, morals, lessons, or themes in the text.

Directions As you read the selection, use your background knowledge and clues from the text to make inferences. Use the chart below to show how you made your inferences. Then write a statement that summarizes the theme, moral, or lesson from the selection.

What I Know	Information from the Text	What I Infer

Statement that summarizes the theme, moral, or lesson _____

_____

_____

Selection Title _____ **Author** _____

Strategic readers **monitor** their understanding of what they've read and use fix-up strategies to **clarify** understanding. Ways to monitor and clarify include the following.

• Ask questions during and after reading and summarize to check your understanding.

• Adjust your reading rate, read on, or reread the section that caused confusion.

• Visualize what you are reading.

• Use text features and illustrations to help clarify the text.

Directions As you read, write down the page numbers of places that you had trouble understanding. Then describe the fix-up strategy you used to clarify the meaning.

Where in the text I had trouble: _____ _____ _____

_____ _____ _____

Fix-Up Strategies I Used

_____

_____

_____

_____

_____

Selection Summary

Write a two- or three-sentence summary of the selection. Use a separate sheet of paper if you need more space.

_____

_____

_____

_____

Name _____

Selection Title _____ **Author** _____

When we **summarize** and **paraphrase,** we capture the important ideas or events of a selection in a few sentences. Paraphrasing is putting what we've read into our own words. Good readers summarize and paraphrase what they've read to check understanding and improve comprehension. Keeping important ideas and events in a logical order also improves comprehension. To summarize or paraphrase, do the following.

- In fiction, look for the important events of the plot, including the climax.

- In nonfiction, look for the important ideas that the author presents.

- Jot notes as you read to help you summarize or paraphrase, keeping events in a logical order.

- Restate important pieces of information in your own words.

Directions As you read the selection, use the chart below to write down any important ideas or plot events. Remember to record events in a logical order. When you're finished reading, use your notes to summarize or paraphrase the selection.

Important Ideas or Events

_____

_____

_____

_____

_____

Summary

_____

_____

_____

_____

_____

Name _____

Selection Title _____ Author _____

Good readers ask questions as they read. **Questioning** helps us monitor our comprehension and clarify anything that's confusing. Questioning also helps to make inferences, interpret the texts we read, and promote discussion. As you read, use the following questioning strategy.

- Preview the selection and think about any questions you have about the topic.

- Read with a question in mind and make notes when you find information that addresses the question.

- Write down other questions that come up as you read and look for answers in the text.

- Remember that not all questions are answered in the text. Sometimes we have to make inferences or interpretations based on the information the author provides.

Directions As you read the selection, use the chart below to write down any questions that you have about the text in the column on the left. Write down any answers you find or inferences you make in the right hand column.

Questions	Answers, Inferences, Interpretations

Name _____

Selection Title _____ Author _____

Important ideas in nonfiction texts are the main ideas and details about a topic that the author wants the reader to understand. You can do the following to help identify important ideas and details as you read.

- Preview the selection and read the title, headings, and captions.
- Look for words in special type such as italics, boldface, and bulleted lists.
- Watch for signal words and phrases such as *for example* and *most important*.
- Use text features including photographs and illustrations, diagrams, charts, and maps.

Directions As you read the selection, use the chart below to write down any important ideas and details that you find. List any text features or signal words you used to locate these ideas. Use the important ideas and details to write a short summary of the selection.

Important Ideas	Details

Write a Summary _____

_____

_____

Selection Title _____ **Author** _____

Text structure refers to the way an author organizes a text. Cause and effect and compare and contrast are two types of text structure. Knowing how a text is structured can improve our comprehension. Here are ways to identify text structure.

- Before you read, preview the text. Make predictions, ask questions, and use titles, headings, and illustrations to try to identify the structure.

- As you read, look for language that gives clues to the organization.

- After reading, recall the organization and summarize the text.

Directions As you preview and read the selection, write down features of the text that help you identify the text structure. Remember to ask questions, use text features, and look for language clues to identify the text structure. After reading, write the name of the text structure and a brief summary of the selection.

Before Reading _____

_____

_____

_____

During Reading _____

_____

_____

_____

Text Structure/Summary _____

_____

_____

_____

© Pearson Education, Inc., 5

Name _____

Selection Title _____ Author _____

Myths are old stories that have been passed down through word of mouth for hundreds of years. Some myths have many different versions depending on the culture. Characteristics of myths include the following.

- The beliefs of a particular culture are reflected in the story.
- Characters are usually gods, goddesses, and humans interacting with natural forces.
- The plot often centers around events that try to explain a force of nature.

Directions As you read *King Midas and the Golden Touch,* look for examples of a particular culture, characters such as gods, goddesses, and humans, and events that try to explain nature that make this story a myth. Write those examples below.

Culture _____

_____

_____

Characters _____

_____

_____

Events _____

_____

_____

Explore the Genre

Think about the culture, characters, and events in another story you've read that's a myth. What similarities and differences do you find between that story and *King Midas and the Golden Touch*? Write about it. Use a separate sheet of paper if you need more space.

_____

Name _____

Selection Title _____ Author _____

When we **predict,** we tell what we think might happen in a selection. Predictions are based on our preview or what we've already read. We **set a purpose** to guide our reading. We can do the following to predict and set a purpose.

- Read the title and the author's name. Look at the illustrations and other text features.
- Think about why you're reading and set a purpose.
- Use your prior knowledge—what you already know—to make a prediction.
- As you read, check and change your prediction based on new information.

Directions Preview the selection. Make a prediction and set a purpose for reading the selection. As you read, check your predictions and set a new purpose as necessary. When you finish reading, write a summary of the selection.

Before Reading
Make a Prediction _____

_____

Purpose for Reading _____

_____

During Reading
Check and Change Prediction _____

_____

Set a New Purpose _____

_____

After Reading
Write a Summary _____

_____

_____

_____

Selection Title _____ Author _____

Background knowledge is what we already know about a topic. Using background knowledge can help us better understand what we're reading. Activate your background knowledge by doing the following.

• Preview the selection to find out what it's about.

• Think about what you already know about the topic.

• Connect the selection to your own world—to people, places, and events you already know.

Directions Use the KWL chart below to chart your background knowledge about the selection. List what you already know in the K column. Then list what you want to learn in the W column. After reading, list what you learned in the L column. Write a brief summary of the selection on a separate sheet of paper.

What We Know	What We Want to Know	What We Learned

Book Talk Tips

- Speak clearly.
- Make eye contact.
- Talk about a book YOU liked reading.
- Don't give away the ending.
- Talk for 2–4 minutes, sharing amusing or important information from the book.

Directions Use the talking points below to help organize your book talk.

1. What is the title of the book?

2. Who is the author?

3. What is the genre?

4. What other book has the author written?

If your book is fiction…

5. What is the most exciting part of this book? The plot, characters, theme? Explain why.

6. Briefly describe a setting, scene, or character from this book.

If your book is nonfiction…

7. What important information did you learn from this book?

8. Briefly describe an interesting part of the book.

9. Do you have a personal connection with the story or topic? Explain.

10. Explain why your listeners should read this book.

Before writing

- Help your partner brainstorm ideas for writing.

- Discuss the writing topic with your partner. Does he or she need to narrow the topic or expand it?

After the first draft

- Before you exchange papers, tell your partner what you would like him or her to look for when reading your writing.

- Using sticky notes or a piece of notebook paper, note any questions or comments you have about your partner's writing.

- Point out the information or ideas that are well written.

- Discuss any information that seems unneeded or confusing, but make sure your comments are helpful and considerate.

Revision

- Read your partner's paper out loud to listen for strengths as well as places for improvement.

- Always tell your partner what you think works well in his or her paper.

- Start with a compliment, or strength, and then offer suggestions for improvement. For example, "I liked how you _____. What if you also _____?"

- Remember also to look for correct spelling and grammar.

Other areas you might comment on:

- Title

- Introduction

- Conclusion

- Descriptions

- Examples

- Use of verbs, nouns, adjectives or adverbs

Name _____

Name of Writing Product _____

Directions Review your final draft. Rate yourself on a scale from 4 to 1 (4 is a top score) on each writing trait. After you fill out the chart, answer the questions below.

Writing Traits	4	3	2	1
Focus/Ideas				
Organization				
Voice				
Word Choice				
Sentences				
Conventions				

1. What is the best part of this piece of writing? Why do you think so?

_____

_____

_____

_____

2. Write one thing you would change about this piece of writing if you had the chance to write it.

_____

_____

_____

_____

Plot and Character

- The **plot** is the pattern of events in a story.
- The person or animal who most affects a story's plot is the **main character.**
- A plot includes (1) a problem or **conflict** the **main character** will experience, (2) **rising action** as the conflict builds, (3) a **climax,** when the main character faces the conflict, and (4) **a resolution,** when the problem or conflict is solved.

Directions Read the following passage. Then complete the diagram by filling in the elements of the story.

Rafael was doing chores in the barn when his radio stopped. He walked into his house and discovered the lights wouldn't turn on. The power was out! Rafael knew all the milk in the refrigerator would spoil if it stayed warm too long. His family's dairy farm couldn't afford to lose that milk.

Then he remembered how his father kept soft drinks cold when they went fishing. Rafael carried 23 gallons of milk to the edge of the stream and placed them in the shallow water almost up to their caps. He knew the cool water would keep the milk chilled until the power came back on.

Main Character
1. _____

↓

Rising Action
2. _____

↓

Problem or Conflict
3. _____

↓

Climax
4. _____

↓

Resolution
5. _____

Home Activity Your child analyzed the plot of a short passage. Discuss a story with your child identifying characters, the problem or conflict, rising action, and resolution.

Writing · Written Directions

Key Features of Written Directions

- explains a process in steps and describes steps in order
- often are numbered or have clue words that show order

Planting Flower Seeds

Flowers on a window sill add a nice touch to any home. Planting flower seeds in a cup or a small pot is a simple activity that brings great rewards. With the proper care, in a short time your seeds will sprout and become beautiful flowers.

To begin, you need a package of flower seeds, a flower pot, small rocks, potting soil, a spoon or scoop, and water. First, place small rocks at the bottom of your pot. These will help water drain away from the roots of your plant each time you water it. If a pot does not drain properly, the roots sit in too much water and could rot. Next, scoop soil into your pot. Fill it a little more than halfway to the top.

You are now ready to plant. Open your packet of seeds and sprinkle seeds into the soil. Since every plant will be different, read the instructions on your seed packet to find out how many seeds you can plant and how close together they should be. Press your seeds into the soil. Be sure that they are completely covered. Add more soil if you need to. Finally, water your seeds to make sure the soil is moist but not too wet. Be careful not to water your plant too much. There should not be puddles of water at the top of the pot.

When your seeds are planted, place your pot in a sunny area of your home. A window sill can work very well. Check your soil daily to make sure it does not dry out. If all goes well, by the end of the week you should begin to see small sprouts. If your flowers outgrow the original pot, you can either move them outside or move them to a bigger pot.

1. Read the directions. What process do these directions explain? What is the first step in the process?

_____

_____

2. What is the second step in the process? What clue word tells you the order of step two?

_____

_____

Vocabulary

Directions Choose the word from the box that best matches each definition. Write the word on the line shown to the left.

_____ **1.** in a way that demands attention

_____ **2.** muttered unhappily

_____ **3.** extremely small

_____ **4.** pushes or presses against something

_____ **5.** regularly or usually the case

Directions Choose the word from the box that best completes the sentences below. Write the word on the line shown to the left.

_____ **6.** Since the car was in ____, it didn't move when she pressed the gas pedal.

_____ **7.** I didn't hurt her feelings on purpose, or ____, but my words were careless.

_____ **8.** The workers ____, or muttered, when the boss told them they had to work faster.

_____ **9.** The child tugged at my dress ____, wanting another cookie.

_____ **10.** The rescue worker applied fifteen ____ to the man's chest, then breathed into his mouth twice.

Write a Letter of Complaint

Pretend that you have returned from a store where you had a terrible experience. The clerks were so rude that you may never shop there again! On a separate piece of paper, write a letter to the store's manager describing the event. Use as many vocabulary words from this week as you can.

Home Activity Your child identified and used words from the story *Red Kayak*. Review the definitions of each of the vocabulary words with your child and work together to use the words in sentences.

Four Kinds of Sentences

Each kind of sentence begins with a capital letter and has a special end mark.

A **declarative sentence** makes a statement. It ends with a period.
The creek goes through dense forests.

An **interrogative sentence** asks a question. It ends with a question mark.
Do you see a red kayak?

An **imperative sentence** gives a command or makes a request. It ends with a period.
The subject (*you*) does not appear, but it is understood.
Look in the marsh.

An **exclamatory sentence** shows strong feeling. It ends with an exclamation mark.
The water is freezing!
What a cold day it is!

Directions Rewrite each sentence. Make any needed corrections in capitalization and punctuation.

1. the creek is dangerous in winter?

   _____

2. he's not breathing.

   _____

3. do you know how to perform CPR.

   _____

Directions Complete each sentence with words from the box. Then write whether the sentence is *declarative, interrogative, imperative,* or *exclamatory.*

> think I see something!   make boating dangerous.
> the opposite shore.   wear life jackets?

4. Strong winds and tides _____

5. Did the boaters _____

6. Drive toward _____

7. Gosh, I _____

Home Activity Your child learned about four kinds of sentences. Have your child write about an event at school using one example of each kind of sentence.

Short Vowel VCCV, VCV

Spelling Words

distance	method	anger	problem	butter
petals	enjoy	perhaps	figure	channel
admire	comedy	husband	tissue	mustard
shuttle	advance	drummer	regular	denim

Words in Context Complete each sentence with a list word.

1. The ____ keeps the rhythm of the band.

2. Most people ____ the skills of talented artists.

3. Watching a ____ makes people laugh.

4. The ____ bus is the fastest way to get there.

5. I like ____ on my hot dog.

6. Her ____ was forty years old.

7. The shortest ____ between two points is a straight line.

8. The ____ fell off the flower one by one.

9. ____ we can have ice cream after dinner.

10. The skater practiced ____ eights on the ice.

1. _____

2. _____

3. _____

4. _____

5. _____

6. _____

7. _____

8. _____

9. _____

10. _____

Word Meanings Write the list word that has nearly the same meaning.

11. handkerchief

12. canal

13. lard

14. technique

15. like

16. proceed

17. rage

18. jeans

19. usual

20. difficulty

11. _____

12. _____

13. _____

14. _____

15. _____

16. _____

17. _____

18. _____

19. _____

20. _____

Home Activity Your child wrote words that have short vowels. Dictate words and have your child say and spell each word.

Steps in a Process

Process _____

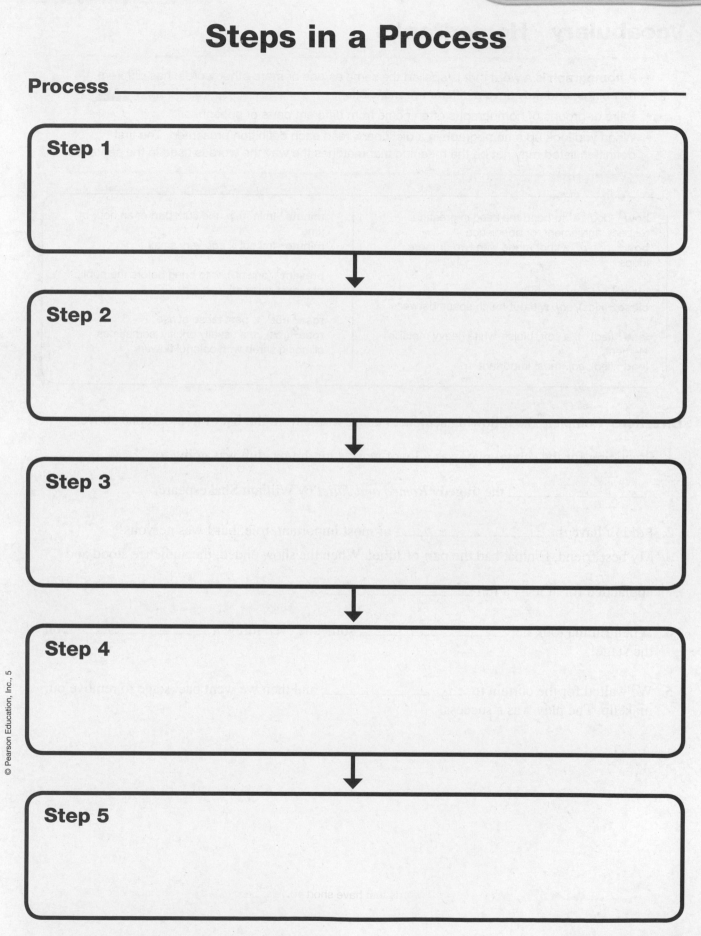

Step 1

Step 2

Step 3

Step 4

Step 5

Vocabulary · Homographs

- A **homograph** is a word that is spelled the same as one or more other words, has different meanings, and may have a different pronunciation.
- Pairs or groups of homographs often come from different parts of speech.
- When you look up a homograph in a dictionary, read each definition presented. The first definition listed may not be the meaning that matches the way the word is used in the sentence.

---

bow[1] (bou), *v.* to bend the head in greeting, respect, agreement, or obedience
bow[2] (bō), *n.* a knot made with two or more loops

close[1] (klōz), *v.* to shut
close[2] (klōs), *adj.* without much space between

lead[1] (led), *n.* a soft, bluish-white heavy metallic element
lead[2] (lēd), *adj.* most important

minute[1] (min´it), *n.* the 60th part of an hour of time
minute[2] (mī nüt´), *adj.* very small

present[1] (priz nt´), *v.* to bring before the public
present[2] (prez´nt), *n.* a gift

rose[1] (rōz), *v.* past tense of *rise*
rose[2] (rōz), *n.* a usually prickly, sometimes climbing shrub with colorful flowers

Directions Complete the following sentences using words from the list of homographs above.

1. Practicing for the school play was a lot of work. Our drama club was going to

   _____ the tragedy *Romeo and Juliet* by William Shakespeare.

2. I didn't have the _____, or most important, role, but I was nervous!

3. My best friend, Emma, had the part of Juliet. When the show ended, the audience stood and

   applauded for at least a full _____.

4. When Emma took her _____, someone even threw a _____ on the stage!

5. We waited for the curtain to _____, and then we went backstage to remove our makeup. The play was a success.

Dictionary/Glossary

- A **dictionary** lists words in alphabetical order and gives their meanings, pronunciations, and other helpful information, including parts of speech—noun, verb, adjective, or adverb.

- A **glossary** is a list of important words and their meanings that are used in a book. Glossaries are located at the back of a book. Some glossary entries include a page reference noting the first appearance of the word in the book.

- When you see an unfamiliar word, and context clues do not help you figure out its meaning, you can use a dictionary or glossary to learn what it means.

Directions Read the dictionary and glossary entries.

Dictionary Entry

rep•u•ta•tion (rep' ye ta' shen) **1.** *n.* what people think and say the character of someone or something is; character in the opinion of others; name; repute: *This store has an excellent reputation for fair dealing.* **2.** good name; good reputation: *Cheating ruined his reputation.* **3.** fame: *an international reputation.*

Glossary Entry

Ice Age *n.* a cold period in which huge ice sheets spread outward from the polar regions, the last one of which lasted from about 1,600,000 to 10,000 B.C. (p. 107)

Directions Answer the questions below.

1. In the dictionary entry, what does the initial bold entry for the word *reputation* tell you?

_____

2. In the dictionary entry, what does the representation of the word in parentheses tell you?

_____

3. Why do you think the dictionary provides sentence examples in the definition of the word?

_____

4. How many definitions does this dictionary list for *reputation*? Which is the most commonly used definition?

_____

5. What does the italicized *n.* stand for in both entries?

_____

6. What two things do you notice are missing from a glossary entry that you find in the dictionary entry?

_____

7. What is the page number listed at the end of the glossary entry for?

_____

8. What information do you get in both a dictionary and glossary entry?

_____

9. If you were reading a book about life in the desert, would you expect to find *Ice Age* in the glossary? Why or why not?

_____

_____

10. If you were reading a story and came across a word you did not know, where would be the first place you would look for a definition—a glossary or a dictionary?

_____

_____

© Pearson Education, Inc., 5

Home Activity Your child learned how to use a dictionary and a glossary. Make a list of all the possible times you might use a dictionary or glossary.

Short Vowel VCCV, VCV

Proofread a Poster Sarah made a poster for the school fair. Circle seven spelling errors. Find one capitalization error. Write the corrections on the lines.

Come too the village fair!
See the funny comady team show.
Milk a cow and churn some buttar at the farm exhibit.
Sample hot dogs with twenty choices of musterd!
Make tisseu flower bouquets.
Decorate your denim jeans with a special new art method.
Enjoy fifty booths of crafts, fun, and games.
park at the Town Hall parking lot.
Ride the special shuttal bus to the fairgrounds.
Discount tickets are on sale in advanse.

1. _____   2. _____

3. _____   4. _____

5. _____   6. _____

7. _____

8. _____

Proofread Words Circle the correct spelling of the word.

9. channal	chanel	channel
10. drummer	drumer	drummor
11. metod	methid	method
12. parhaps	perhaps	pirhaps
13. figure	figger	figour
14. petles	petels	petals
15. problam	problem	problim

Spelling Words

distance
method
anger
problem
butter
petals
enjoy
perhaps
figure
channel

admire
comedy
husband
tissue
mustard
shuttle
advance
drummer
regular
denim

Frequently Misspelled Words

and
to
too

Home Activity Your child found misspelled list words with VCCV and VCV patterns. Select a list word and ask your child to spell it.

© Pearson Education, Inc., 5

Four Kinds of Sentences

Directions Read the passage. Then read each question. Circle the letter of the correct answer.

The Storm

(1) The storm came up suddenly? (2) In a few short minutes, the sky turned dark. (3) Danny and Sherry were out in their sailboat within view of land! (4) Before they could reach harbor, however, the wind changed. (5) Sherry and Danny struggled to take down the sail. (6) The wind was too strong! (7) How could the pair get the boat to safety.

1 What change, if any, should be made in sentence 1?

  A Change *came up* to **come up**

  B Change *suddenly?* to **suddenly.**

  C Change *The storm* to **Storm**

  D Make no change

2 What change, if any, should be made in sentence 2?

  A Change *minutes* to **minute's**

  B Change the period to a question mark

  C Remove the comma

  D Make no change

3 What change, if any, should be made in sentence 3?

  A Change *were* to **was**

  B Change the exclamation mark to a question mark

  C Change the exclamation mark to a period

  D Make no change

4 What change, if any, should be made in sentence 4?

  A Remove *however*

  B Change *Before* to **before**

  C Change the period to a comma

  D Make no change

5 What change, if any, should be made in sentence 7?

  A Change the period to a question mark

  B Change the period to an exclamation mark

  C Change *How* to **How?**

  D Make no change

© Pearson Education, Inc., 5

Home Activity Your child prepared for taking tests on kinds of sentences. Have your child read part of a story to you and identify each sentence as declarative, interrogative, imperative, or exclamatory.

Cause and Effect

- A **cause** is what makes something happen. An **effect** is what happens as a result of the cause.
- If there are no clue words, ask yourself, "What made this event happen? What happened as a result of this event?"
- An effect may become the cause of another effect.

Directions Read the following passage and complete the diagram below.

By the third day of non-stop rain, no one on our street could keep the water out of their homes. The homes that had basements were hit hardest. Basements were flooded in spite of efforts to pump the water out. Toys, washing machines, and furniture in basements were soaked through completely.

Our neighbor, Mrs. Chan, was so sad because all her photographs of her grandchildren had been in her basement. Her granddaughter May was my best friend, and I had May's school picture in my wallet. I wrapped it in a plastic bag, put on my raincoat, and ran to Mrs. Chan's house. Just as I handed Mrs. Chan May's picture, a ray of sun peeked out from behind a cloud.

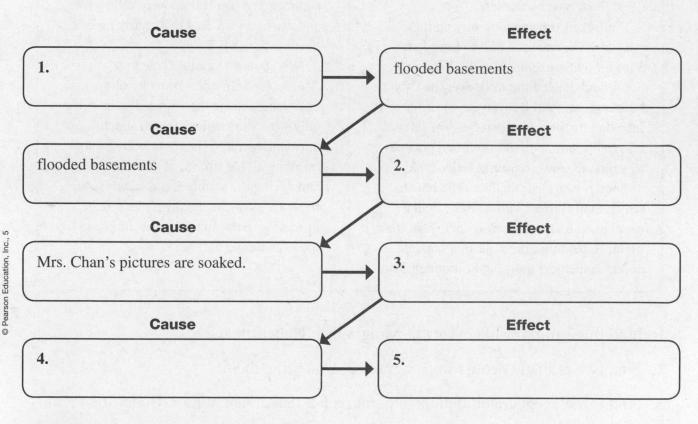

Cause	Effect
1.	flooded basements
flooded basements	2.
Mrs. Chan's pictures are soaked.	3.
4.	5.

Home Activity Your child identified causes and effects in a short passage. While working around the house, have your child explain to you the effects of one of the chores. Then ask your child to figure if the effect becomes the cause of another effect.

Writing • Writing for Tests

The Winter of Blue Snow

It was the coldest winter Paul Bunyan had ever seen. It was so cold that the fish moved south, the trees begged to be cut down, and even the snow turned blue. The nights were so frosty that when Sourdough Sam called Paul Bunyan and the other lumberjacks to dinner, his words froze solid and hung in the air, so nobody heard him and the lumberjacks went hungry until morning.

To get his mind off his starving belly, Paul Bunyan went for a walk. He was just about to eat a valley-sized handful of blue snow when he heard a strange sound—like the snort of a bear crossed with the bleat of a lamb. Peering into his hands, Paul Bunyan saw the sorriest sight: a tiny baby ox, stained blue by the snow.

Well, Paul Bunyan took pity on the poor little ox and took him to Sourdough Sam for a few gallons of milk. While old Sourdough heated the milk over the fifty-burner stove, Paul Bunyan ate the dinner intended for fifty lumberjacks—he left not one spiral ham, bushel of mashed potatoes, or gallon of gravy on the massive table.

Soon it was clear that the little blue ox, which Paul Bunyan named Babe, had it in mind to take after its new owner. That first night, Babe drank the milk of a hundred cows, so the next morning Sourdough Sam had to make oatmeal for breakfast with melted blue snow. Babe soon grew so big that Paul Bunyan had to build an extra large barn to keep him in. When Babe was a week old, he started helping Paul Bunyan by hauling a hundred logs at a time by the strength of his massive neck.

The only trouble between Babe and Paul Bunyan was that Babe loved the winter and hated summer, so Paul Bunyan had to be mighty creative to keep Babe hauling logs in the summer heat. He even painted the roads white to make Babe think that they were covered in snow. Finally, Paul Bunyan hit on a grand idea: he introduced Babe to Bessie, the yellow cow. Bessie was almost a big as Babe and as beautiful as a summer day. She had a lovely yellow hide and warm brown eyes that nearly melted the blue right off Babe.

Now, being a summer cow and Sourdough Sam's best provider of milk and cream during the winter, Bessie could only work during the summer months. So during the winter, Babe hauled logs alone, thinking all the time about his Bessie, and during the summer, Babe and Bessie hauled logs together, which made Babe grow to love the summertime almost as much as Bessie did.

1. Find three improbable events in paragraph 1. Underline them.

2. Find two realistic details in paragraph 2. Underline them.

3. Find three exaggerated details in paragraph 5 that create humor. Underline them.

Name_____

Vocabulary

Directions Choose the word from the box that best matches each definition. Write the word on the line.

_____ 1. blood vessels that carry blood to the heart from all parts of the body

_____ 2. song for singing to a child

_____ 3. stealing

_____ 4. a thick, black, sticky substance made from tar or turpentine

_____ 5. fitted together; built

Directions Choose the word from the box that best completes the sentences below. Write the word on the line shown to the left.

_____ 6. The rancher _____ his cattle with the symbol from his ranch so nobody else could claim them.

_____ 7. The cracks in the roof were sealed with _____ .

_____ 8. Grandma and Grandpa danced elegantly, or _____, in time with the music's gentle beat.

_____ 9. When no one else could think of how to solve the school's litter problem, Marisa impressed the principal with her_____ idea.

_____ 10. The tornado caused a lot of _____, or destruction, when it whipped through town and ripped several homes from their foundations.

Write a Friendly Letter

On a separate sheet of paper, write a friendly letter to someone living out of town about an event that happened where you live. Use as many vocabulary words as you can.

Home Activity Your child identified and used vocabulary words from *Thunder Rose*. Work with your child to learn the words and their definitions. Have your child create colorful flash cards to do so.

Subjects and Predicates

Every sentence has a subject and a predicate. The words that tell whom or what the sentence is about are the **complete subject.**

    <u>Many families</u> moved west in the 1840s.

The words that tell what the subject is or does are the **complete predicate.**

    The trip <u>could take up to six months.</u>

A **nominative** is a noun or pronoun that means the same as the subject. It explains or identifies something about the subject.

    Joe was an experienced cowboy.   The nominative is *cowboy.*

A **fragment** is a group of words that lacks a subject or a predicate.

    Had to carry everything with them.   This fragment lacks a subject.

A **run-on** is two or more complete sentences run together.

    The settlers needed food they needed tools.

Directions Underline each complete subject once. Underline each complete predicate twice.

1. A tornado's shape is like a funnel.

2. The deadly funnel measures up to a mile wide.

3. They are unpredictable in their movements.

4. Settlers feared the awful twister.

Directions Write *F* after a fragment. Write *R* after a run-on. Then correct the sentence errors. Write a simple sentence or a compound sentence on the lines.

5. The wind inside a tornado _____

_____

_____

6. A tornado can be called a twister it is also sometimes called a cyclone. _____

_____

_____

Home Activity Your child learned about subjects and predicates. Talk about a storm you and your child have experienced. Have your child write several sentences about the storm and identify the complete subjects and predicates in each sentence.

Long Vowel VCV

Spelling Words				
fever	broken	climate	hotel	basic
vocal	native	silent	labor	spider
label	icon	agent	motive	vital
acorn	item	aroma	ego	solo

Words in Context Complete each sentence with a list word.

1. From a small ____, a large oak tree grows.

2. When you are sick, you may have a ____.

3. Your ____ is what you think of yourself.

4. Flying ____ means doing something alone.

5. A desert ____ may produce too little rain to support crops.

6. The two people were loud and ____ as they cheered.

7. The travel ____ helped plan a vacation.

8. We want to stay in the ____ that has a pool.

9. Have you ever watched a ____ spin its web?

10. The clothing ____ itches the back of my neck.

1. _____
2. _____
3. _____
4. _____
5. _____
6. _____
7. _____
8. _____
9. _____
10. _____

Antonyms Write the list word that has the opposite or nearly the opposite meaning.

11. fixed   11. _____

12. advanced   12. _____

13. alien   13. _____

14. noisy   14. _____

15. unimportant 15. _____

Synonyms Write the list word that has the same or nearly the same meaning.

16. work   16. _____

17. reason   17. _____

18. object   18. _____

19. scent   19. _____

20. image   20. _____

Home Activity Your child wrote words with the long vowel VCV pattern. Have your child tell you one synonym or one antonym for a list word.

Scoring Rubric: Tall Tale

	4	3	2	1
Focus/Ideas	Exaggerated character and events	Somewhat exaggerated character and events	Character and events hardly exaggerated	Character and events not exaggerated
Organization/ Sequence	Clear order of events	Mostly clear order of events	Confused order of events	No order of events
Voice	Engaging and original voice	Generally engaging voice	No clear original voice	Voice is not engaging or original
Word Choice	Writer uses strong sensory details	Writer uses good sensory details	Writer uses weak sensory details	Writer does not include sensory details
Sentences	Clear, complete sentences	Most sentences clear and complete	Some sentences unclear and incomplete	Many sentences incomplete
Conventions	Subjects and predicates used correctly	Most subjects and predicates used correctly	Some mistakes with subjects and predicates	Many errors with subjects and predicates

Vocabulary · Context Clues

- **Homonyms** are words that are spelled the same but have different meanings.
- Look for **context clues**—words and sentences around a word—to figure out which meaning is being used in the sentence.

Directions Read the following passage about a hurricane. Then answer the questions below. Look for homonyms as you read.

As Pedro scaled the ladder to the roof, he felt the blood in his veins pumping through his body. He was the first person to get a look at the destruction the hurricane had created. He looked at the roof and reminded himself to bring up a bucket of pitch next time to repair the new cracks. Looking out over the countryside, he saw that many buildings would need to be constructed again. He started gathering broken branches to pitch, or throw, down to the ground below. Then he paused and took a deep breath, thinking about what this disaster had done to his community. He knew that none of his neighbors would have to pitch tents and live in their yards while repairs were made to their homes. The people of his town would help each other find shelter, and everyone would be fine.

1. *Vein* can mean "a blood vessel" or "a crack in a rock filled with a mineral deposit." How is it used in the passage? How can you tell?

_____

2. What does *pitch* mean in the third sentence of this passage? What clues help you understand the meaning used in this sentence?

_____

3. What does *pitch* mean in the fifth sentence of this passage? What clues help you understand the meaning used in this sentence?

_____

4. To *scale* something can mean "to climb up something" or "to measure something." How is it used in this passage? How can you tell?

_____

5. What does *pitch* mean in the second-to-last sentence of this passage? What clues help you understand the meaning used in this sentence?

_____

Home Activity Your child read a short passage and used context clues to understand homonyms, words that are spelled the same but have different meanings. With your child, make a list of homonyms. Challenge your child to make up a sentence using each meaning.

© Pearson Education, Inc., 5

Almanac

An **almanac** is a yearly book that contains calendars, weather information, and dates of holidays. Almanacs also contain charts and tables of current information in subject areas such as populations of cities and nations, and lists of recent prize winners in science, literature, and sports.

Directions Read this almanac entry about the United States Census. Use the information to answer the questions on the next page.

United States Census

Every ten years, the federal government conducts a census, or count, of the number of people who live in the United States. According to the federal Constitution, a census must be completed every ten years to determine the number of representatives each state may send to the U.S. House of Representatives.

The census shows how the populations of cities, regions, and states compare. This data helps government officials decide how and where to spend federal money. Traditionally, a census not only counts the number of citizens, but it also gathers other information, such as:

- the ethnic background of citizens
- the number of adults and children
- the number of employed people and unemployed people
- the income level of citizens and their type of housing

For many decades, the three largest cities have remained New York City, Los Angeles, and Chicago. However, other cities are growing more quickly than any of these three. Many sociologists, economists, and government officials find the growth rates of cities the most interesting information in the census. In recent years, the trend has been for great numbers of people to move from the North to the South—especially to states in the Southwest.

The federal government collects data every year, not just every decade. For instance, the chart below shows data from the 2000 census in one column, but it also includes data collected by the government in 2002. This chart shows the ten fastest growing cities of 100,000 people or more in the United States.

CITY	2000 Population	2002 Population	Numerical Change	Percentage Change
Gilbert, AZ	109,920	135,005	25,085	22.8
North Las Vegas, NV	115,488	135,902	20,414	17.7
Henderson, NV	175,750	206,153	30,403	17.3
Chandler, AZ	176,652	202,016	25,364	14.4
Peoria, AZ	108,685	123,239	14,554	13.4
Irvine, CA	143,072	162,122	19,050	13.3
Rancho Cucamonga, CA	127,743	143,711	15,968	12.5
Chula Vista, CA	173,566	193,919	20,353	11.7
Fontana, CA	128,938	143,607	14,669	11.4
Joliet, IL	106,334	118,423	12,089	11.4

© Pearson Education, Inc., 5

Name_____

1. According to the U.S. Constitution, what is the maximum number of years that can pass between federal censuses?

_____

2. What is the purpose of conducting a federal census, according to the U.S. Constitution?

_____

_____

3. In addition to population, what are two examples of other data a census provides?

_____

_____

4. What types of people consult the federal census?

_____

_____

5. What are the three largest cities in the United States?

_____

6. Which state has the most listings among the fastest-growing cities on the 2002 census?

_____

7. Would an almanac be a good place to find information on why nine of ten fastest-growing U.S. cities are located in the Southwest or West? Why or why not?

_____

_____

8. Which city had the highest numerical increase in population between 2000 and 2002?

_____

9. Which city had the highest population in 2002? How much higher is its population than that of the city listed below it?

_____

_____

10. Between 2000 and 2002, Los Angeles (population 3,503,532) saw a numerical increase in population of 104,239. Why do you think Los Angeles isn't listed on this chart?

_____

Home Activity Your child learned about the contents of almanacs and analyzed data from an almanac. Together, look up information about your town or area of the country in an almanac. Read about population, weather forecast, historical sites, and so on. Discuss how the information in the almanac helps you better understand your own geographical area.

Long Vowel VCV

Proofread a Postcard Yolanda wrote a postcard to her friend. Circle six spelling errors and one capitalization error. Write the corrections on the lines.

Spelling Words

fever
broken
climate
hotel
basic
vocal
native
silent
labor
spider

label
icon
agent
motive
vital
acorn
item
aroma
ego
solo

dear Margaret,

 I'm having a great time at the hotle. There are lemon trees everywhere and the eroma from the blossoms is awesome. Today, I'm going to by some gifts. There are many nateve crafts to choose from. It's very calm and silant here. The only noise comes from the wind and the ocean. Thank your travel agant for suggesting this place. It's now a family favorite!

                              Your friend,
                              Yolanda

1. _____   2. _____

3. _____   4. _____

5. _____   6. _____

7. _____

Proofread Words Circle the correct spelling of the word.

Frequently Misspelled Words

favorite
buy

8. vocle   vocal   vocel

9. label   laebel   labal

10. brokin   brokan   broken

11. basec   basic   basuc

12. ikon   icon   ican

13. motive   motife   motove

14. akorn   acern   acorn

15. fever   fevar   feaver

16. eego   ego   egho

Home Activity Your child identified misspelled list words in a paragraph. Ask your child to name one list word with the long *a* sound and one with the long *o* sound.

© Pearson Education, Inc., 5

Subjects and Predicates

Directions Read the passage. Then read each question. Circle the letter of the correct answer.

Cowboys of Texas

(1) Cowboys of Texas herded cattle to Kansas on the Abilene Trail. (2) The great herds moved along slowly. (3) These large animals must graze for hours each day. (4) They needed a vast supply of water. (5) Lean, tanned cowboys (6) They crossed dangerous rivers and slept under the light of the moon. (7) A cowboy's horse was his friend and co-worker.

1 What is the complete subject of sentence 1?

 A Cowboys

 B Cowboys of Texas

 C Kansas

 D the Abilene Trail

2 What is the complete predicate of sentence 2?

 A moved

 B moved along

 C moved along slowly

 D The great herds

3 What is the complete subject of sentence 3?

 A These large animals

 B large animals

 C hours each day

 D animals must graze

4 How can you best describe sentence 5?

 A Has a subject and predicate

 B Run-on sentence

 C Has a complete subject

 D Sentence fragment

5 In sentence 6, what is the complete subject?

 A They

 B They crossed

 C They crossed dangerous rivers

 D rivers

Home Activity Your child prepared for taking tests on subjects, predicates, fragments, and run-ons. Circle a paragraph in the newspaper. Have your child identify the subject and predicate of each sentence in the paragraph.

Theme and Setting

- The **theme** is the underlying meaning of a story. It is often not stated. You can figure out a theme from events and other evidence in the story.

- The **setting** is where and when the story takes place. Writers use details, such as sights and sounds, to describe it.

Directions Read the following passage. Then complete the diagram with the sights, sounds, smells, or feelings expressed in the passage.

I love to go to the beach in the summer because a beach can excite the senses. I might hear the roaring waves or the squawk of seagulls. I might feel the gritty warmth of the sand underfoot. Even the mix of odors on the breeze—an airy freshness with a hint of rotting fish—can stay with me long after I've left the water's edge. When I look out toward the vast horizon over the water, I feel as free as the birds darting and diving above my head, and as small as the grains of sand blowing across my toes.

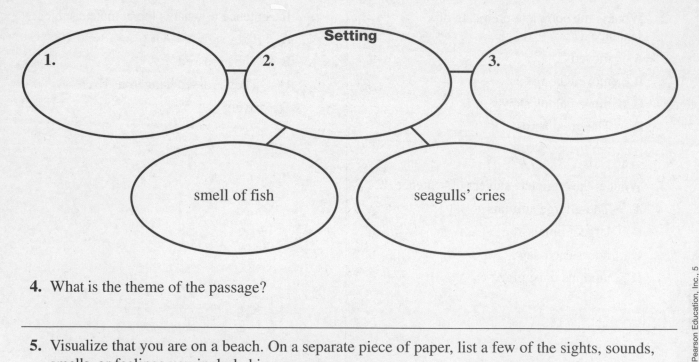

Setting

1.

2.

3.

smell of fish

seagulls' cries

4. What is the theme of the passage?

_____

5. Visualize that you are on a beach. On a separate piece of paper, list a few of the sights, sounds, smells, or feelings you included in your scene.

_____

School + Home **Home Activity** Your child identified the setting and theme in a fictional passage. Sit with your child in a familiar place and identify its sights, sounds, and smells.

© Pearson Education, Inc., 5

Name _____

Writing • Invitation

Key Features of an Invitation
- may be informal or formal
- gives important information about an event or plan
- sometimes asks for a response

Beach Party!

Dear Melissa,

To celebrate the last few days of summer, I'm going to have a beach party! Here are the details:

What: Beach Party!

Where: Kaiser Beach, 1409 Lakefront Way

When: 12:00 P.M., Saturday, August 22

This is the best beach in town! It's really big, so it's not usually too crowded.

To get to the beach, take a right off Sandy Point Rd. and go three blocks. We'll have a spot set up near the lifeguard stand on the beach. Look for the yellow beach umbrella.

Here are a few items you might want to bring with you:
Swimsuit
Sunscreen
Towel

Please tell me if you will be able to make it or not. You can call me at home. (222) 567-1234

Your friend,
Emily

1. Tell what the event is, where it is taking place, and when it is happening.

_____

2. Name three types of additional details the writer includes.

_____

© Pearson Education, Inc., 5

Vocabulary

Directions Choose a word from the box that best matches each clue. Write the word on the line.

_____ 1. This is a good place to build a
   lighthouse.

_____ 2. Some call it seaweed, others call
   it this.

_____ 3. This could be considered a secret
   hiding spot.

_____ 4. This is what the rabbit did to
   the carrot.

_____ 5. This works with your muscle to
   help you move.

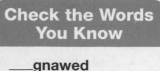

**Check the Words
You Know**

___gnawed
___headland
___kelp
___lair
___ravine
___shellfish
___sinew

Directions Choose the word from the box that best completes each sentence. Write the word on
the line.

The fox slowly emerged from its, den, or **1.** _____. Having **2.** _____

the last bone from an earlier meal, the fox headed down the hill toward the **3.** _____,

or canyon, in search of more food. While foxes will occasionally eat **4.** _____,

they much prefer the **5.** _____ and muscle of birds or small mammals.

Write a Letter

On a separate sheet of paper, write a letter you might send off in a bottle if you were stranded on an
island. Use as many vocabulary words as you can.

Home Activity Your child identified and used vocabulary words from *Island of the Blue Dolphins.* With your
child, work together to tell a story incorporating the vocabulary words. Take turns adding sentences to the
story until all the words have been used.

© Pearson Education, Inc., 5

Name _____

Independent and Dependent Clauses

A related group of words with a subject and a predicate is called a **clause.** A clause that makes sense by itself is an **independent clause.** A clause that does not make sense by itself is a **dependent clause.** A **complex sentence** contains an independent and a dependent clause.

    Independent Clause   They came to the island in canoes.
    Dependent Clause   even though it was a long trip

If the dependent clause comes first, set it off with a comma: *Until they were attacked, Native Americans lived on the island.* If the independent clause is first, no comma is needed: *Native Americans lived on the island until they were attacked.*

Directions Write *I* if the underlined group of words is an independent clause. Write *D* if it is a dependent clause.

1. If you live on an island, you become independent. _____

2. Natives made their own clothes because they could not buy them. _____

3. Since there were no stores, they hunted for food. _____

4. A seal provided meat while people used its hide for clothes. _____

5. A hunting party paddled boats out to sea so that they could catch fish. _____

6. Women gathered berries and roots before winter came. _____

7. Because they needed containers for the food, they made baskets out of grasses. _____

Directions Underline the dependent clause in each sentence.

8. Because they cooked with fire, the natives kept live coals.

9. After food was prepared, they covered the embers with ashes.

10. While they slept through the night, the coals stayed warm.

11. The coals smoldered until morning came.

12. When the cook blew on the coals, they glowed brightly.

13. She fed wood to the coals so that the fire would catch again.

14. If her husband had caught fish that morning, they would eat well for breakfast.

© Pearson Education, Inc., 5

Home Activity Your child learned about independent and dependent clauses. Ask your child to write a sentence about Native Americans using an independent clause and a dependent clause and explain the difference between the two.

Long Vowel Digraphs

Spelling Words

coast	feast	speech	wheat	Spain
paint	arrow	needle	charcoal	praise
faint	maintain	crease	grain	breeze
willow	appeal	bowling	complain	sneeze

Words in Context Complete each sentence with a list word.

1. I am dizzy and may ____.

2. A perfect ____ score is 300.

3. I had multi-____ bread in my sandwich.

4. High ____ tells you that you did a great job.

5. Make a ____ in the paper to fold it in half.

6. Food grilled over a ____ fire tastes great.

7. It is generally better to be positive than to ____.

8. A sailboat needs a strong ____ to go fast.

9. Antique car owners spend time and money to ____ their vehicles so they will continue to run.

10. Two countries that border ____ are Portugal and France.

1. _____

2. _____

3. _____

4. _____

5. _____

6. _____

7. _____

8. _____

9. _____

10. _____

Classifying Write the list word that belongs in each group.

11. bow, feather, ____

12. sew, thread, ____

13. glide, cruise, ____

14. cold, cough, ____

15. corn, barley, ____

16. talk, lecture, ____

11. _____

12. _____

13. _____

14. _____

15. _____

16. _____

Synonyms Write the list word that has the same or nearly the same meaning.

17. request

19. tree

17. _____

19. _____

18. banquet

20. color

18. _____

20. _____

© Pearson Education, Inc., 5

Home Activity Your child wrote words with long vowel digraphs. Have your child tell you two ways to spell long *e*.

Four-Column Chart

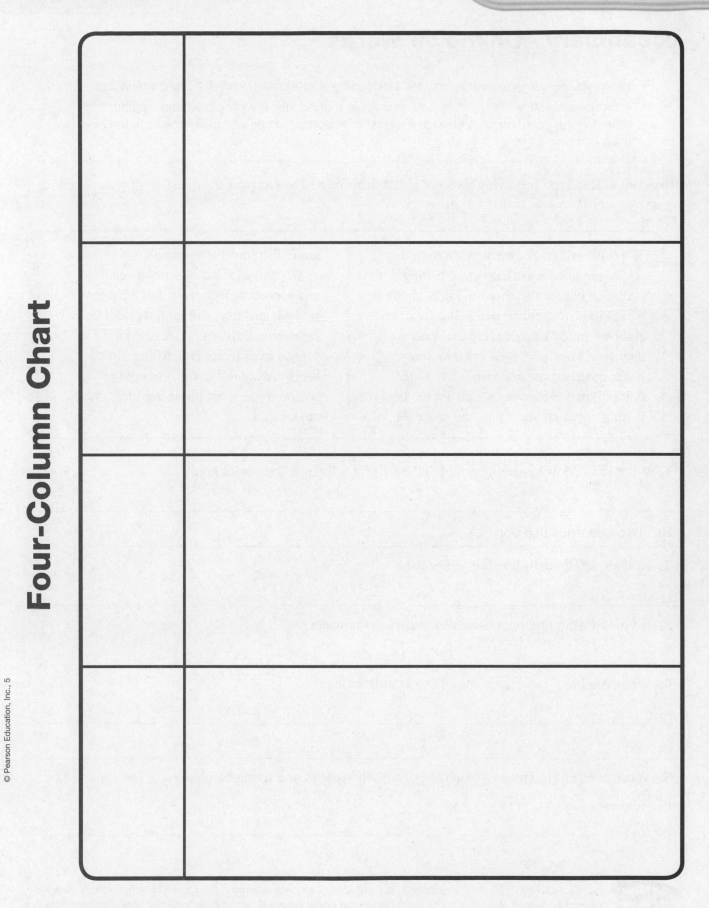

Vocabulary • Unknown Words

- When you see an unknown word, use a dictionary or glossary to learn the word's meaning.
- A **dictionary** lists words in alphabetical order and gives their meanings, pronunciations, and other helpful information. A **glossary** is a list of important words and their meanings that are used in a book.

Directions Read the following passage about fishermen. Then answer the questions below. Look up unknown words in a dictionary or glossary.

People who make their living from the ocean need more than good fishing skills. Of course they need to know about what kinds of shellfish live in the area, and how much kelp floats in the waters they fish. They also need to know about water quality: how brackish is the water? Is it polluted? Knowing which are the best fishing coves and how near the shore the larger fish travel is essential.

We view a coastline from a headland and appreciate its beauty, but a fisherman sees a completely different world. He or she sees a deep-sea ravine, the lair of a myriad of different fish. Many fishing decisions are left to the brain of the person fishing, not his or her luck, muscle, or sinew.

1. What is *kelp?* Why should people who fish for a living know about kelp?

_____

_____

2. How do *shellfish* differ from other fish?

_____

3. If you are standing on a *headland,* where is the water?

_____

4. What is a *lair?* How does it apply to schools of fish?

_____

_____

5. What does *myriad* mean? Would a person who fishes for a living be pleased to see a myriad of fish?

_____

© Pearson Education, Inc., 5

Home Activity Your child identified and used vocabulary words from a passage about fishermen. Read a nonfiction article with your child. Have him or her point out unknown words. Together, look up the words in a dictionary or glossary.

SPQ3R

SPQ3R is an acronym for a set of study skills that can help you when you read any text. It is especially helpful when reading nonfiction. Here's what it means: **Survey:** Look at the title, author name, chapter headings, and illustrations to get an idea of what you are about to read. **Predict:** Imagine what the story you're going to read is about. **Question:** Generate questions you want answered when reading the story. **Read:** Read the story, keeping your predictions and questions in mind. **Recite:** Recite or write down what you learned from reading the story. **Review:** Look back at the story, the predictions you made, the questions you posed, the answers you found in the text, and the information you learned from your reading.

Directions Use SPQ3R in reading the passage and answering the questions that follow.

Hawaii: A Remote State

Hawaii is a group of volcanic islands in the central Pacific Ocean some 2,300 miles west of San Francisco, California. Hawaii became the fiftieth state in the United States in 1959. It is an important military location of the U.S. because of its location in the ocean. Because it is so beautiful, it is also one of the most popular vacation spots for Americans even though the flight to Hawaii is long.

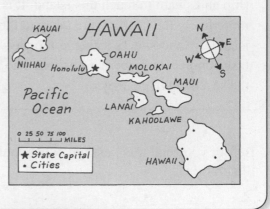

1. Before you read this passage, what could you tell about the passage by surveying the map?

_____

2. Before you read this passage, what did you predict the passage would be about?

_____

3. What was a question you wanted the passage to answer before you read it?

_____

4. When did Hawaii become a state? What is one of the things that Hawaii is known for?

_____

5. Write a brief review of what you learned from this passage. In your review, discuss whether your questions were answered and whether your prediction was true.

_____

_____

© Pearson Education, Inc., 5

Directions Use SPQ3R in reading the passage and answering the questions that follow.

Assateague Island's Wild Horses

Assateague Island is a 37-mile-long barrier island, a thin strip of land that helps to protect Maryland's shoreline. It has been an outpost for the U.S. Coast Guard for nearly 50 years. What is most unique about the island is the horses that roam freely on the beaches and marshland. While the origin of the horses is unclear, the popular myth claims the horses jumped from a sinking Spanish ship and swam to reach this island. It is more likely the horses were taken to the island by landowners trying not to pay taxes on livestock, perhaps as long ago as the seventeenth century.

1. Before you read this passage, what could you tell about the passage by surveying the illustration?

_____

2. Before you read this passage, what did you predict the passage would be about?

_____

3. Before you read this passage, what questions did you want the passage to answer?

_____

4. What is most unique about Assateague Island?

_____

5. Write a brief review of what you learned from this passage. In your review, discuss whether your questions were answered and whether your prediction was true.

_____

_____

_____

© Pearson Education, Inc., 5

Home Activity Your child learned about the SPQ3R study skill and applied it to two nonfiction passages. Have your child explain the study skill to you. Then, with your child, apply it to a newspaper or magazine article.

Name _____

Long Vowel Digraphs

Proofread a Report Miguel wrote about his family's trip. Circle six spelling errors. Find one punctuation error. Write the corrections on the lines.

This summer, my family traveled to Spain. We felt very lucky to stay in a hotel right on the caost. The weather was always beautiful with a light breaze blowing in off the ocean. Outside my window, the branches of a wilow tree dipped into a small pond. The sky was the same color as the baby blue color in my pante box. On our last night we had a wonderful feest. I thought I would fante at the sight of so much food! Everything was really delicious? My stomach hurt before we got to dessert. Is that anything to complain about?

© Pearson Education, Inc., 5

Spelling Words
coast
feast
speech
wheat
Spain
paint
arrow
needle
charcoal
praise
faint
maintain
crease
grain
breeze
willow
appeal
bowling
complain
sneeze

1. _____   2. _____

3. _____   4. _____

5. _____   6. _____

7. _____

Proofread Words Circle the correct spelling of the word.

8.	weat	wheet	wheat
9.	charcole	charcoal	charcol
10.	maintain	maintane	mantain
11.	boling	bolling	bowling
12.	complain	complane	complan
13.	creese	creaze	crease
14.	arow	arrow	arro

Frequently Misspelled Words
Halloween
really

Home Activity Your child corrected misspelled list words in a paragraph and selected the correctly spelled word in a group of words. Select three list words and ask your child to spell them.

Name _____

Independent and Dependent Clauses

Directions Read the passage. Then read each question. Circle the letter of the correct answer.

Ancient Tools

(1) Natives used different kinds of natural materials as tools. (2) Carved to a point, a rock could serve as a knife. (3) Bones of some animals became tools too. (4) Because bone is so hard, it can pass through leather. (5) Artists might carve bone if the weather was bad. (6) Deerskin made soft, warm clothing after it was tanned. (7) They used every part of an animal so that nothing was wasted.

1 What is the independent clause in sentence 2?

  A Carved to a point

  B a rock

  C a rock could serve

  D a rock could serve as a knife

2 What is the dependent clause in sentence 3?

  A Bones of some animals

  B some animals

  C became tools

  D None of the above

3 In sentence 4, which word identifies a dependent clause?

  A Because

  B hard,

  C , it

  D leather.

4 What is the independent clause in sentence 6?

  A Deerskin

  B Deerskin made soft, warm clothing

  C it was tanned

  D after it was tanned

5 In sentence 5, what is the dependent clause?

  A if the weather was bad

  B the weather

  C Artists might carve

  D None of the above

Home Activity Your child prepared for taking tests on independent and dependent clauses. Say a dependent clause (*after we eat dinner, before we leave home, when we go to the store*). Have your child add an independent clause to make a sentence.

Name _____

Fact and Opinion

- A **statement of fact** can be proved true or false.
- A **statement of opinion** is what someone thinks or feels. Statements of opinion often contain words that make judgments, such as *interesting* or *beautiful.*
- A single sentence might contain both a statement of fact and a statement of opinion.

Directions Read the following passage.

Jackie Robinson was the first African American baseball player to play in the modern major leagues. I think he was very brave to do so. He played in the Negro Leagues until 1947 when he was signed to the Brooklyn Dodgers. Despite controversy about Robinson breaking the color barrier, he was an immediate success. At the end of his first season, Robinson was named Rookie of the Year. During his third season, he won the league's batting title and was later named the league's Most Valuable Player. He was probably the most valuable player of the entire twentieth century.

For each statement, circle *F* or *O* to tell whether it is a fact or an opinion. Circle the words in the sentence that tell you the statement is an opinion.

F   O   **1.** I think Jackie Robinson was very brave to play in the major leagues.

F   O   **2.** Jackie Robinson was the first African American baseball player to play in the modern major leagues.

F   O   **3.** Jackie Robinson was probably the most valuable player of the twentieth century.

F   O   **4.** Jackie Robinson was named the league's Most Valuable Player.

F   O   **5.** The Brooklyn Dodgers signed Jackie Robinson.

© Pearson Education, Inc., 5

Home Activity Your child read a short passage and identified whether statements were facts or opinions. Read a newspaper article and an editorial about the same current event with your child. Have your child analyze which statements are facts and which are opinions.

Writing • Newsletter Article

Key Features of a Newsletter Article

- presents basic facts, and then adds details
- typically tells about an event, idea, or person
- includes direct quotations to enhance the article
- answers the questions: *Who? What? Where? When? Why? How?*

Muhammad Ali

Muhammad Ali is a legendary fighter. He began boxing when we was twelve, and in 1960 he won a gold medal at the Olympics in Rome. After that, he became a professional boxer.

Ali's career is legendary, and with good reason: Not only did he not lose a professional fight until 1971, but Ali was a great showman. He taunted opponents and relied on his quick reflexes to dodge punches in the ring. He once spoke of an opponent, "Frazier is so ugly that he should donate his face to the US Bureau of Wild Life."

In 1964, Ali defeated Sonny Liston to become the heavyweight champion of the world. He lost few fights after that and truly earned his reputation as one of our country's greatest athletes. He had many fans of all races at a time when it was hard for black Americans to rise above racial discrimination. He once said, "I wish people would love everybody else the way they love me. It would be a better world."

Though he faced countless tough opponents during his boxing career, Ali faced his biggest challenge when he was diagnosed with Parkinson's disease. Parkinson's is a disease that affects the central nervous system and causes people to lose control of their movements. While the disease may have silenced Ali (he speaks rarely because of the way in which Parkinson's affects his voice), it has not stopped him from fighting for what he believes. He continues to battle against Parkinson's disease as well as other problems, such as world hunger, poverty, and human rights' abuses. Even in the face of his greatest challenge, Muhammad Ali remains a champion.

1. Read the article. Who is the article about? What is he known for?

_____

_____

2. Name three important events in Muhammad Ali's life.

_____

_____

Vocabulary

Directions Draw a line to match each word on the left with its definition on the right.

1. fastball   firm belief in yourself

2. unique   a pitch thrown at high speed

3. weakness   laughing at; making fun of

4. confidence   having no like or equal

5. mocking   a weak point; slight fault

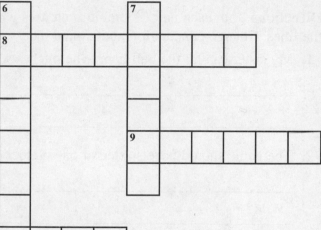

Check the Words You Know

___confidence
___fastball
___mocking
___outfield
___unique
___weakness
___windup

Directions Choose the word from the box to complete each clue and fill in the crossword puzzle.

DOWN

6. We have full _____ in his hitting.

7. Motions the pitcher makes before throwing the ball is called a _____.

ACROSS

8. If the ball is hit out of the diamond, it's in the _____.

9. A standout hitter like Hank Aaron is _____ among players.

10. Running too slowly is a player's major _____.

Write a News Report

On a separate sheet of paper, write a brief television news report about a baseball game, using as many vocabulary words as you can.

Home Activity Your child identified and used vocabulary words found in the biographical story *Satchel Paige.* Look in the sports pages of a newspaper and read a description of a sporting event with your child. See if you can identify any of the vocabulary words in the article.

Compound and Complex Sentences

A **simple sentence** expresses a complete thought. It has a subject and a predicate.
   The Negro League formed in 1920.

A **compound sentence** contains two simple sentences joined by a comma and a conjunction such as *and, but,* or *or.*
   The athletes played several games a day, and they traveled on a bus.

A **complex sentence** contains an independent clause, which can stand alone, and a dependent clause, which cannot stand alone. The clauses are joined by a word such as *if, when, because, until, before, after,* or *since.* In the following sentence, the independent clause is underlined once; the dependent clause is underlined twice.
   Many years would pass before the major leagues were integrated.

Directions Join each pair of simple sentences with *and, but,* or *or.* Write the compound sentence on the lines. Change punctuation and capital letters as necessary.

 1. My sister can hit the ball hard. She pitches well too.

   _____

   _____

 2. The game should have started at one o'clock. A thunderstorm began at 12:45.

   _____

   _____

 3. The teams will make up the game next Sunday. They will wait until the end of the season.

   _____

   _____

Directions Write *compound* after each compound sentence. Write *complex* after each complex sentence. Underline the word that joins the two clauses in each sentence.

 4. All players are important to a team, but the pitcher may be most important. _____

 5. If a pitcher strikes out batters, the opposing team cannot score. _____

 6. Outfielders must catch the ball when the batter hits a pop fly. _____

 7. The game was tied, and no one left the bleachers. _____

 8. The pitcher struck out two batters, but the third batter hit a home run. _____

School + Home **Home Activity** our child learned about compound and complex sentences. Have your child write a paragraph about a baseball game, using at least one compound sentence and one complex sentence.

Adding -ed, -ing

Spelling Words				
supplied	supplying	denied	denying	decided
deciding	included	including	admitted	admitting
occurred	occurring	qualified	qualifying	identified
identifying	delayed	delaying	satisfied	satisfying

Word Pairs Write the best list words to complete each sentence pair.

Were you **(1)**____ with lunch? I found the food very **(2)**____.

1. _____   2. _____

David **(3)**____ that he lost his key. **(4)**____ guilt was the best thing to do in his case.

3. _____   4. _____

Did you see the eclipse as it was **(5)**____? Last time one **(6)**____, I missed it.

5. _____   6. _____

The runners lined up for the **(7)**____ race. After that race, only three runners **(8)**____ for the team.

7. _____   8. _____

My lost cat has an **(9)**____ number tattooed on her skin. She was easily **(10)**____ as mine when she was found.

9. _____   10. _____

I have so much trouble **(11)**____ between piano or karate lessons. Have you **(12)**____ on a choice yet?

11. _____   12. _____

The coach used many **(13)**____ tactics, such as time-outs, during the game. Then the final quarter was **(14)**____ by the rain.

13. _____   14. _____

The school closet was fully **(15)**____ with pencils. Do you think the school will be **(16)**____ pencils for the big test?

15. _____   16. _____

Stop **(17)**____ that you broke the window! Even though you **(18)**____ it, we all saw your ball break the window.

17. _____   18. _____

Are you **(19)**____ olives on your shopping list? I've **(20)**____ carrots, celery, and pickles on my list.

19. _____   20. _____

Home Activity Your child wrote words with *-ed* and *-ing* endings. Select a list word and ask your child to tell you its meaning.

© Pearson Education, Inc., 5

Five-Column Chart

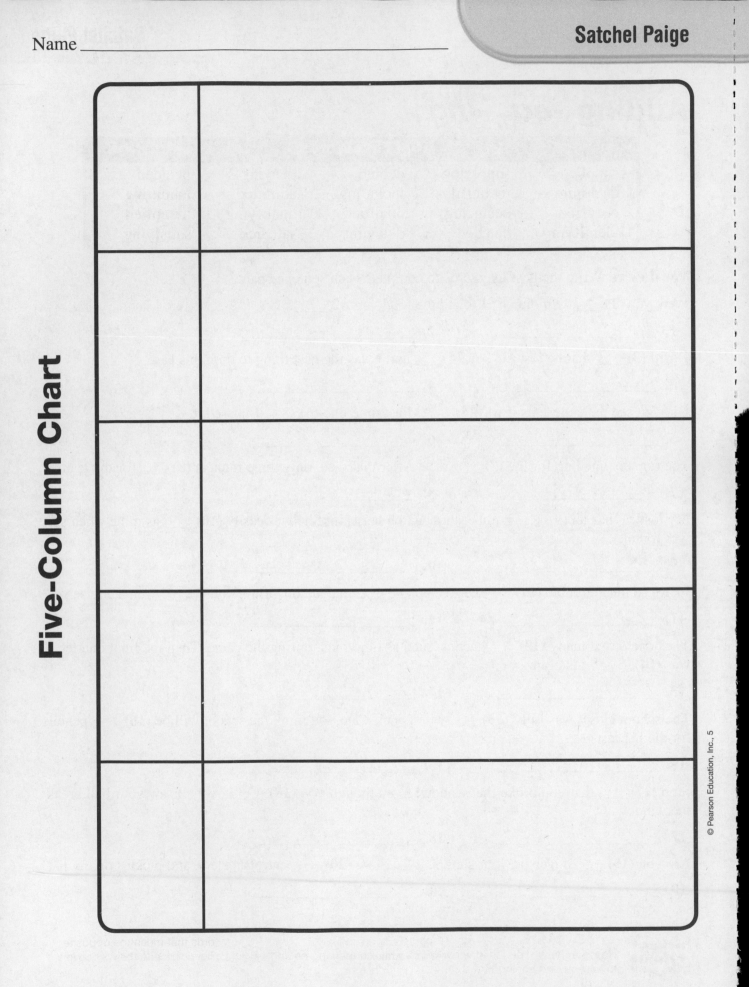

Vocabulary • Antonyms

- An **antonym** is a word that means the opposite of another word.
- Words such as *unlike, but,* and *instead* may indicate the presence of antonyms.
- A **thesaurus**, a book that lists words and their antonyms and synonyms (words that mean the same thing), may help bring *clarity,* instead of *confusion,* to your writing and reading.

Directions Read the following passage about an athlete. Then circle the words in the list below that complete antonym pairs. Use a thesaurus to help you.

Although Pete was born without legs, he refused the idea that his disability should slow him down. Unlike people who accepted misfortune as an excuse to give up, Pete tried to live life to the fullest. It was true that his wheelchair sometimes made him feel confined at school. But on the weekends, his favorite sport, rock climbing, made him feel completely free.

Pete always used caution when fastening his ropes and caring for his equipment. Two hundred feet above the rocky bottom of a canyon was no place for recklessness! Starting at the base of a cliff, he would pull his way up to the pinnacle. After straining for hours, he would reach the top, exhausted. Pete didn't feel that school was boring, but it didn't match the exhilarating feeling that came from the physical and mental challenge of rock-climbing.

1. **refused**	disability	excuse	accepted
2. **free**	confined	completely	favorite
3. **caution**	recklessness	rocky	caring
4. **base**	cliff	reach	pinnacle
5. **boring**	mental	feeling	exhilarating

Home Activity Your child read a short passage and identified antonyms, words that mean the opposite of each other. Have your child describe a familiar person, place, or thing using words and their antonyms, using a dictionary, glossary, or thesaurus for help.

Newspaper/Newsletter

- A **newspaper** is a daily (or weekly) periodical that contains timely news and information on current events and issues. Daily newspapers use various text features in providing local, regional, national, and international news. Most newspapers organize information from most important to least important. There are three basic kinds of articles found in a newspaper: news stories, editorials (opinions pieces), and feature stories.

- A **newsletter** is a brief publication by a group or organization that contains news of interest to that group's members.

Directions Read the newspaper page and answer the questions below.

HOMETOWN NEWS

JULY 17, 2004   **Cloudy, 72°**

BARR HITS FOR THE CYCLE–AGAIN

Hometown hero Billy Barr has been having the kind of week baseball players can only dream of. Last night, for the third game in a row, Barr hit for the cycle, which means he hit a single, a double, a triple, and a home run.

"I guess my grandfather was looking out for me tonight," said Barr after the game, referring to his grandfather Alan Barr, one of the first Negro League players to break into Major League baseball in the 1950s. Billy Barr frequently makes reference to his grandfather, who inspired his grandson to play baseball.

The last time a Major League player hit for the cycle in three consecutive games was in 1971, when Sal Bando did it for the Oakland Athletics.

Where do you find the date on a newspaper's front page?

_____

2. ow does the headline give you a clue to what the article will be about?

_____

3. Mo newspapers give the daily weather forecast somewhere on the front page. What is the fore st for this day?

_____

4. Why d the writer mention the last time this event occurred at the very end of the article?

_____

5. Which of three basic types of articles is this one?

_____

Directions Read the selection from the newsletter and answer the questions below.

EVANSTON SOCCER NEEDS VOLUNTEERS

Hello Evanston soccer families!

The new season starts soon, and we're busy getting our teams and coaches organized and ready to play. As you can imagine, it's a lot of work. So once again we are asking for volunteers to help us out for the new season. We are an all-volunteer organization. In 2006 we won the Regional Youth Soccer Organization of the year award because of the great support our volunteers gave us. We want to make it two in a row for this year!

Volunteering only requires a few hours of your time each week. Currently, we need about forty parents to volunteer to be coaches, referees, and board members.

We know how busy everyone's lives are, but our organization can only succeed if everyone pitches in. We hope you'll consider volunteering this year!

---

6. To whom is this newsletter story directed?

_____

7. Who do you think would receive a copy of this newsletter?

_____

_____

8. Name two things this newsletter specifically asks soccer parents to volunteer to do.

_____

9. Based on this newsletter article, who runs this youth soccer organization?

_____

10. If you wanted to find out about a big event happening in your city, where would you go to find out the information—a newspaper or a newsletter? Why?

_____

_____

_____

© Pearson Education, Inc., 5

Home Activity Your child answered questions about newspapers and newsletters. With your child, sketch out the front page of a newspaper based on your family's activities for the day.

Adding -ed, -ing

Proofread a Newspaper Article This is an article from a local weekly newspaper. Circle six spelling errors. Write the sentence with a punctuation error correctly. Write the corrections on the lines below.

Three Caught After Holdup
by Rosy Redeye

   The crime ocurred after midnight. The store's videotape identifyed three suspects. The store owner supplyed the license plate number to the police department. Geting the results took no time. The police quickly located the car and suspects They had trouble admiting their wrongdoing. However, in front of the judge, they deceided to admit everything. The police were satisfied that they had solved the case.

1. _____   2. _____

3. _____   4. _____

5. _____   6. _____

7. _____

Proofread Words Circle the correct spelling of the word.

8. occured	occurred	ocured
9. cluded	includid	includ
10. qualifed	qualifide	qualified
11. decded	decided	decieded
12. satesing	satisfying	satisfiying
13. admitted	admited	admetted
14. suppliing	sapplying	supplying

Home Activity Your child identified misspelled list words. Select three list words and ask your child to spell them.

Compound and Complex Sentences

Directions Read the passage. Then read each question. Circle the letter of the correct answer.

Just For Fun

(1) Every day Ted and I play catch, or we join our friends in a game. (2) We love the game, but we aren't the best players. (3) They say that if you practice every day, you will do better. (4) Today, our game was fun because the crowd cheered us on. (5) Although our team played well, we still lost. (6) Because we have fun, we don't mind an occasional loss. (7) We keep score, but we really play just for fun.

1 In sentence 1, *Every day Ted and I play catch* is what?

    A   Dependent clause

    B   Independent clause

    C   Compound sentence

    D   Complex sentence

2 In sentence 2, which word is a conjunction?

    A   We

    B   aren't

    C   but

    D   best

3 Sentence 4 is which type of sentence?

    A   Compound sentence

    B   Complex sentence

    C   Simple sentence

    D   Exclamatory sentence

4 What is the dependent clause in sentence 5?

    A   our team lost

    B   we still lost

    C   our team played well

    D   Although our team played well

5 Sentence 7 is which type of sentence?

    A   Compound sentence

    B   Complex sentence

    C   Simple sentence

    D   Exclamatory sentence

Home Activity Your child reviewed compound and complex sentences. Ask your child to explain how a game is played using some compound and complex sentences.

Cause and Effect

- A **cause** is what makes something happen. An **effect** is what happens as a result of the cause.
- An effect may have more than one cause, and a cause may have more than one effect.

Directions Read the following passage and complete the diagram below.

Colonists came to America seeking opportunities unavailable to them in Europe. England viewed America as a source of revenue and raw materials for its growing economy. As the colonies flourished, laws were enacted forcing them to buy finished products from England rather than allow colonists to make and sell their own. Laws including new taxes on tea, textiles, and sugar, made colonists resent the meddling in their everyday lives, and they felt restrained. When they protested, the king sent troops to enforce the laws and keep order. In response, colonists formed their own government and signed the Declaration of Independence. The king didn't accept this call for self-government, and soon the American Revolution began.

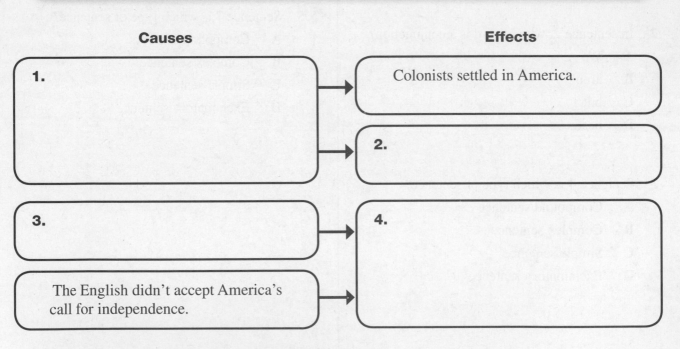

Causes

1.

Effects

Colonists settled in America.

2.

3.

4.

The English didn't accept America's call for independence.

5. Summarize the passage in one or two sentences.

_____

_____

© Pearson Education, Inc., 5

Home Activity Your child read a short passage and identified causes and effects. Look up an event in the U.S. Revolutionary War and discuss causes and effects described in the selection.

Writing • Expository Composition

Key Features of an Expository Composition
- tells about real people and events
- provides a description or explanation of something
- includes a topic sentence, a body, and a closing sentence

Education for All

Since our country's beginning, leaders of the United States have wanted to provide education for all citizens. When our nation was newly formed, schools were run by private groups and religious organizations. Thomas Jefferson thought that a government-run educational system was a good idea. Other leaders agreed.

The idea was a good one, but it seemed to be an impossible task. Who would pay for the schools and teachers? How would schools deal with the large numbers of immigrants that were coming into the U.S.? It was a difficult and confusing time, both politically and economically. Schools continued to serve only those students from wealthy families who could afford an education.

It was not until the 1800s that the modern idea of public education began to take shape. Horace Mann, of Massachusetts, was one of the first to reform the American educational system. He supported a public school system that provided education for all children. He extended the school year and worked to train teachers.

Over the years, other people worked to provide equal education for all students. Catherine Beecher worked to provide more educational opportunities for women. Booker T. Washington worked to provide education for African Americans.

Although today's educational system still faces challenges, we have come a long way since the Declaration of Independence. Students of every kind come together in schools and have the opportunity to receive an education. The impossible challenge of education for all has been overcome.

1. Circle the introduction and conclusion.

2. Underline the main idea of each body paragraph.

Vocabulary

Directions Choose the word from the box that best completes each sentence. Write the word on the line.

The wagon **1.** _____ forward, swaying and

almost throwing me out the back. My father and mother sat on the

driver's bench, **2.** _____ the foothills of the

Sierra Nevada Mountains below us. Like many immigrant families,

we traveled west over miles of dry, **3.** _____ lands.

Everything we could take from our past, or

4. _____, life back in Boston was now in our

covered wagon. We were headed to California to try our luck

5. _____ gold from the earth to make our fortune.

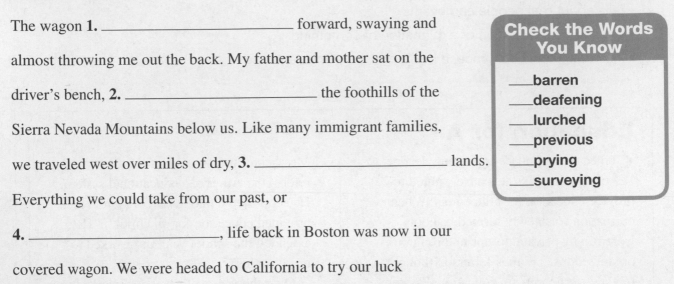

Check the Words You Know

___barren
___deafening
___lurched
___previous
___prying
___surveying

Directions Circle the word that has the same or nearly the same meaning as the first word in each group.

6. prying	extracting	attempting	bragging
7. surveying	wondering	planning	measuring
8. lurched	fumbled	staggered	belched
9. deafening	loud	empty	dry
10. previous	sinister	related	earlier

Journal Entry

On a separate piece of paper, write a journal entry as if you have just moved to another country. Use as many vocabulary words as you can.

Home Activity Your child identified and used vocabulary words from *Ten Mile Day*. Together with your child, read an article about life in another country. Talk with your child about what it might be like to live in that country.

Name _____

Common, Proper, and Collective Nouns

The names of particular persons, places, and things are **proper nouns.** Capitalize the first word and each important word of a proper noun.

I like Brady Parks in the book by Priscilla Cummings.

All other nouns are **common nouns**. They are not capitalized.

That author has written several exciting novels.

Capitalize the first word and all important words in a title.

Reflections on a Gift of Watermelon Pickle

Capitalize days of the week and months of the year.

Saturday, October 14

Capitalize the first letter of an abbreviated proper noun. Abbreviations often occur in addresses, titles and initials in names, and names of days and months. Most abbreviations end with a period. In addresses, state names are abbreviated using two capital letters and no period.

The envelope went to Mr. L. Cho, 11 E. 3rd St., Rochester, MN 55901.
It was postmarked Mon., Nov. 6.

A **collective noun** names a group, such as *family* or *class*.

Directions Write the proper noun from the box that matches each common noun. Add capital letters where they are needed.

sears tower	*my side of the mountain*
argentina	president jefferson
rebecca	"america the beautiful"

Common Noun   **Proper Noun**

1. girl _____

2. president _____

3. country _____

4. book _____

5. building _____

6. song _____

Home Activity Your child learned about common, proper, and collective nouns. Take a walk with your child. Have him or her pick out collective and proper nouns on signs and buildings in your community and practice speaking and writing them using proper capitalization.

Contractions

Spelling Words				
they're	you've	weren't	needn't	there'd
they've	mustn't	what'll	doesn't	hadn't
could've	would've	should've	might've	wouldn't
who've	shouldn't	who'd	this'll	couldn't

Contractions Write the contraction that can be made from the underlined words.

1. <u>They are</u> going on a school trip to the museum.

2. The students <u>need not</u> bring lunch because the museum has a cafeteria.

3. <u>This will</u> be an educational and fun trip.

4. Students <u>must not</u> bring umbrellas or backpacks.

5. Those <u>who have</u> taken the tour can go to the bookstore.

6. Those <u>who would</u> rather not go, please report to Room 303.

7. Students <u>should not</u> talk during the tour.

8. We <u>could not</u> hear the tour guide.

9. Anyone who <u>does not</u> behave will not be allowed to go on the next trip.

10. Students <u>would not</u> want to disappoint their teacher.

1. _____
2. _____
3. _____
4. _____
5. _____
6. _____
7. _____
8. _____
9. _____
10. _____

Questions Write the contraction that completes each answer.

11. Do they have any ice cream at the stand? No, ____ sold out.

12. Would they have eaten popcorn instead? Yes, they ____.

13. Should I have thrown the ball? Yes, you ____.

14. Could I have handed in my project yesterday? Yes, you ____.

15. Had the students worn these coats before? No, they ____.

16. Would there be another party? Yes, ____ be another party at a later date.

17. Might they have joined in the fun? They ____, but they had to go home.

18. Do you know what will happen tomorrow? No one knows ____ happen tomorrow.

19. Were the boys at the game? No, they ____ there.

20. Do you have my book? No, ____ put it in your locker.

11. _____
12. _____
13. _____
14. _____
15. _____
16. _____
17. _____
18. _____
19. _____
20. _____

School + Home

Home Activity Your child wrote contractions. Say two words and have your child combine them into a contraction and spell the word.

Web B

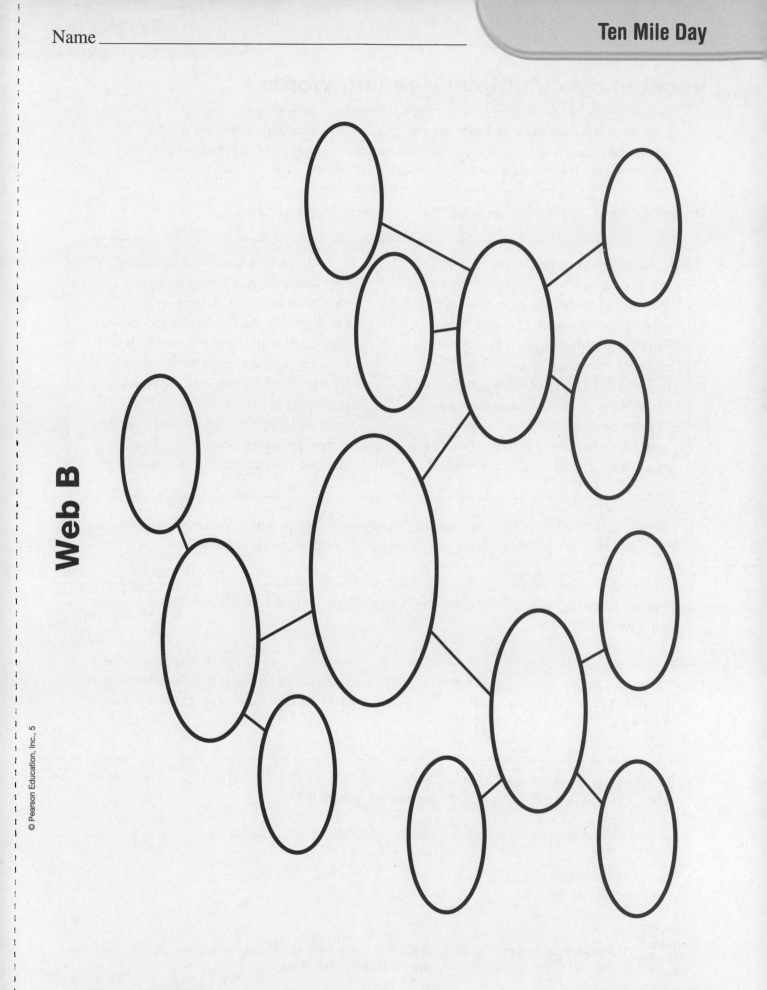

Vocabulary • Multiple-Meaning Words

- Some words have more than one meaning. They are called **multiple-meaning words.**
- **Context clues,** words and phrases near the multiple-meaning word, may help identify what a word means in a particular context, or situation.

Directions Read the following passage. Then answer the questions below.

Many things surprised Svetlana when she arrived with her family in America. Mostly, she was surprised at how many cars were on the road. Plenty of people had cars in Bulgaria, of course, but everyone here seemed to enjoy being mobile all the time. The sidewalks were clean and wide, but people would refuse to use them, even on sunny days. She noticed her neighbors getting in their cars just to go a half mile instead of walking.

In Bulgaria, when Svetlana needed to go somewhere a few miles away, she would usually ride her bicycle. Occasionally, she would ride the moped she shared with her whole family. It used little gas, and she could park it anywhere. To what did Svetlana attribute people's addictions to their automobiles? She supposed they believed owning a car was a sign of success. She took pride in the exercise she got walking and bicycling!

1. *Mobile* can mean "capable of motion" or "a hanging sculpture whose parts are moved by air currents." How do you think these two meanings are related to one another?

_____

2. *Refuse* can mean "indicate unwillingness" or "garbage." Which of these definitions is meant in the fourth sentence?

_____

3. *Moped* can mean "acted as if drained of energy by sadness" or "a small two-wheeled vehicle that has both an engine and pedals." Use a dictionary to find out how to pronounce *moped*. Which meaning uses two syllables?

_____

4. *Attribute* can mean "characteristic, quality, or trait" or "explain by suggesting a source or cause." Which definition is meant in the second paragraph?

_____

Home Activity Your child identified words with multiple meanings in a fictional passage. With your child, make a list of words you often use that have different meanings.

© Pearson Education, Inc., 5

Electronic Encyclopedia

An **encyclopedia** gives general information about many different subjects. An electronic encyclopedia can be found on a CD-ROM or on the Internet. They often have interactive graphics and maps, as well as audio files. They are organized alphabetically by **entries,** which are the topics. You can locate topics by using **keyword searches.** Keyword searches give you a list of topics to choose from. Cross-referencing is represented by hotlinks, which are underlined words.

Directions Read the entry from an online encyclopedia and answer the questions below.

Online Student Encyclopedia   🏠 home

Keyword Search [   ]

Print Article   E-Mail Article to Friend   Bookmark Article

Ellis Island
Ellis Island is located in New York Harbor. It was named after its owner in the 1770s, Samuel Ellis. Sixteen million immigrants to the United States passed through Ellis Island between 1892 and 1954. In 1965 the island became part of the Statue of Liberty National Monument. The immigration processing center is no longer used; however, it was made into a museum in 1990. The museum houses 400 years' worth of documents and artifacts about American immigration.

See also **Immigration**.

Back to top

1. How would you search for information about Samuel Ellis in this online encyclopedia?

_____

_____

2. Can you e-mail this article to a friend? Why do you think e-mailing an article would be useful?

_____

_____

3. Why do you think you would bookmark this page?

_____

_____

4. When was Ellis Island made into a museum?

_____

5. What is a simple way you could learn more about immigration?

_____

Directions Read the entry from an online encyclopedia and answer the questions below.

Online Student Encyclopedia 🏠 home

Keyword Search [_____]

<u>Print Article</u>   <u>E-Mail Article to Friend</u>   <u>Bookmark Article</u>

Ethnic Diversity

Most contemporary societies are, to some extent, ethnically diverse. History has played a part in making societies more diverse. Conquerors brought people from different societies to live under their rule. Sometimes people were brought to a new society as slaves. When they are not forced to move, people are often motivated to move to new societies to pursue economic improvement or to flee political and religious persecution. See also <u>ethnicity</u>, <u>immigration</u>.

Assimilation occurs when a newly arrived group takes on some (or all) of the customs and values of the dominant group. Assimilation can occur voluntarily or it can be forced by the dominant group.

Back to top

---

6. This selection is part of a larger topic entitled *Ethnic Groups*. What keywords would you use if you wanted to learn about how the Irish moved to America?

_____

7. If you wanted to learn about people who moved to flee religious persecution, what words would you use in the keyword search?

_____

8. How would you print this article?

_____

_____

9. According to the entry, what are three reasons people leave their native lands?

_____

_____

10. What is the difference between a dictionary and an encyclopedia?

_____

_____

_____

Home Activity Your child answered questions about electronic encyclopedias. With your child, search an encyclopedia for information about your family's ancestors and their native land or lands.

© Pearson Education, Inc., 5

Contractions

Proofread a Conversation Jack wrote this conversation between a waiter and a diner. Circle six spelling errors and one punctuation error. Write the corrections on the lines.

> "Whatll you have for lunch?" asked the waiter.
>
> "I'm not sure," said the diner.
>
> "Maybe this'll tempt you—lima bean casserole!" said the waiter.
>
> "Who'ud eat that for lunch?" asked the diner.
>
> "That's a very popular dish around here," said the waiter. "Theyr'e already lining up outside the door for the beans."
>
> "You were'nt kidding about a long line," said the diner. You mustn't miss this tasty treat," said the waiter.
>
> "Okay, I wouldn't want to miss your special dish!" said the diner. "Hey, this doesnt taste too bad at all!"
>
> "See what you would've been missing if you had'nt tried our special dish!" said the waiter.

Spelling Words

they're
you've
weren't
needn't
there'd
they've
mustn't
what'll
doesn't
hadn't

could've
would've
should've
might've
wouldn't
who've
shouldn't
who'd
this'll
couldn't

1. _____ 2. _____

3. _____ 4. _____

5. _____ 6. _____

7. _____

_____

Frequently Misspelled Words

that's
you're
doesn't

Proofread Words Circle the correct spelling of the word.

8. wood've   woud've   would've

9. dosn't   doesn't   dosen't

10. weren't   wearn't   wheren't

11. coudn't   culdn't   couldn't

12. might've   mihgt've   mitgth've

13. whatll   whatl'l   what'll

14. who'd   who'ld   whod'd

Home Activity Your child identified misspelled list words. Select contractions and ask your child to tell you how they were formed.

Common, Proper, and Collective Nouns

Directions Read the passage. Then read each question. Circle the letter of the correct answer.

The Railroad

(1) Grenville Dodge was the chief engineer of the Transcontinental Railroad.
(2) The book *the transcontinental railroad* tells how the railroad was built.
(3) The Union Pacific laid its first rails in july 1865. (4) Dr. Thomas c. Durant
ran that railroad. (5) Groups of workers were brought from China and Ireland.
(6) They began in Iowa and met the Central Pacific workers in Promontory, Utah.
(7) Hundreds of miles of these tracks remain today.

1 What change, if any, should be made in sentence 1?

  A Change *chief engineer* to **Chief Engineer**

  B Change the period to an exclamation mark

  C Change *engineer* to **engineer,**

  D Make no change

2 What change, if any, should be made in sentence 2?

  A Change *the transcontinental railroad* to **The Transcontinental Railroad**

  B Change *the book* to the **book,**

  C Capitalize railroad

  D Make no change

3 What is the collective noun in sentence 5?

  A Groups

  B brought

  C China

  D Ireland

4 What change, if any, should be made in sentence 3?

  A Change *Union Pacific* to **union pacific**

  B Change *july* to **July**

  C Change *its* to **it's**

  D Make no change

5 What change, if any, should be made in sentence 4?

  A Change the period to a question mark

  B Change *Dr. Thomas c. Durant* to a collective noun

  C Change *Dr. Thomas c. Durant* to **Dr. Thomas C. Durant**

  D Make no change

Write your own sentences about railroads using common, proper, and collective nouns. Read the sentences aloud.

Home Activity Your child prepared for taking tests on common, proper, and collective nouns. Have your child read an interesting magazine or newspaper article. He or she can circle the proper nouns, underline the common nouns, and put a box around collective nouns.

Short Vowel VCCV, VCV

Spelling Words				
distance	method	anger	problem	butter
petals	enjoy	perhaps	figure	channel
admire	comedy	husband	tissue	mustard
shuttle	advance	drummer	regular	denim

Alphabetize Write the twelve list words below in alphabetical order.

method	comedy
denim	anger
distance	enjoy
perhaps	advance
admire	figure
channel	regular

1. _____
2. _____
3. _____
4. _____
5. _____
6. _____

7. _____
8. _____
9. _____
10. _____
11. _____
12. _____

Hidden Words Each of these small words can be found inside one of the list words. Write the list word that contains the small word.

13. sue _____
14. rob _____
15. drum _____
16. pet _____

17. ban _____
18. shut _____
19. but _____
20. tar _____

Home Activity Your child learned to spell longer words with short vowel sounds. Find words with short vowel sounds in a magazine or newspaper and ask your child to spell them.

Four Kinds of Sentences

Directions Write *D* if the sentence is declarative. Write *IN* if the sentence is interrogative. Write *IM* if the sentence is imperative. Write *E* if the sentence is exclamatory.

1. Keesha's family took a kayak trip in Alaska. _____

2. How do you make a kayak go? _____

3. A kayaker uses a long paddle. _____

4. Please find out who invented kayaks. _____

5. Eskimos used kayaks thousands of years ago. _____

6. Eskimo kayaks were made of sealskins. _____

7. A kayak weighs as little as 32 pounds. _____

8. Wow, that is really light! _____

9. Can you ride a kayak in rapids? _____

10. Kayaking is so much fun! _____

Directions Complete each sentence with words from the box. Then write *D, IN, IM,* or *E* to identify the kind of sentence.

> can participate in races.   kayaking can be dangerous?
> include kayak races.   me how to kayak.
> exciting the rapids are!

11. Don't you think _____
    _____

12. Good kayakers _____
    _____

13. How _____
    _____

14. Please teach _____
    _____

15. The Olympic Games _____
    _____

Long Vowel VCV

Spelling Words				
fever	broken	climate	hotel	basic
vocal	native	silent	labor	spider
label	icon	agent	motive	vital
acorn	item	aroma	ego	solo

Analogies Write the word that completes each comparison.

1. Mouth is to taste as nose is to _____.

2. Loud is to deafening as quiet is to _____.

3. Cold is to chill as hot is to _____.

4. Robin is to bird as black widow is to _____.

5. Two is to duet as one is to _____.

6. Cottage is to house as inn is to _____.

7. Vine is to grape as oak tree is to _____.

8. Smart is to intelligent as self-esteem is to _____.

9. Friend is to enemy as stranger is to _____.

10. Sleep is to rest as work is to _____.

Word Clues Write the list word that fits each clue.

11. This includes a place's temperatures and rainfall. _____

12. You'll find one of these sewn into a piece of clothing. _____

13. You can't use something described as this. _____

14. An actor or athlete might employ this person. _____

15. A person who speaks up is described this way. _____

16. This explains why you did something. _____

17. This describes something that is absolutely necessary. _____

18. You can click on one of these on a Web site. _____

19. This is another word for a thingamajig. _____

20. This describes something that is not advanced. _____

Home Activity Your child learned to spell longer words with long vowel sounds. To practice at home, make up clues about words with long vowel sounds and ask your child to spell them.

© Pearson Education, Inc., 5

Subjects and Predicates

Directions Draw a line between the complete subject and the complete predicate in each sentence. Circle the simple subject and the simple predicate.

1. Many useful tools are made from metal.

2. Steel is an important metal for buildings and tools.

3. This alloy contains a mixture of iron and carbon.

4. An iron bar will rust over time.

5. Oxygen from the air mixes with the metal.

6. That orange deposit on the outside surface is called rust.

Directions Underline each simple subject once. Underline each simple predicate twice.

7. Many ranchers mend fences regularly.

8. The shiny thin wires are stretched from post to post.

9. Someone hammers the wire to the post.

10. The wooden posts stretch in a straight line.

11. This job is certainly hard work.

12. A work crew will repair the old fence today.

Directions Write *F* after a fragment. Write *R* after a run-on. Write *S* after a complete sentence.

13. Has been replaced by plastic in many products. _____

14. Plastic is hard and durable at the same time, it is lighter than metal. _____

15. Many parts of today's trucks and automobiles. _____

16. Plastic is not only lighter than metal it is cheaper too. _____

17. Just think about all the uses for plastic! _____

18. Many new materials from recycled products. _____

© Pearson Education, Inc., 5

Long Vowel Digraphs

Spelling Words

coast	feast	speech	wheat	Spain
paint	arrow	needle	charcoal	praise
faint	maintain	crease	grain	breeze
willow	appeal	bowling	complain	sneeze

Word Search Circle ten hidden list words. Words are down, across, and diagonal. Write the words on the lines.

```
F  B  W  S  P  P  A  D  E  Y
N  J  O  I  C  F  A  I  N  T
A  L  A  W  E  R  B  I  P  O
G  Q  W  I  L  L  O  W  N  M
R  T  U  A  E  I  S  U  G  T
A  E  S  P  A  I  N  N  W  Y
I  B  N  P  S  P  E  G  F  T
N  W  H  E  A  T  E  N  O  P
E  K  S  A  I  k  Z  E  N  l
H  E  E  L  C  R  E  A  S  E
```

1. _____   6. _____

2. _____   7. _____

3. _____   8. _____

4. _____   9. _____

5. _____   10. _____

Scramble Unscramble the list words and write them on the lines.

11. elende _____   16. timinana _____

12. worar _____   17. shepec _____

13. sarpie _____   18. larhocca _____

14. zerbee _____   19. stafe _____

15. ascto _____   20. aclimpon _____

Home Activity Your child learned to spell words with long vowel digraphs. Ask your child to give examples of and spell words with *ea, ee, ai, oa,* and *ow.*

Name _____

Independent and Dependent Clauses

Direction Write *I* if the underlined group of words is an independent clause.
Write *D* if it is a dependent clause.

1. <u>We visited the seashore</u> when we went to California. _____

2. <u>After we walked on the beach</u>, we swam in the ocean. _____

3. Although the sun was warm, <u>I shivered with cold</u>. _____

4. The water seemed even colder <u>because our skin was hot</u>. _____

5. <u>If you look far out</u>, you can see dolphins swimming. _____

6. <u>They leap out of the water</u> as if they are playing. _____

7. While I was resting on the sand, <u>I spied something</u>. _____

8. <u>When I looked through binoculars</u>, I saw seals. _____

9. As I watched, <u>some of them slid into the water</u>. _____

10. <u>Since I saw them</u>, I have read more about seals. _____

Directions Complete each sentence by adding a clause from the box. Underline the dependent clause in each sentence.

> it is the exception to the rule   while a seal has none   it can weigh up to 8,800 pounds
> because walruses are usually much bigger   you will remember it

11. You can tell a walrus and a seal apart _____

_____

12. In addition, a walrus has two large ivory tusks _____

_____

13. Because an elephant seal can grow very large, _____

_____

14. If you run into an elephant seal, _____

_____

15. When a male elephant seal is full grown, _____

_____

© Pearson Education, Inc., 5

Name _____

Adding *-ed, -ing*

Spelling Words				
supplied	supplying	denied	denying	decided
deciding	included	including	admitted	admitting
occurred	occurring	qualified	qualifying	identified
identifying	delayed	delaying	satisfied	satisfying

Antonyms Write the list word ending in *-ed* that has the opposite or nearly the opposite meaning.

1. unhappy   _____
2. on time   _____
3. denied   _____
4. excluded   _____
5. unsure   _____

Synonyms Write the list word ending in *-ed* that has the same or nearly the same meaning.

6. happened   _____
7. named   _____
8. furnished   _____
9. confessed   _____
10. able; competent   _____

Word Clues Write the list word that fits each clue.

11. what a lawbreaker is doing to avoid getting in trouble   _____
12. what an athlete is doing in a regional track meet   _____
13. what trucks full of food are doing at the supermarket   _____
14. what a jury is doing after a trial   _____
15. what an event is doing while it is underway   _____
16. what a detective is attempting by looking at fingerprints   _____
17. what a school is doing when it lets students in   _____
18. what an airline is doing to passengers when running late   _____
19. what a delicious meal is doing for your hunger   _____
20. what you are doing when you put everything in   _____

Home Activity Your child learned to spell words with *-ed* and *-ing*. To practice at home, name three verbs that describe after-school activities. Ask your child to spell each word with an *-ed* ending and with an *-ing* ending.

Name _____

Compound and Complex Sentences

Directions Write *compound* if the sentence is a compound sentence. Write *complex* if the sentence is a complex sentence.

1. Great athletes seem superhuman, but they often begin humbly. _____

2. After they learned the basics, they practiced hard. _____

3. If they had failures, they did not give up. _____

4. They kept at it for years, and they steadily improved. _____

Directions Combine each pair of simple sentences using the conjunction in ( ). Write the compound sentence on the line.

5. I like swimming. My dad coaches track. (but)

_____

6. I can jump like a rabbit. I can run like a racehorse. (and)

_____

7. I could choose one sport. I could do both. (or)

_____

8. According to Mom, I should decide. She is usually right. (and)

_____

Directions Write the word in ( ) that best connects the clauses. Underline the dependent clause in the complex sentence.

9. The players are tired _____ they have played two games. (because, if)

10. _____ they finish their games, they sleep on the bus. (Although, After)

11. They may travel for hours _____ they reach the next town. (before, since)

12. The driver will not wake them _____ the bus gets to the hotel. (after, until)

© Pearson Education, Inc., 5

Name _____

Contractions

Spelling Words				
they're	you've	weren't	needn't	there'd
they've	mustn't	what'll	doesn't	hadn't
could've	would've	should've	might've	wouldn't
who've	shouldn't	who'd	this'll	couldn't

Words in Context Complete each sentence with a list word.

1. The students want to raise money, so _____ selling fruit.

2. James had been to big cities, but he _____ ever been to Chicago.

3. I had never met anyone _____ been to Africa.

4. The electricity is out, so _____ we do about dinner?

5. We have practiced for weeks, so _____ be the best school play ever.

6. We'll go to the zoo after lunch since it _____ open until noon on Monday.

7. Several players _____ at the first soccer practice.

8. If there were a big storm, _____ be many people without food and water.

9. You may help chop vegetables, but you _____ cut yourself.

10. It's raining; I knew I _____ brought my umbrella.

11. I just realized I _____ left my spelling book at home.

12. You need to bring a pillow to camp, but you _____ bring a sleeping bag.

13. _____ you like to go swimming?

14. Sophia tried, but she _____ open the jar.

15. The Scotts aren't home; _____ gone to Florida for two weeks.

16. It may rain Saturday, but it _____ affect our plans.

17. Put the dressing on the salad after _____ mixed it well.

18. If I _____ found my cap, I would've worn it to the game.

19. I admire people _____ climbed high mountains.

20. Our team _____ won the game if we'd gotten one more goal.

 Home Activity Your child learned to spell contractions. Ask your child to give examples of and spell contractions formed with the words *are*, *not*, *have*, and *will*.

© Pearson Education, Inc., 5

Common, Proper, and Collective Nouns

Directions Write the proper noun from the box that matches each common noun. Add capital letters where they are needed.

> empire state building   mount everest   aunt lucinda
> *the dark is rising*   ms. simpson

Common Noun	Proper Noun
1. teacher	_____
2. building	_____
3. mountain	_____
4. book	_____
5. relative	_____

Directions Rewrite each sentence. Capitalize all proper nouns.

6. Americans in new york had good train service.

_____

7. People in san francisco and other parts of california needed better transportation.

_____

_____

8. A group of workers from china was led by mr. charles crocker.

_____

_____

9. The eastern and western tracks were joined in promontory, utah, on may 10, 1869.

_____

_____

10. The tracks met near aunt joan's house: 491 e. 1st st., ogden, ut 84404.

_____

_____

Notes for a Personal Narrative

Directions Fill in the graphic organizer with information about the event or experience that you plan to write about.

Summary

What happened? _____

When? _____

Where? _____

Who was there? _____

Details

Beginning

Middle

End

Words That Tell About *You*

Directions How did you feel about the challenge facing you at the beginning, middle, and end of your experience? Choose one or two words from the word bank to describe each part of your experience. Then add details that *show* readers each feeling.

anxious	thrilled	proud	inspired
disappointed	excited	contented	determined
dismayed	fearful	delighted	upset

Beginning _____

_____

_____

_____

_____

Middle _____

_____

_____

_____

_____

End _____

_____

_____

_____

_____

Combining Sentences

You can improve your writing by combining short simple sentences to make compound or complex sentences. This will create a smoother flow of ideas in your writing. The two sentences you combine must make sense together. You can create compound sentences by combining short sentences using the words *and, but,* or *or.* You can create complex sentences by combining short sentences with *if, because, before, after, since,* or *when.*

Directions Use the word in ( ) to combine the two sentences. Remember to capitalize the first word of the new sentence and to replace the first period with a comma.

1. (but) My big sister could climb the pine tree in the pasture. I had not tried.

   _____

   _____

2. (because) The first limbs were so high. I thought it was too hard.

   _____

   _____

3. (when) She boosted me up. I could just reach the lowest limb.

   _____

   _____

4. (and) The rough bark scratched my skin. Sticky pine resin oozed onto my hands.

   _____

   _____

5. (but) I was scared. I climbed to the very top of that pine.

   _____

   _____

Editing 1

Directions Edit these sentences. Look for errors in spelling, grammar, and mechanics. Use proofreading marks to show the corrections.

Proofreading Marks	
Delete (Take out)	ᴖ
Add	∧
Spelling	⬭
Uppercase letter	≡
Lowercase letter	/

1. A person who is born deaf generaly does not speak, but they have ways to communicate.

2. Like many deaf people, I use sign language, which includes hand signs, jestures,

   facial expressions and body movements.

3. Did you know the first school for the deaf was started in Hartford, connecticut, in 1817.

4. Laurent Clerc a founder of the school who knew a french form of sign language.

5. Users added to and adapted Clerc's sign language untill it become

   the sign language that we use today.

6. Hearing parents often learn sign language, they taught it to their deaf children.

7. I tell everyone that time and effort is neccesary to learn sign language.

8. Sign language helps people who cant here deal with communication challenges.

Now you'll edit the draft of your personal narrative. Then you'll use your revised and edited draft to make a final copy of your narrative. Finally, you'll share your written work with your audience.

Name_____

Compare and Contrast

- To **compare** and **contrast** two or more things is to show how things are alike and different.
- Some clue words are: *as, like, but,* and *however.*
- Sometimes writers do not use clue words when they compare and contrast things.

Directions Read the following passage. Fill in the columns below based on Alex's observations about the differences between the ocean and the lake back home.

Alex had never been to the ocean before, so he was excited when Joel invited him to go with Joel's family to Rhode Island. As they walked across the sand, Joel asked Alex if he knew anything about a "riptide," a strong flow of water near the shore. Afraid to admit he knew nothing about the sea, Alex told Joel he knew all about riptides. As he swam, Alex noticed several differences between lakes and oceans. Both were cold. Salty ocean water, however, seemed to allow him to float more easily. Ocean waves were also much larger than freshwater ones.

In the lake Alex remembered that small fish swam around his feet. In the ocean, crabs crawled over them. Suddenly, Alex and Joel heard a whistle blow. A lifeguard was ordering swimmers out of the water. Alex heard the lifeguard explain to a man that the riptides had become too strong and had pulled a young girl hundreds of feet from shore. She had almost drowned. Alex gulped. He knew he had put himself in danger by not being honest about his ignorance.

Lake	Ocean
fresh water	1.
2.	3.
4.	5.

Home Activity Your child compared and contrasted details from a short passage. Discuss with your child two places that you have gone for enjoyment. Ask your child to make a list of the similarities and differences.

© Pearson Education, Inc., 5

Comprehension 109

Writing • Description

Key Features of a Description

- vivid language helps readers visualize a scene
- can be part of a longer story
- often provides details that tell what something smelled, felt, or tasted like, as well as how something looked or sounded

Remembering Grandpa

When my grandfather died, I learned that I could keep his memory alive through objects he left behind. I went to his house after the funeral and looked through the shelves and closets. They were filled with items from my past.

His coat still smelled like his cologne. I felt the soft material and inhaled the musky, sweet scent. I looked through stacks of photographs to remember his smile. We used to drink root beer together, so I looked in the refrigerator. He still had root beer! I took one and carried it around with me. It tasted so good. It made me happy to remember sharing root beer with Grandpa.

It started to rain outside. As I listened to the sound of the soft rain and my parents talking in the living room, I realized that Grandpa can still be alive in my heart. I can be sad and happy at the same time. I took his coat and some photographs home with me. When I wear his coat, I remember him with pride.

1. List three sensory words from the selection.

_____

2. What is the writer like? How do you know?

_____

_____

Vocabulary

Directions Choose the word from the box that best matches each definition. Write the word on the line.

_____ 1. handheld, usually small tool used for pinching or grasping

_____ 2. put out of sight; hidden

_____ 3. harsh, firm, or strict

_____ 4. wood floating in a body of water or washed upon the shore of one

_____ 5. any of a group of aquatic organisms ranging in size from microscopic to hundreds of feet

Check the Words You Know

___algae
___concealed
___driftwood
___hammocks
___lamented
___sea urchins
___sternly
___tweezers

Directions Choose the word from the box that best completes each sentence. Write the word on the line to the left of the sentence.

_____ 6. The underwater divers harvested dozens of the spiny _____ at the ocean floor to sell to a local restaurant featuring Japanese specialties.

_____ 7. The brother and sister swung lazily in _____, side by side under a tree, discussing how to spend the last summer day before school started.

_____ 8. He hid, or _____, his glee at winning the match, trying at least to appear to have a sense of good sportsmanship.

_____ 9. The puppy's ears drooped and her tail stopped wagging as I _____ lectured her about not chewing on the furniture.

_____ 10. The pop music star _____, or complained about, the loss of his youth and fame, sadly wondering if another fan letter would ever arrive in the mail.

Write a Description

On a separate sheet of paper, write a description of what life might be like as a dolphin, living in the ocean. Use as many of the vocabulary words as you can.

Home Activity Your child identified and used vocabulary words from *At the Beach*. With your child, write a story about making the choice to be honest with someone.

Name _____

Regular and Irregular Plural Nouns

Plural nouns name more than one person, animal, place, or thing.
- Add *-s* to form the plural of most nouns.
  swing/swings   animal/animals
- Add *-es* to nouns ending in *ch, sh, x, z, s,* and *ss*.
  fox/foxes   bush/bushes   church/churches
- If a noun ends in a vowel and *y*, add *-s*.
  monkey/monkeys   toy/toys
- If a noun ends in a consonant and *y*, change *y* to *i* and add *-es*.
  blueberry/blueberries   pony/ponies   penny/pennies
- Some nouns have **irregular plural** forms. They change spelling.
  woman/women   tooth/teeth   ox/oxen
- For most nouns that end in *f* or *fe*, change *f* to *v* and add *-es*.
  wife/wives   wolf/wolves   thief/thieves
- Some nouns have the same singular and plural forms.
  salmon   trout   sheep

Directions Underline the plural nouns in each sentence.

1. Some seals live on those beaches.

2. The fishermen in boats near shore caught many salmon.

3. You will see crabs, shells, and driftwood near the water.

4. Don't burn your feet on the hot sand.

5. Clumps of seaweed float on the waves.

Directions Cross out each incorrectly spelled plural noun. Write the correct spelling above the word you crossed out.

6. You can find blueberrys on the bushs near those beaches.

7. The skys over the shore were clear, but we saw cloudes in the distance.

8. The four woman prepared the picnic, and the children played with beach toyes.

Home Activity Your child learned about regular and irregular plural nouns. Take a walk and have your child identify people, places, animals, and things in groups. Ask him or her to spell these plural nouns correctly.

© Pearson Education, Inc., 5

Digraphs *th*, *sh*, *ch*, *ph*

Spelling Words				
shovel	southern	northern	chapter	hyphen
chosen	establish	although	challenge	approach
astonish	python	shatter	ethnic	shiver
pharmacy	charity	china	attach	ostrich

Word Meanings Write the list word that has the same or nearly the meaning as the underlined words.

1. We are raising money for a <u>worthy cause</u>.

2. The <u>drugstore</u> filled the prescription for the medicine.

3. The United States is made up of many people from different <u>cultural</u> groups.

4. The restaurant chain wants to <u>set up</u> a diner in the community.

5. We set the table with our best <u>glass dishes</u>.

6. The best way to succeed is to constantly <u>test</u> yourself.

7. The cool breeze sent a <u>quiver</u> down my back.

8. I never would have <u>selected</u> those blue jackets.

9. The plane was on its final <u>move</u> toward the runway.

10. The magic trick was crafted to <u>amaze</u> the unsuspecting audience.

1. _____
2. _____
3. _____
4. _____
5. _____
6. _____
7. _____
8. _____
9. _____
10. _____

Classifying Write the list word that belongs in each group.

11. even if, while, ___

12. cobra, rattler, ___

13. fasten, join, ___

14. spade, scoop, ___

15. episode, part, ___

16. smash, break, ___

17. peacock, swan, ___

18. dash, line, ___

11. _____
12. _____
13. _____
14. _____
15. _____
16. _____
17. _____
18. _____

© Pearson Education, Inc., 5

Home Activity Your child matched list words with synonyms. Name two list words and see if your child can give a synonym for each.

Web A

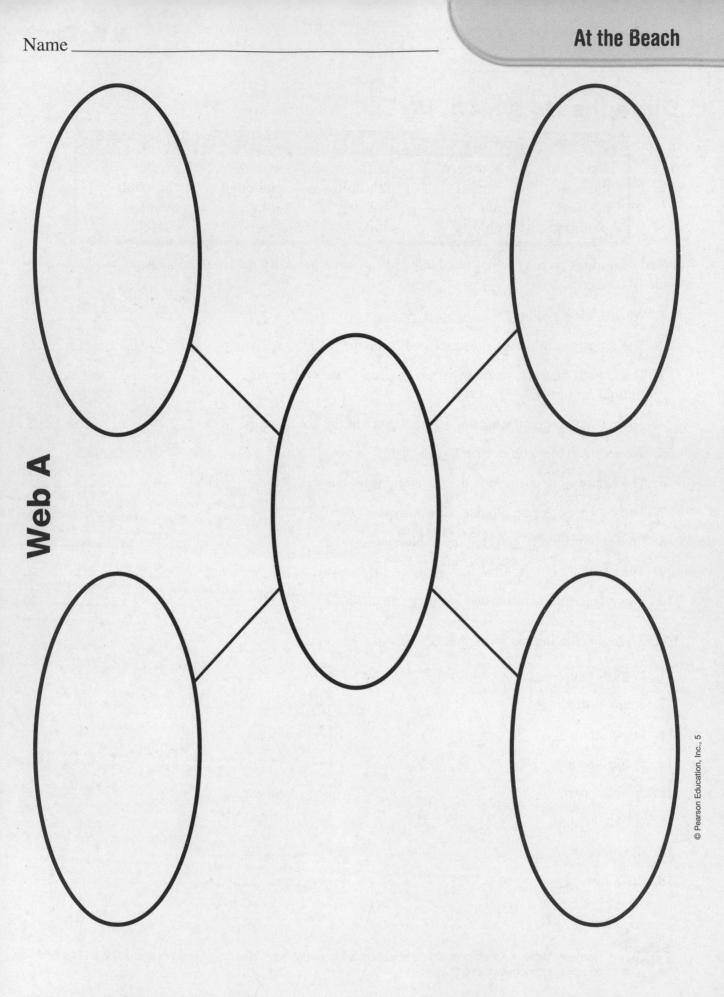

Vocabulary · Unfamiliar Words

- **Dictionaries** provide alphabetical lists of words and their meanings.
- Sometimes looking at the words around an unfamiliar word can't help you figure out the word's meaning. If this happens, use a dictionary to find the meaning.

Directions Read the following passage. Look for unfamiliar words and nearby clues as to their meaning. Use a dictionary to look up words you do not know. Then answer the questions below.

The smell of brine was heavy in the air as Dr. Jansen dipped the glass vial into the brackish water of the salt marsh. She was collecting the samples from the grassy place by the shoreline to test for pollution. Many species of animals depended on the ecosystem of the marsh to remain healthy.

She held up the last vial and peered through the grass as she screwed the plastic cap on the top. She smiled, knowing that even though the water seemed to be absent of life, tiny organisms swam through the cloudy, muddy water. Glancing out over the waves in the distance, Dr. Jansen smiled. The seagulls whirling above the sand, swooping and diving in circles, always seemed to act as if there might be bread crumbs in Dr. Jansen's laboratory bag.

1. Smell can travel a long way in the air. What does *brine* smell like? How do you know?

_____

2. Find a word in the passage whose meaning cannot be guessed by context clues nearby. Look up the word in a dictionary and provide the definition.

_____

3. What might the word *vial* mean, based on the context clues in the paragraph? Use a dictionary to check your answer.

_____

4. What might the word *whirling* mean, based on the context clues in the paragraph? Use a dictionary to check your answer.

_____

5. The word *organism* is not easily guessed by context clues in the passage. Look the word up in a dictionary and provide its definition.

_____

Home Activity Your child identified unfamiliar words that could be defined using a dictionary or glossary. Work with your child to identify unfamiliar words in a newspaper or magazine article. Ask your child if he or she needs to use a dictionary to find the meaning of the words. If so, ask your child to look up at least one definition in a dictionary or glossary.

Reference Book

A **reference book** is a type of **manual.** Manuals usually contain instructions, either for immediate use or for reference. A grammar reference book is a manual for using language. Like other manuals, it usually has a table of contents, an index, sections, illustrations, and explanations. Be sure to consult a grammar reference book whenever you have questions about grammar.

Directions Use the following chart from a grammar book to answer the questions below.

Quick Reference Chart for Using Apostrophes

Use an apostrophe

1. to show possession

   John's dad collects bottle caps.

2. with *s* to show the plural of letters

   b's   j's   t's

3. to show the omission of a letter, letters, or numbers

   We'll   class of '05   won't

Study the following contractions and notice the letter or letters that have been omitted to form the contraction.

they're — they are   *she'll — she will*

we've — we have   *let's — let us*

o'clock — of the clock   *aren't — are not*

---

1. What is the title of the chart?

   _____

2. Which of the ways the apostrophe is used would apply if you were describing ownership of something?

   _____

3. How would you use an apostrophe to contract the words *must* and *not*?

   _____

4. How many different uses does the chart show for an apostrophe?

   _____

5. Insert apostrophes where needed in the following sentence: *Ill take my moms casserole over to the neighbors house at 6 oclock.*

   _____

   _____

Directions Use the following table of contents from a grammar book to answer the questions below.

6. Which chapter would you look in for a usage question about the word *theirs*?

_____

7. Why do you think grammar books are organized by individual parts of speech?

_____

_____

8. What kind of words might you find in the section on "Personal Pronouns"?

_____

9. If you were having trouble writing a word that showed ownership, in which section of the grammar book would you look?

_____

10. Why might the short essays at the end of each chapter be included in a grammar book?

_____

_____

© Pearson Education, Inc., 5

Home Activity Your child answered questions about grammar reference books and manuals. With your child, find a manual to an item in your house (computer, refrigerator, television, phone, etc.) and read through the table of contents to see how it is organized. Does it make sense? Could you easily find an answer to a question or a problem by using the manual?

Digraphs *th, sh, ch, ph*

Proofread a Poster Circle five spelling errors. Find one sentence with a punctuation error. Write the corrections on the lines.

Come to the charaty auction for the
new recreation center.

Help dig the building site. Buy a chance to
shovle some earth.

Bid on and buy, wonderful prizes from around the world!

Challange yourself in contests and games.

Bid on lovely china figures and platters.

Sample delicious northurn and southern cooking!

Time: Saturday, from 9 A.M. to 6 P.M.

Place: The old pharmecy building

1. _____   2. _____

3. _____   4. _____

5. _____

6. _____

_____

Proofread Words Circle the correct spelling of the word.

7. The ending of the book will _____ you.
   astonish   astonesh   astonash

8. I need a stapler to _____ the poster to the bulletin board.
   attatch   attach   atach

9. Music is my _____ field of study.
   chosen   chozen   choicen

10. I want to read a _____ a day.
    chaptar   shapter   chapter

11. Numbers, such as sixty-five, are written with a _____.
    hiphen   hyphen   hipfen

12. The _____ in the zoo was 12 feet long.
    pythn   python   pithon

Home Activity Your child identified misspelled list words. Select words with two different digraph sounds and ask your child to spell them.

© Pearson Education, Inc., 5

Regular and Irregular Plural Nouns

Directions Read the passage. Then read each question. Circle the letter of the correct answer.

Ocean Life

(1) There are interesting creatures at the beach. (2) Many bunchs of tiny fish swim near shore. (3) Seashells once covered the bodies of some animals. (4) Some loud geese fly overhead in autumn. (5) Many varieties of animals live in the ocean. (6) You might see sharks with sharp teeth. (7) Whales enjoy long lives in the deep sea's.

1 In sentence 1, *creatures* is which type of noun?

  A Regular plural

  B Irregular plural

  C Proper

  D Collective

2 What change, if any, should be made in sentence 2?

  A Change the period to an exclamation mark

  B Change *bunchs* to **bunches**

  C Change *shore* to **shore,**

  D Make no change

3 How many plural nouns are in sentence 3?

  A 1

  B 2

  C 3

  D 4

4 What are the irregular plural nouns in this paragraph?

  A geese, seashells, bunches

  B bodies, animals, varieties

  C bodies, geese, varieties

  D geese, teeth, lives

5 What change, if any, should be made in sentence 7?

  A Insert a comma after *lives*

  B Change *sea's* to **seas**

  C Capitalize *deep sea's*

  D Make no change

Home Activity Your child prepared for taking tests on regular and irregular plural nouns. Have your child make flash cards with singular and plural forms of nouns on opposite sides. Use the cards to help him or her learn plural forms.

Sequence

- The **sequence** of events is the order in which they take place, from first to last.
- Clue words such as *first, next,* and *then* may show sequence in a story or article, but not always. Other clues are dates and times of day.
- Sometimes two events happen at the same time. Clue words that show this are *meanwhile* and *in that same year.*

Directions Read the passage and complete the time line below.

On July 1, 1863, a small group of Union cavalry troops fought off a larger force of Confederate soldiers near Gettysburg, Pennsylvania. By the next day, most of both armies had arrived. That day, the Confederates attacked both sides of the Union forces. However, the Union troops held them off. The third day, the Confederates attacked the middle of the Union forces with more than 12,000 soldiers. The attack was called Pickett's Charge. Again, the Union forces held. The Confederates had to retreat.

The Battle of Gettysburg was the turning point of the Civil War. After it, the Union victories began to mount. In November, President Lincoln visited the battle site and delivered a speech to honor those who fought there. The speech was called the *Gettysburg Address.*

1. _____ 2. _____ 3. _____ 4. _____

5. Was Pickett's charge a success? Explain.

_____

_____

School + Home **Home Activity** Your child read a short passage and answered questions about the sequence of events described in it. Read a newspaper or magazine article with your child and discuss the sequence of events it describes.

Writing • Informal Letter

Key Features of an Informal Letter

- contains a heading, salutation, and closing
- has a casual tone
- usually written to someone you know well
- contains a body, or the paragraphs that make up the main part of the letter

April 12, 2011

Dear Patrick,

Has the news hit Texas yet? It turns out that I'm a big hero! I fearlessly braved dazzling heights in order to save a precious member of the Scales family. Okay, so I'm exaggerating a little, but let me tell you the story.

I was on my way home from soccer practice when I found Melissa crying in front of her house. You remember Melissa, right? She is in the grade below us, and her family lives two houses down from mine. I asked why she was upset, and she said the family's pet rat had escaped. It was on the outer ledge that surrounds the second-story windows.

"Good riddance," I thought. "Who wants a pet rat?" But Melissa was so upset that I knew I had to help. I told her to get a ladder, and I would see what I could do.

Now you know how I feel about heights. I'm not going to say I'm a wimp, but heights are personally terrifying to me. Nevertheless, I asked Melissa to hold the base of the ladder steady, and I boldly faced my fear.

My foot was shaking as I placed it on the first step. I tightly gripped the rung above me with each new step I took. When I got to the top, all I could think about was the sound my body would make as it hit the ground. I saw the rat shivering near the corner of the ledge. I grabbed it quickly and stuck it in my pocket. I don't think anybody in the history of the world has ever come down a ladder as fast as I did that day!

Melissa was overjoyed. Her family invited me to dinner to thank me for saving their favorite pet. I sure wish you could have been there to see it! Things haven't been the same since you moved away. Even a big rat adventure is not as fun without my best pal. Hope you can visit soon.

Your friend,

Eric

1. Read the letter. Circle and label the date, greeting, and closing.

2. What is the relationship between Eric and Patrick? Underline clue words that help you know.

Vocabulary

Directions Choose the word from the box that best matches each definition. Write the word on the line.

_____ 1. great praise and honor

_____ 2. a male horse

_____ 3. a small container for carrying water or other drinks

_____ 4. a joining of two or more people or things into one

_____ 5. a fight with words

_____ 6. a group of countries or states working together

_____ 7. a fight against your own government

> ## Check the Words You Know
>
> ___canteen
> ___confederacy
> ___glory
> ___quarrel
> ___rebellion
> ___stallion
> ___union

Directions Choose the word from the box that best matches the underlined words in the sentences.

8. Some soldiers earn <u>valor</u> on the field of battle.

_____

9. A soldier or a scout might carry a <u>water bottle</u>.

_____

10. A cavalry trooper would ride a <u>horse</u> into battle.

_____

Write a Newspaper Article

On a separate sheet of paper, write a newspaper article announcing that the United States has gone to civil war. Use as many vocabulary words as you can.

© Pearson Education, Inc., 5

Home Activity Your child identified and used vocabulary words from *Hold the Flag High*. With your child, discuss the meaning of each word from the vocabulary list. Help your child use each word in a sentence.

Name _____

Possessive Nouns

A **possessive noun** shows ownership. A **singular possessive noun** shows that one person, animal, place, or thing has or owns something. A **plural possessive noun** shows that more than one person, animal, place, or thing has or owns something.

- To make a singular noun show possession, add an apostrophe (') and -s.
  a bird's song
- To make a plural noun that ends in -s show possession, add an apostrophe (').
  several weeks' work
- To make a plural noun that does not end in -s show possession, add an apostrophe (') and -s.
  the women's papers

Directions Write each noun as a possessive noun. Write *S* if the possessive noun is singular. Write *P* if the possessive noun is plural.

1. friends _____ _____

2. story _____ _____

3. freedom _____ _____

4. mornings _____ _____

5. children _____ _____

6. milk _____ _____

Directions Add an apostrophe (') or an apostrophe (') and -s to make each underlined word possessive. Write the sentence on the line.

7. A <u>soldier</u> life can be difficult.

_____

8. Would the <u>Union</u> flag fly in the South?

_____

 Home Activity Your child learned about possessive nouns. Have your child look at some sale ads and make up sentences about them using possessive nouns.

Irregular Plurals

Spelling Words

staffs	ourselves	pants	scissors	loaves
volcanoes	chiefs	buffaloes	flamingos	beliefs
echoes	shelves	quizzes	sheriffs	dominoes
thieves	measles	avocados	chefs	pianos

Words in Context Write a list word to complete each sentence.

1. When people get sick with ____, they get red spots all over their bodies.   1. _____

2. The ____ of many people's voices bounced around the canyon walls.   2. _____

3. At the assembly today, two people played ____ for the students.   3. _____

4. Do you like fresh ____ in your salad?   4. _____

5. The ____ were caught red-handed with the loot.   5. _____

6. The old ____ were sagging under the weight of the books.   6. _____

7. It took eight different ____ to prepare the huge banquet.   7. _____

8. When ____ erupt, clouds of ash can travel many miles.   8. _____

9. These ____ are made with waterproof material.   9. _____

10. We have ____ for everyone who needs to cut ribbons.   10. _____

Classifying Write the list word that belongs in each group.

11. deputies, detectives, ___   11. _____

12. checkers, chess, ___   12. _____

13. values, opinions, ___   13. _____

14. cranes, herons, ___   14. _____

15. deer, cattle, ___   15. _____

16. employees, workers, ___   16. _____

17. breads, buns, ___   17. _____

18. us, we, ___   18. _____

19. leaders, bosses, ___   19. _____

20. tests, examinations, ___   20. _____

Home Activity Your child wrote list words that are irregular plurals to complete sentences and word groups. Name two list words and ask your child to use each in a sentence.

© Pearson Education, Inc., 5

Story Sequence A

Title _____

Beginning

Middle

End

Vocabulary • Dictionary/Glossary

- As you read, you may find unknown words, or words you do not understand. You can use a **dictionary** or a **glossary** to look up the word.
- Dictionaries and glossaries provide alphabetical lists of words and their meanings.
- A dictionary is a book of words and their meanings, and a glossary is a short dictionary at the back of some books.
- An **entry** shows the spelling of a word and comes before the definition.

Directions Read the passage. Then answer the questions below using a dictionary or your glossary.

John Sharp took a drink from the canteen as he looked over his army's campsite. It seemed to stretch for miles. Campfires, canvas tents, and blue uniforms were everywhere. This was the Army of the Potomac, the army of General Grant and President Lincoln. Most of the soldiers John knew were not here for glory. Most did not have a quarrel with individual Southerners, either. No, most of the men he knew were there to save that most precious union—the United States of America. For that reason, all of them knew they must give everything to stop the Southern rebellion.

1. What is the definition of *quarrel*? Put it in your own words.

_____

_____

2. What is a canteen? What part of speech is it?

_____

_____

3. What is the meaning of *union*? Use it in a sentence.

_____

_____

4. Look for the word *glory* in a dictionary. What other words could you use to replace *glory* in the passage?

_____

_____

5. Explain why a dictionary would give more complete information for an entry than a glossary.

Home Activity Your child used a dictionary to find out the meanings of unknown words. Choose a few words that your child does not know. Have your child use a dictionary to find their meanings.

© Pearson Education, Inc., 5

Parts of a Book

The **parts of a book** include its **cover, title page, copyright page, table of contents, chapter titles, captions, section heads, glossary,** and **index.** Examining the parts of a book can give you clues about a book and help you to learn as much as you can from it.

Directions Read the following copyright page and answer the questions below.

A Three-Minute Speech: Lincoln's Remarks at Gettysburg

Text copyright © 2003 Jennifer Armstrong
Illustration copyright © 2003 Albert Lorenz

First Aladdin Paperbacks
An imprint of Simon and Schuster Children's Publishing Division
1230 Avenue of the Americas
New York, NY 10020
All rights reserved, including the right of reproduction, in whole or in part in any form.

Library of Congress Control Number 2002107413
ISBN: 0-689-85622-9

---

1. What is the purpose of a copyright page in a book?

_____

2. The owner of the copyright is listed after the symbol © and the year of publication. Who owns the copyright for the text of this book?

_____

3. What do you think it means to own the copyright to a book?

_____

_____

4. Who published this book? When was the book published?

_____

5. How might numbers such as the Library of Congress number or ISBN number be used?

_____

_____

Directions Study the following table of contents page. Then answer the questions below.

CONTENTS

Forming a Government
for the United States of America

6. What does the title tell you this book will be about?

_____

_____

7. What do the numbers on the right side of the page represent? Where would you find a chapter about checks and balances?

_____

8. What can you learn about a book by studying its table of contents before you read?

_____

9. How many chapters are in the book? What is the purpose of chapter titles?

_____

_____

10. What other sections can you find in this book besides chapters?

_____

Home Activity Your child learned about the parts of a book. Pick out several kinds of books around your home (nonfiction, a reference book, a work of fiction) and examine the parts of the different books together.

Story Sequence A

Title _____

Beginning

Middle

End

© Pearson Education, Inc., 5

Irregular Plurals

Proofread a List Circle six spelling errors and one capitalization error.
Write the corrections on the lines.

> six scissers
>
> three sets of metal shelfes
>
> twenty sets of dominos
>
> ten waterproof pants
>
> one dozen avacadoes
>
> three toy pianos
>
> twenty-five loavs of bread
>
> three pink Lawn flamingoes

staffs
ourselves
pants
scissors
loaves
volcanoes
chiefs
buffaloes
flamingos
beliefs

echoes
shelves
quizzes
sheriffs
dominoes
thieves
measles
avocados
chefs
pianos

1. _____   2. _____

3. _____   4. _____

5. _____   6. _____

7. _____

Proofread Words Circle the correct spelling of the word.

8. Almost everyone used to get ____ as a child.

  meesles   measels   measlcs

9. We had pop ____ in math and science today.

  quizes   quizzes   quizzez

10. People are entitled to their own ____.

  beliefs   believes   beleifs

11. We have no one to blame except ____.

  ourselfs   hourselves   ourselves

12. The music school has three ____ for students to use.

  pianos   pianoes   painos

Frequently Misspelled Words

know
knew

Home Activity Your child identified misspelled list words. Select three words from the list and ask your child to spell them to you.

© Pearson Education, Inc., 5

Possessive Nouns

Directions Read the passage. Then read each question. Circle the letter of the correct answer.

In the Officers' Tent

(1) Ending the battle, the generals men fled from the Southern soldiers. (2) Back at camp, the men ate, rested, and inspected the gear. (3) A soldier's shoes wore out quickly, and his rifle needed daily care. (4) Success often depended on an army's supplies. (5) In the officers' tent, we talked about these little details that were so important. (6) Later, I took out my children's letters. (7) I read them quietly while the enlisted men wrote letters home.

1   What change, if any, should be made in sentence 1?

   A   Change the period to an exclamation mark

   B   Change *generals* to **general's**

   C   Change *soldiers* to **soldier's**

   D   Make no change

2   What is the possessive noun in sentence 2?

   A   camp

   B   gear

   C   men

   D   None of the above

3   In sentence 3, what type of noun is *soldier's*?

   A   Singular possessive

   B   Plural possessive

   C   Irregular plural

   D   none of the above

4   What are the plural possessive nouns in this paragraph?

   A   officers', children's

   B   soldier's, officers', children's

   C   army's, officers', children's

   D   officers', children's, his

5   What change, if any, should be made in sentence 7?

   A   Insert a comma after *them*

   B   Change *letters* to **letter's**

   C   Change *enlisted men* to **enlisted men's**

   D   Make no change

Home Activity Your child prepared for taking tests on possessive nouns. Have your child write several sentences describing a favorite toy or game using possessive nouns (such as *the bear's nose* or *the pieces' shapes*).

© Pearson Education, Inc., 5

Possessive Nouns

Directions Read the passage. Then read each question. Circle the letter of the correct answer.

In the Officers' Tent

(1) Ending the battle, the generals men fled from the Southern soldiers. (2) Back at camp, the men ate, rested, and inspected the gear. (3) A soldier's shoes wore out quickly, and his rifle needed daily care. (4) Success often depended on an army's supplies. (5) In the officers' tent, we talked about these little details that were so important. (6) Later, I took out my children's letters. (7) I read them quietly while the enlisted men wrote letters home.

1 What change, if any, should be made in sentence 1?
   A Change the period to an exclamation mark
   B Change *generals* to **general's**
   C Change *soldiers* to **soldier's**
   D Make no change

2 What is the possessive noun in sentence 2?
   A camp
   B gear
   C men
   D None of the above

3 In sentence 3, what type of noun is *soldier's*?
   A Singular possessive
   B Plural possessive
   C Irregular plural
   D none of the above

4 What are the plural possessive nouns in this paragraph?
   A officers', children's
   B soldier's, officers', children's
   C army's, officers', children's
   D officers', children's, his

5 What change, if any, should be made in sentence 7?
   A Insert a comma after *them*
   B Change *letters* to **letter's**
   C Change *enlisted men* to **enlisted men's**
   D Make no change

Home Activity Your child prepared for taking tests on possessive nouns. Have your child write several sentences describing a favorite toy or game using possessive nouns (such as *the bear's nose* or *the pieces' shapes*).

Irregular Plurals

Proofread a List Circle six spelling errors and one capitalization error.
Write the corrections on the lines.

> six scissers
> three sets of metal shelfes
> twenty sets of dominos
> ten waterproof pants
> one dozen avacadoes
> three toy pianos
> twenty-five loavs of bread
> three pink Lawn flamingoes

1. _____   2. _____

3. _____   4. _____

5. _____   6. _____

7. _____

Proofread Words Circle the correct spelling of the word.

8. Almost everyone used to get _____ as a child.

   meesles   measels   measles

9. We had pop _____ in math and science today.

   quizes   quizzes   quizzez

10. People are entitled to their own _____.

    beliefs   believes   beleifs

11. We have no one to blame except _____.

    ourselfs   hourselves   ourselves

12. The music school has three _____ for students to use.

    pianos   pianoes   painos

Spelling Words
staffs
ourselves
pants
scissors
loaves
volcanoes
chiefs
buffaloes
flamingos
beliefs
echoes
shelves
quizzes
sheriffs
dominoes
thieves
measles
avocados
chefs
pianos

Frequently Misspelled Words
know
knew

Home Activity Your child identified misspelled list words. Select three words from the list and ask your child to spell them to you.

Compare and Contrast

- When you **compare and contrast** things you tell how they are similar and how they are different.
- Sometimes clue words point out comparisons and contrasts, but not always.
- You can compare and contrast different things you read about with one another and also with what you already know.

Directions Read the following passage.

In Japan during the Middle Ages, samurai warriors followed a code of honor called bushido. Following the code meant being a fierce fighter, an athlete, a kind and honest person, and living a simple life. During the same time in Europe, knights were expected to follow the code of chivalry. Chivalry meant you were loyal to a lord (the landowner who hired the knight), brave in battle, and honorable in all deeds. They wore different armor. Samurai primarily wore protective leather gear, and knights wore heavy metal armor.

Directions Complete the following graphic organizer. List similarities and differences between *chivalry* and *bushido*. Then compare them with a code with which you are familiar.

Similarities in Text	Differences in Text	Compared with What I Know
1.	3.	4.
2.	Samurai wore leather gear, and knights wore metal armor.	5.

Home Activity Your child read a short passage and made comparisons and contrasts. Read two of your child's favorite stories and compare and contrast the main characters.

Writing • Poem

Key Features of a Poem

- uses verse to communicate ideas
- may use poetic techniques, rhyme, or sound patterns
- often includes sensory details or vivid language

The Day I Learned to Fish

I learned how to fish last May.
My sister wanted me to play.
She took a look at my thick book
And made me trade it for a hook.

We took our poles and bags of bait
To the pond beyond the gate.
We flung our lines, sat really still,
And leaned back flat against the hill.

Splash splash went my fish!
I caught a big one for my dish.
But I put mine back anyway
To catch again another day.

1. Circle the rhymes in each stanza.

2. Underline the words that show the use of onomatopoeia.

3. List one example of assonance.

_____

Vocabulary

Directions Draw a line to connect each word on the left with its definition on the right.

1. astonished   thankfulness

2. procession   to suggest favorably

3. behavior   surprised greatly

4. gratitude   way of acting

5. recommend   something that moves forward

Directions Choose a word from the box that best completes each sentence. Write the word on the line to the left.

_____ 6. The unequal ____ of food caused some people to be hungry.

_____ 7. Without the generosity of his supporter, or _____, Guillermo would not be able to afford to go to art school.

_____ 8. In some cultures, animals are highly valued and considered ____, or holy.

_____ 9. Our family's holiday____ are passed from generation to generation.

_____ 10. I was surprised by the contest results, but the winner was truly ____.

Write a Thank-You Note

On a separate sheet of paper, write a thank-you note to someone who has helped you in some way. Use as many vocabulary words as you can.

Home Activity Your child identified and used vocabulary words from the story *The Ch'i-lin Purse*. With your child, read a story about someone who performed an act of kindness. Look for words in the story that describe that person.

Action and Linking Verbs

A complete sentence has a subject and a predicate. The main word in the predicate is a **verb**. An **action verb** tells what the subject does.
  The little boy *cried* often.

A **linking verb** links, or joins, the subject to a word or words in the predicate. It tells what the subject is or is like.
  He *seemed* very quiet. He *was* a good sport.

- Action verbs show actions that are physical (*hike, build*) or mental (*remember, approve*).
- Common linking verbs are forms of the verb *be* (*am, is, are, was, were*).
- These verbs can be linking verbs: *become, seem, appear, feel, taste, smell,* and *look.* (*The cake appears fresh. It looks tasty.*) However, some of them can also be used as action verbs. (*A boy appeared suddenly. He looked at the food.*)

Directions Write the verb in each sentence of the paragraph. Then write *A* if the verb is an action verb. Write *L* if it is a linking verb.

1. Are you a spoiled child? **2.** A spoiled child always gets his or her way. **3.** He or she seems selfish. **4.** Parents pamper the child too much. **5.** This treatment often leads to misery. **6.** The world responds better to a kind, unselfish person. **7.** Compassion is good for the giver and the receiver. **8.** The most unselfish people appear happiest.

1. _____ _____   5. _____ _____

2. _____ _____   6. _____ _____

3. _____ _____   7. _____ _____

4. _____ _____   8. _____ _____

Directions Write a verb from the box to complete each sentence. On the line after the sentence, write *A* if the verb is an action verb. Write *L* if it is a linking verb.

> combine   is   showed   are

9. The dragon _____ popular in Chinese culture. _____

10. In ancient China, people _____ great respect for dragons. _____

11. Dragons _____ not real animals. _____

12. They _____ traits of many animals. _____

Home Activity Your child learned about action and linking verbs. Read a story together. Have your child point out several action verbs and linking verbs.

Name _____

Vowel Sounds with *r*

Spelling Words				
snore	tornado	spare	appear	career
square	report	prepare	pioneer	chair
beware	smear	repair	sword	ignore
order	engineer	resort	volunteer	declare

Words in Context Write the list word to complete each sentence.

1. I ____ loudly when I sleep.

2. Have you heard the saying "The pen is mightier than the ____"?

3. The ____ fixed the machine.

4. It was hard to ____ the loud sirens outside.

5. The mayor will ____ a holiday.

6. I have to bring my worn shoes to the shop for ____.

7. We have guests staying in our ____ bedroom.

8. A triangle has three sides; a ____ has four sides.

9. The father told his small child to ____ of traffic.

10. Did the weather ____ forecast rain?

1. _____
2. _____
3. _____
4. _____
5. _____
6. _____
7. _____
8. _____
9. _____
10. _____

Word Groups Write the list word that best completes the group.

11. cyclone, twister, ___

12. show up, materialize, ___

13. job, employment, ___

14. lead the way, be the first, ___

15. get ready, make, ___

16. offer, give aid, ___

17. ask for, send for, ___

18. blur, spread, ___

19. vacation spot, dude ranch, ___

20. seat, bench, ___

11. _____
12. _____
13. _____
14. _____
15. _____
16. _____
17. _____
18. _____
19. _____
20. _____

© Pearson Education, Inc., 5

School + Home **Home Activity** Your child wrote list words that have vowel sounds with *r*. Select three words and ask your child what they mean.

Name _____

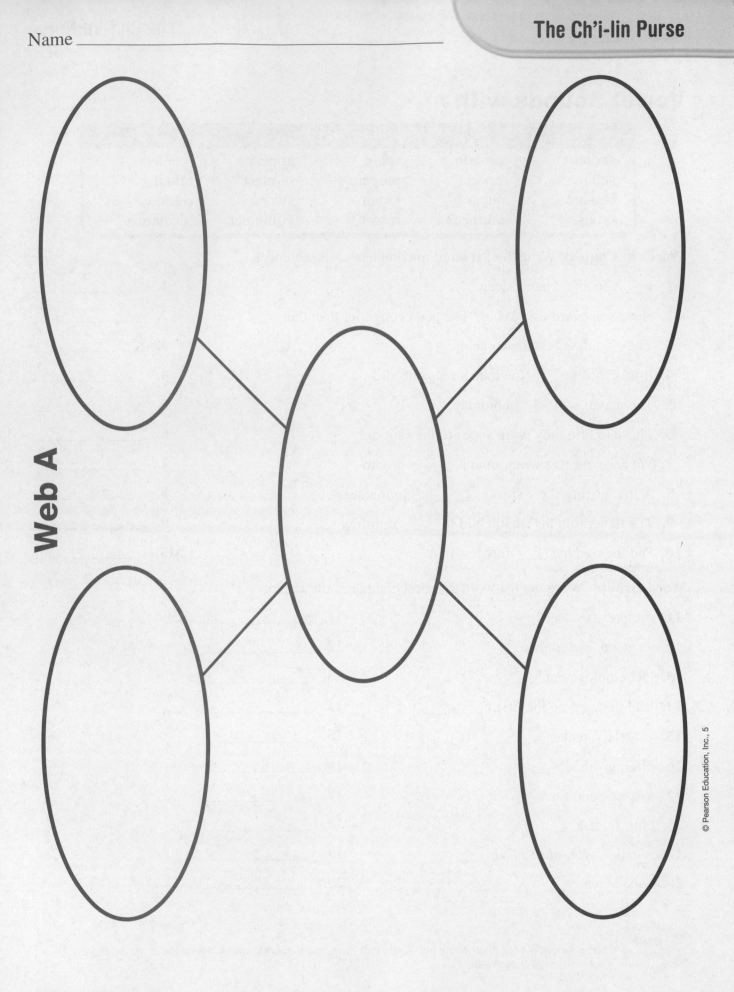

Web A

Vocabulary • Greek and Latin Roots

- **Greek and Latin roots** are used in many English words.
- When you find a word you don't know, recognizing the root can help you figure out its meaning.
- The Latin word *bene* means "well" or "good," as in *beneficial, benefit,* and *benefactor.*
  The Latin word *gratus* means "pleasing," as in *gratitude* and *grateful.*

Directions Read the following passage. Then answer the questions below.

I always wanted to be a singer, and I worked very hard. I was grateful to be able to do something that I loved. However, it was difficult to make enough money to pay for lessons. One day, I was singing in a procession to celebrate the holidays. Afterward, my mother found me and she was very excited.

"This is Mrs. Kazarian. She is a benefactor for young artists and wants to pay for your lessons at the school of music," my astonished mother said.

"I'd like to recommend a teacher who works with young singers," Mrs. Kazarian told us. A month later, I was practicing with my new teacher. Each day, I am filled with gratitude that I am the beneficiary of Mrs. Kazarian's generosity. Without her support, I would not have had this chance.

1. What is the Latin root in *grateful*? How does the root help you understand its meaning?

_____

_____

2. What is the Latin root in *benefactor*? How does the root help you understand its meaning?

_____

_____

3. What do you think *beneficiary* means? How does the root help you understand its meaning?

_____

_____

4. How does the root in *gratitude* help you understand its meaning?

_____

5. Write a sentence using a new word with either the root *bene* or *gratus*.

_____

Home Activity Your child read a short passage and used Latin roots to identify the meanings of unfamiliar words. Look in a dictionary with your child to find other words that use the Latin roots *bene* and *gratus*.

Textbook/Trade Book

A **textbook** usually teaches one subject, such as social studies or math. Textbooks contain **chapter titles, headings, subheadings,** and **vocabulary words.** A **trade book** is any book that is not a textbook, a periodical, or a reference book.

Directions Study the following table of contents from a textbook. Then answer the questions below.

1. What subject do you think this textbook is for? Why?

_____

_____

2. Based on the table of contents, how are the sections of this textbook organized?

_____

_____

3. In what chapter and section can you learn about the city of Tokyo?

_____

4. In what section would you find a summary of the whole chapter?

_____

5. What do you think is included in the sections in italics? How can you tell?

_____

_____

Directions Read the back cover of this trade book. Then answer the questions below.

The Chinatown Dragon
The Day My Little Sister Was Eaten by a Paper Dragon

THE UPDATED AND EXPANDED TENTH ANNIVERSARY EDITION

It has been ten years since Lori Liu first gave us her collection of stories about her childhood growing up in San Francisco's Chinatown. That edition let people from all over the world get a close-up glimpse of a Chinatown few outsiders are able to see. Readers eagerly immersed themselves in sights and sounds, like the time her little sister ran straight into the mouth of a block-long paper dragon during a parade!

Since then, Ms. Liu has captured new tales full of music, action, humor, and good food to add to the original collection. This edition celebrates the original collection and expands it in a way that will delight her long-time readers.

"Lori Liu's stories are full of the laughter and tears common to everyone's childhood."
    —Mario Michelin, *San Jose Post*

"If you have ever enjoyed an afternoon's visit to Chinatown, you will love Lori Liu's collection of stories, *The Chinatown Dragon*. You will feel like a resident rather than a visitor."
    —Beatrice Kelly, *San Francisco News*

---

6. What kind of book is this?

_____

7. What is the book's title? What do you think the subtitle, which is in italics, means?

_____

8. What is special about this edition of the book?

_____

_____

9. Why are quotes included on the back cover?

_____

10. If you wanted to look up information about the history of Chinese New Year, would you look in a textbook or a trade book? Why?

_____

_____

Home Activity Your child read a short passage and then answered questions about textbooks and trade books. With your child, look at a trade book and a textbook. Ask your child to explain the difference between the two types of books.

© Pearson Education, Inc., 5

Vowel Sounds with *r*

Proofread a Story Ramon wrote this story about sharing a room with his brother. Circle six spelling errors. Find one sentence with a punctuation error. Write the corrections on the lines.

snore
tornado
spare
appear
career
square
report
prepare
pioneer
chair

beware
smear
repair
sword
ignore
order
engineer
resort
volunteer
declare

My Brother

Mom asked my brother and me to voluntier to give up our rooms for our visiting grandparents. So, we're sharing the spair attic room, but it's no fun. My brother snores, and it's hard to ignoure it. Just as I was falling asleep, he snored like a tornadoe. That was it I threw my pillow at him. It knocked over the lamp, which hit the chare with a loud pop. This did not apear to disturb him at all. I gave up and slept in the hallway as a last resort.

1. _____   2. _____

3. _____   4. _____

5. _____   6. _____

7. _____

Proofread Words Circle the correct spelling of the word.

8. A ____ is someone who leads the way for others.

   pioneer   pioner   pieneer

9. The knight wore a brightly polished ____ on his hip.

   swoard   sword   sworde

10. The ____ is a wind funnel.

    tornado   tornardo   tornadoe

11. Be careful or you'll ____ the fresh paint.

    smear   smere   smeer

12. I asked the bike shop to ____ my flat tire.

    ripare   repair   repare

© Pearson Education, Inc., 5

Home Activity Your child identified misspelled list words in a paragraph. Ask your child to tell you the six patterns used in the list words to spell vowel sounds with *r*.

Action and Linking Verbs

Directions Read the passage. Then read each question. Circle the letter of the correct answer.

The Three Letters

(1) In ancient China, the Three Letters were important to a marriage. (2) The Betrothal Letter formally announced the engagement. (3) After that, a Gift Letter was <u>necessary</u>. (4) The letter listed gifts for the wedding. (5) The Wedding Letter _____ the third formal document. (6) The groom's family <u>presented</u> it to the bride's family. (7) This letter formally accepted the bride into the groom's family.

1 What kind of verb is *were* in sentence 1?

  A Action verb (physical)

  B Action verb (mental)

  C Linking verb

  D Not a verb

2 What kind of verb is *announced* in sentence 2?

  A Action verb (physical)

  B Action verb (mental)

  C Linking verb

  D Not a verb

3 In sentence 3, what type of verb is the underlined word?

  A Action verb (physical)

  B Action verb (mental)

  C Linking verb

  D Not a verb

4 In sentence 6, what type of verb is the underlined word?

  A Action verb (physical)

  B Action verb (mental)

  C Linking verb

  D Not a verb

5 Which linking verb best completes sentence 5?

  A were

  B was

  C are

  D become

© Pearson Education, Inc., 5

Home Activity Your child prepared for taking tests on action and linking verbs. Read a newspaper article with your child. Have your child circle action verbs and underline linking verbs in the article.

Author's Purpose

- The **author's purpose** is the reason or reasons the author has for writing.
- An author may write to persuade, to inform, to entertain, or to express himself or herself.

Directions Read the passage. Then answer the questions below.

Dirty beaches are disgusting. I hate to see the shore of a lake or ocean dotted with candy wrappers, soda bottles, or other bits of garbage. Garbage on beaches is more than an eyesore. It also kills wildlife. Animals such as fish and turtles may eat drifting garbage they find in the water. If they do, they may choke. The plastic six-pack yokes from soda cans are dangerous to birds. Birds often become tangled in the plastic and die. To help keep beaches clean, you can volunteer on clean-up days. People who clean beaches help protect the environment and are definitely doing the right thing!

Directions Fill in the diagram below based on the passage.

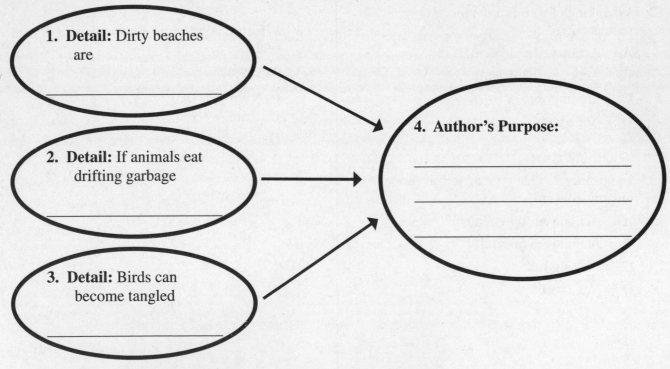

1. **Detail:** Dirty beaches are
_____

2. **Detail:** If animals eat drifting garbage
_____

3. **Detail:** Birds can become tangled
_____

4. **Author's Purpose:**
_____
_____
_____

5. How do the details provided help support the author's purpose?

_____

_____

© Pearson Education, Inc., 5

Home Activity Your child analyzed the author's purpose in a passage about beaches. Challenge him or her to read an editorial from a newspaper and explain the author's purpose for writing the editorial. Ask your child to explain who the author is trying to persuade or convince.

Name _____

Writing • Personal Narrative

Key Features of Personal Narratives

- uses the first-person point of view *(I, me)*
- tells a story about a real event in your life
- shares thoughts and feelings about an event or time

Mom or Me

I knew it was going to be the best birthday party I'd ever been to. Maria's parents really wanted to celebrate her turning ten years old. They planned out an entire day of fun for her and her friends, including me!

We were going to begin the day with breakfast at a great restaurant called Good Morning. After that, we would go to a water park to ride the water slides and swim in the wave pool. Then, we would go back to Maria's house for a cookout, including hot dogs and hamburgers. Later that night we would roast marshmallows and make s'mores while we sat by the campfire. It was a day full of my favorite things!

The party was still a month away when I found out the date—August 2, my mom's birthday! Every year, my mom asked for only one gift from her family for her birthday. She asked that we all be there with her to celebrate. We usually had dinner together and either went to see a movie or rented movies to watch at home. How could I go to Maria's all-day birthday party and still be there for my mom's birthday dinner?

When I revealed my problem to my mom, she smiled and told me that it was okay for me to miss her birthday this year. But she looked sad. I know how she liked having her whole family together. I knew what I had to do.

Everyone had a great time at Maria's birthday party except for me—but that's because I wasn't there! I surprised my mom by staying home to celebrate her birthday with her and our family. She was so happy that she cried. She told me that I gave her the best present she had ever gotten. I showed her just how important she is to me.

1. Reread the selection. What difficult decision does the writer face? How does he or she solve the problem?

_____

_____

2. What are the writer's thoughts and feelings about the friend's birthday party?

_____

Vocabulary

Directions Choose a word from the box that best matches each clue. Write the word on the line.

_____ 1. shoved or pushed against someone roughly

_____ 2. a member of a group of Native Americans living mainly in New Mexico, Arizona, and Utah

_____ 3. a band or chain worn for ornament around the wrist or arm

_____ 4. a high, steep hill that has a flat top and stands by itself

_____ 5. a clear blue or greenish blue precious stone, used in jewelry

_____ 6. a dwelling used by the Navajo Indians of North America

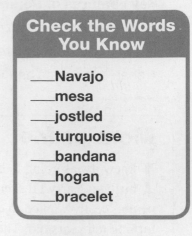

Check the Words You Know

___Navajo
___mesa
___jostled
___turquoise
___bandana
___hogan
___bracelet

Directions Choose the word from the box that best completes each sentence. Write the word on the line.

The southwestern United States is home to Native Americans such as the

7. _____. A typical member might have lived in a 8. _____. He or

she may have worn a head scarf, such as a 9. _____. Navajos also wore jewelry

made of 10. _____.

Write About a Character

On a separate sheet of paper, write a description of one character from the story. Describe the character's appearance and personality. Use as many vocabulary words as you can.

© Pearson Education, Inc., 5

School + Home **Home Activity** Your child identified and used vocabulary words from *A Summer's Trade*. With your child, find out information on Native Americans in Texas. Use the vocabulary words to discuss them.

Main and Helping Verbs

Verbs that are made up of more than one word are **verb phrases.** In a verb phrase, the **main verb** names the action. The **helping verb** helps tell the time of the action. Some common helping verbs are *has, have, had, am, is, are, was, were, do, does, did, can, could, will, would,* and *should.*

- The main verb is always the last word in a verb phrase. (The horse is <u>looking</u> at me.)
- There may be more than one helping verb in a verb phrase. (She <u>has been riding</u> horses a long time.)
- Helping verbs such as *is* and *are* show that action is happening in the present. (Annamae *is reading* about the Navajo.) *Was* and *were* tell that the action happened in the past. (The class *was reading* about the Navajo last month.) *Will* tells that the action is going to happen in the future. (We *will study* the Anasazi next week.)

Directions Underline the verb phrase in each sentence. Put one line under each helping verb and two lines under the main verb.

1. I have ridden horses for years.

2. Right now I am mending my old saddle.

3. Some friends will visit the ranch tomorrow.

4. They have come to the ranch many times.

5. The wind is blowing gently on the range.

6. Within two days, we will have reached the mountains.

7. You can see everything from the mountain.

8. My chores will be waiting for me.

9. My sister is reminding me to take pictures.

10. People from the city should visit the ranch often.

 Home Activity Your child learned about main and helping verbs. Have your child model an activity such as making a sandwich. Ask him or her to explain the job using sentences with verb phrases.

Final Syllables *-en, -an, -el, -le, -il*

Spelling Words				
example	level	slogan	quarrel	scramble
evil	oxygen	wooden	double	travel
cancel	chuckle	fossil	toboggan	veteran
chisel	suburban	single	sudden	beagle

Word Clues Write the list word that matches each clue.

1. a kind of laugh

2. not urban or rural

3. a kind of sled

4. a gas we breathe

5. something made of oak or maple

6. something that has been preserved in stone

7. a small argument

8. two of something

9. only one

10. a kind of hound dog

1. _____

2. _____

3. _____

4. _____

5. _____

6. _____

7. _____

8. _____

9. _____

10. _____

Synonyms Write a list word that has the same meaning as the underlined word.

11. I found a perfect <u>model</u> of my favorite color.

12. Did you <u>mix</u> the eggs for me?

13. The sculptor had to carefully <u>carve</u> the marble bit by bit.

14. One of my goals is to <u>journey</u> around the world.

15. The ground was <u>flat</u> and then it dropped down steeply.

16. The <u>wicked</u> queen tried to poison her enemy.

17. The company's <u>motto</u> was "Right every time!"

18. The politician was <u>an old hand</u> at running elections.

19. I had to <u>call off</u> my dentist appointment today.

20. The storm was <u>swift</u> and unexpected.

11. _____

12. _____

13. _____

14. _____

15. _____

16. _____

17. _____

18. _____

19. _____

20. _____

School + Home

Home Activity Your child matched list words to meanings. Ask your child to tell you the meanings of three list words.

Story Sequence C

Title _____

Characters

Setting

Problem

Events

_____

_____

_____

_____

_____

_____

_____

_____

Solution

Vocabulary · Context Clues

As you read, you will find unfamiliar words. You can use context clues to figure out the meaning of a new word. **Context clues** are found in the words and sentences around an unfamiliar word.

Directions Read the following passage. Then answer the questions below. Look for context clues around unknown words to determine their meanings.

Centuries ago, high on a mesa in the heart of the Great Basin Desert, a man jostled his heavy pack into place on the back of his horse. Nearby, a woman dipped a canteen into a creek. On her arm she wore a bracelet of turquoise, the same color as the sky above. These people were members of the Navajo tribe.

They traveled across the desert to gather with other Navajos. From Arizona to New Mexico, they looked for a peaceful home, free from the aggressive Spaniards who had settled in what is now the southwestern United States. Today, most of northeastern Arizona is home to the Navajo Nation.

1. What does the word *mesa* mean?

_____

2. What context clues can help you understand the meaning of the word *turquoise?*

_____

3. Look at the sentences after the word *Navajo*. How do these sentences give clues to the meaning of *Navajo?*

_____

_____

4. What does *jostled* mean as it is used in this passage?

_____

5. What is the meaning of *bracelet?* How do you know?

_____

© Pearson Education, Inc., 5

Home Activity Your child answered questions about unfamiliar words in a reading passage by using context clues. Explain a process to your child, such as making a complicated meal, using unfamiliar words, and help your child figure out what the new words mean by their context.

Electronic Media

- There are two types of **electronic media**—computer and non-computer. Computer sources include computer software, CD-ROMs, DVDs, and the Internet. Non-computer sources include audiotapes, videotapes, films, filmstrips, television, and radio.
- To find information on the Internet, use a search engine and type in your keywords. Be specific. It's a good idea to use two or more keywords as well as typing "AND" between keywords. To go to a Web site that's listed in your search results, click on the underlined link.

Directions Use the following list of electronic media to answer the questions below.

- *From the Pueblo to the Shoshonean* (Public Television documentary about Native Americans of the Southwest)
- The Navajo Nation (Internet site about the Navajo people)
- *Our Native Tongue* (Podcast of authentic Native American music)
- *The Story of New Mexico* (Documentary about the history of the state of New Mexico)
- *North American Tribes and Nations* (CD-ROM showing the existing Native American tribes in the United States)
- The Sun and the Moon (Internet site showing Native American art, jewelry, and ceramics)

1. Which source would be the most helpful in writing a report on the Navajo?

_____

2. How would you get information from *North American Tribes and Nations?*

_____

3. If you were doing an Internet search, what keywords would you type into the search engine to find the Web site The Sun and the Moon?

_____

_____

4. Which source would be most useful if you wanted to learn about Navajo songs and chants?

_____

5. Which source would you start with if you wanted to learn about the Native Americans of Florida?

_____

Name_____

Directions Use the following Internet search results found on a search engine to answer the questions below.

Search Results

<u>Navajo Nation</u>
   Official site of the Navajo Nation. Describes Navajo history, culture, and traditions.

<u>Native American Indian Heritage Month</u>
   United States Department of the Interior, Bureau of Indian Affairs. Discusses the importance of preserving Native American culture. Lists events across the country, highlighting Native American traditions. Describes Native American customs.

<u>Box of Memories</u>
   One man's effort to record the stories and traditions of Navajo Native Americans in the hope of preserving Navajo culture.

<u>Navajo Traditions</u>
   University of Arizona's study of Navajo traditions and how they have developed over time.

---

6. What does the information below the underlined links tell you?

_____

7. What keywords might have been used to get these search results?

_____

8. Which site is a United States government source?

_____

9. Which site would be least reliable if you were doing a report for school?

_____

10. In what ways might the Navajo Traditions site be valuable if you were doing a report?

_____

_____

_____

Home Activity Your child answered questions about electronic media. With your child, look around your house and see how many different types of electronic media you have on hand. Talk with your son or daughter about how each of the various electronic media sources could be valuable in his or her studies.

Final Syllables *-en, -an, -el, -le, -il*

Proofread a Story Sally wrote this story. There are seven spelling errors and one punctuation error. Circle the errors and write the corrections on the lines.

Spelling Words

example
level
slogan
quarrel
scramble
evil
oxygen
wooden
double
travel

cancel
chuckle
fossil
toboggan
veteran
chisel
suburban
single
sudden
beagle

The Old Woodcarver

We decided to travle to see a veteren woodcarver. My dad wanted him to make a tobaggan like the one Dad owned when he was a child. We drove down a long suburben road. When we got out of the car, a beagel ran from behind the house, followed by the woodcarver. He carried an example of a tiny sled made of metal. "Don't worry," he said with a chuckle, "your sled will be wooden." He pulled a chisle out of his pocket. "Would you like to learn how to carve?" he asked. "I may seem like an old fossel to you," he said. "I'm probably double your father's age, but I'm pretty handy with a chisel."

"Sure," I said, "that's a great idea!

1. _____   2. _____

3. _____   4. _____

5. _____   6. _____

7. _____

8. _____

Proofread Words Circle the correct spelling of the word.

9. oxygin   oxygan   oxygen

10. cancel   cancle   cancil

11. quarril   quarrel   quarele

12. evile   eval   evil

13. slogan   slogen   slogin

14. chukle   chuckle   chuckel

15. suddin   suddan   sudden

16. egsample   example   exsampel

Frequently Misspelled Words

Mom
Dad's
heard

Home Activity Your child identified misspelled words with the final syllables *-en, -an, -el, -le,* and *-il*. Ask your child which words are the most difficult for him or her to spell. Have your child spell them.

Main and Helping Verbs

Directions Read the passage. Then read each question. Circle the letter of the correct answer.

Tempe Wick

(1) Tempe Wick was a spirited girl and have often rode alone. (2) While she <u>was riding</u> one day, Tempe and her horse _____ captured by stray soldiers. (3) The soldiers knew the Wicks were a wealthy family and wanted to take Tempe's horse. (4) Tempe managed to escape the soldiers but knew they <u>would</u> come looking for the horse in the barn. (5) Tempe decided to hide the horse in her bedroom. (6) Who would think to look in a bedroom for a horse? (7) The soldiers never discovered where she <u>had been hiding</u> the horse.

1   What change, if any, should be made in sentence 1?

   A   Change *was* to **were**

   B   Remove helping verb *have*

   C   Change *have* to **has**

   D   Make no change

2   Which describes the underlined words in sentence 2?

   A   Verb phrase

   B   Main verb

   C   Helping verb

   D   None of the above

3   Which helping verb best completes sentence 2?

   A   did

   B   are

   C   was

   D   were

4   Which best describes the underlined word in sentence 4?

   A   Verb phrase

   B   Main verb

   C   Helping verb

   D   None of the above

5   How many helping verbs are in the underlined verb phrase in sentence 7?

   A   0

   B   1

   C   2

   D   3

© Pearson Education, Inc., 5

Home Activity Your child prepared for taking tests on main and helping verbs and verb phrases. Have your child write sentences about his or her day's activities using verb phrases and point out main and helping verbs.

Author's Purpose

- The **author's purpose** is the reason or reasons the author has for writing.
- An author may write to persuade, to inform, to entertain, or to express himself or herself.

Directions Read the following passage and look at the time line to answer the questions below.

The Reverend Martin Luther King Jr. was an important leader of the civil rights movement. In 1948, at the age of 19, King became a minister. During his lifetime, he organized many civil rights protests, including the Montgomery Bus Boycott and the Freedom March on Washington, D.C. Because of his frequent participation in civil rights protests, he was arrested 30 times. King received the Nobel Peace Prize for his work. Dr. King is a truly a hero of freedom in America.

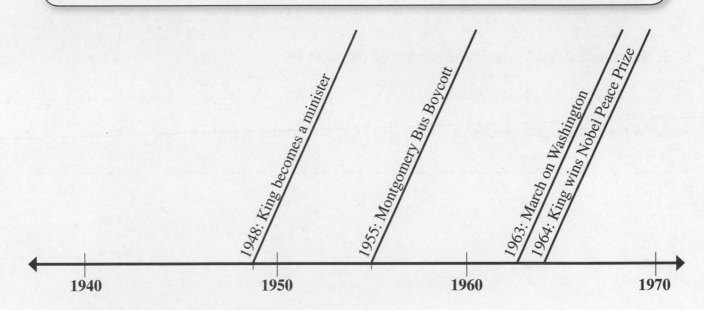

1. For what purpose did the author write this passage?

_____

2. How does the time line support the author's purpose?

_____

3. How many years passed between Dr. King becoming a minister and the March on Washington?

_____

4. What happened first, the Montgomery Bus Boycott or the Freedom March on Washington?

_____

Home Activity Your child analyzed the author's purpose in a nonfiction passage. Look at an article in a newspaper or magazine. Read the article with your child and discuss what you think is the author's purpose.

© Pearson Education, Inc., 5

Comprehension 153

Writing • Writing for Tests

In the Army Now

On a cool October day in seventeen hundred and seventy eight, young Deborah Sampson packs her knapsack and walks to the recruiting post in Billingham, Massachusetts. She finds herself standing in front of a captain, a tired, wiry man with a scruffy red beard.

She hears herself say, "I want to join, I want to fight!" Her voice sounds high and weak. Deborah stands straight and bravely meets the captain's stare. She is wearing pants, a coarse wool vest, and a coat, and a man's hat covers her hair.

"You're but a boy, yet I reckon you'll do," the captain sighs. "The soldiers are waiting. Now, what is your name?"

"Call me Robert," Deborah replies.

"Welcome to the army," says the captain Deborah has just enlisted in the American army as a soldier. Now, she has to keep her true identity a secret.

1. Read the story. What is the setting of the story?

_____

2. Who is the main character in the story? What does she do?

_____

Vocabulary

Directions Choose the word from the box that best completes each sentence. Write the word on the line.

_____ 1. a high-spirited horse

_____ 2. made something look larger

_____ 3. not afraid

_____ 4. a faint, unsteady light

_____ 5. dark or gloomy

Check the Words You Know

___fate
___fearless
___glimmer
___lingers
___magnified
___somber
___steed

Directions Choose a word from the box that best matches each clue. Write the word on the line.

Some have fought for freedom in a **6.** _____ and inspiring way.

The founding fathers **7.** _____ this kind of commitment when they

fought against the British and, some would say, **8.** _____ itself.

The **9.** _____ of hope they fclt eventually became reality when

they defeated the English king's forces. That dedication to the fight for freedom

10. _____, remaining in all Americans to this day.

Write a Conversation

On a separate sheet of paper, write a short conversation between two members of the colonial army in 1775. Use as many vocabulary words as you can.

Home Activity Your child identified and used vocabulary words from the poem *The Midnight Ride of Paul Revere*. With your child, look up information about Paul Revere and his activities as a colonist in the 1700s. Discuss the information, using as many vocabulary words as possible.

Subject-Verb Agreement

The subject and verb in a sentence must **agree,** or work together. A singular subject needs a singular verb. A plural subject needs a plural verb.

Use the following rules for verbs that tell about the present time.

- If the subject is a singular noun or *he, she,* or *it,* add *-s* or *-es* to most verbs.
  The wagon *creaks*. It *lurches* along.

- If the subject is a plural noun or *I, you, we,* or *they,* do not add *-s* or *-es* to the verb.
  The oxen *pull* the wagon. They *strain* uphill.

- For the verb *be,* use *am* and *is* to agree with singular subjects and *are* to agree with plural subjects.
  I *am* hot. Thomas *is* happy. The patriots *are* loyal. We *are* late.

- A **collective noun** names a group, such as *family, team,* and *class.* A collective noun is singular if it refers to a group acting as one: The family *rides* in the wagon. A collective noun is plural if it refers to members of the group acting individually: The family *are arguing* about the tax.

Directions Match each subject with a verb that agrees. Write the letter of the correct verb on the line.

_____ **1.** The colonists   **A.** are training.

_____ **2.** The British king   **B.** is beginning.

_____ **3.** A war   **C.** rebel.

_____ **4.** Troops   **D.** sends his army.

Directions Underline the verb in ( ) that agrees with the subject of each sentence.

5. The American colonies (trade, trades) with England.

6. Two of the colonies' exports (is, are) cotton and indigo.

7. England (tax, taxes) the items imported into the colonies.

8. Tea (is, are) a popular drink in the colonies.

9. The Boston Tea Party (show, shows) the colonists' anger about taxes.

10. Today, Americans (drink, drinks) more coffee than tea.

11. Earlier conflicts (is, are) forgotten.

12. The two countries (consider, considers) themselves close allies.

© Pearson Education, Inc., 5

School + Home **Home Activity** Your child learned about subject-verb agreement. Have your child make up sentences about clothes he or she wears, using both singular subjects (shirt, belt) and plural subjects (socks, shoes) and making sure verbs agree.

Final Syllables -*er*, -*ar*, -*or*

Spelling Words				
danger	wander	tractor	dollar	harbor
eager	eraser	surrender	solar	sticker
locker	helicopter	pillar	refrigerator	caterpillar
rumor	glimmer	linger	sensor	alligator

Definitions Write a list word that means the same or almost the same as the word or phrase.

1. spark   1. _____
2. port   2. _____
3. sun   3. _____
4. gossip   4. _____
5. post   5. _____
6. peril   6. _____
7. cooler   7. _____
8. excited   8. _____
9. 100 cents   9. _____
10. roam   10. _____

Missing Words Write the list word that completes the sentence.

11. I have a habit of chewing on my pencil ____.   11. _____
12. Smart criminals ____ when spotted.   12. _____
13. The farmer drove the ____ across the field.   13. _____
14. I store my schoolbooks in my ____.   14. _____
15. The ____ floated silently across the swampy water.   15. _____
16. The ____ became a beautiful butterfly.   16. _____
17. She pulled the price ____ off the package.   17. _____
18. The news ____ flew over the accident scene.   18. _____
19. I like to ____ in my room instead of watching television downstairs.   19. _____
20. The motion ____ turns on the light when anyone is near.   20. _____

© Pearson Education, Inc., 5

Home Activity Your child wrote words with the final syllables -*er*, -*ar*, and -*or*. Select three list words and ask your child to define them.

Scoring Rubric: Historical Fiction

	4	3	2	1
Focus/Ideas	Excellent, focused historical fiction; interesting and realistic characters and events	Somewhat focused historical fiction; characters and events are believable but not fully described	Some unclear or off focus details; characters and events are not described well	Historical fiction does not have a clear focus; characters and events have not been described
Organization	Plot events follow a clear order	Order of plot events is generally clear	Order of plot events isn't always clear	Unorganized and no clear order of events
Voice	Strongly engages reader	Somewhat engages reader	Not fully engaged	Writer is not engaged
Word Choice	Uses many sensory details to create strong imagery	Uses some sensory details to create imagery	Few or no sensory details to create imagery	No sensory details or imagery
Sentences	Uses simple and compound sentences	Some varied sentence structures	Sentences are not varied	Fragments or run-on sentences
Conventions	Excellent control, few or no errors; correct subject-verb agreement	Good control, few errors; subject-verb agreement generally correct	Errors that hamper understanding; subjects and verbs rarely agree	Many serious errors; subjects and verbs do not agree

Vocabulary • Inflected Endings -s, -ed, -ing

Inflected endings -s, -ed, and -ing are attached to the end of a word to create a new word with a new meaning. If you are unsure about the meaning of a word with an inflected ending, check the dictionary.

Directions Read the following passage about the colonists. Then write the words from the passage that have the inflected ending.

Sometimes your life may seem complicated, but in fact it may be simple compared to a colonist's life. For example, in the 1700s the car had not been invented. Instead of depending on cars for swift travel, people rode horses to get where they needed to go—a very slow method of transportation. The pace was more leisurely than driving a car, but it was still faster than walking.

Walking outside the settlement left a person open to such dangers as wild animals. Since there were no sidewalks or streetlights outside of town, it was best not to linger but to come home quickly. Horses gave colonists an extra measure of safety.

1. *-s* _____

_____

2. *-ed* _____

3. *-ing* _____

Directions Write the following words with inflected endings *-s, -ed,* and *-ing*. Then write a sentence using one of the three new words.

4. depend _____

_____

5. compare _____

_____

Home Activity Your child reviewed the inflected endings *-s, -ed,* and *-ing*. Together, make a list of words from a book or a magazine article that contain these endings. Then help your child write new sentences using those words.

Illustration/Caption

- **Illustrations** or **pictures** can convey information about characters and events in a story. They can help establish mood, dramatize action, reinforce the author's imagery or symbolism, or help explain the text.
- A **caption** is the text explaining the illustration or picture. It usually appears below or to the side of the image.

Directions This illustration appears in a text about Ben Franklin. Look at the illustration and read the caption. Then answer the questions below.

This illustration shows Benjamin Franklin flying a kite in an experiment to relate lightning and electricity.

1. Based on the illustration, in what kind of weather did Franklin fly his kite?

_____

_____

2. Look at the picture. How did Franklin's experiment work?

_____

_____

3. What do the clothes of the people in the illustration tell you?

_____

_____

4. Why do Ben Franklin and his companion look pleased?

_____

5. Can you tell where the event took place by looking at the illustration?

_____

© Pearson Education, Inc., 5

Name_____

Directions This illustration gives additional information in a text about state coins. Look at the illustration and read the caption. Then answer the question below.

This illustration shows the Illinois state quarter, whose design was inspired by the artwork of Thom Cicchelli of Chicago.

6. Look at the illustration of the quarter. Who is pictured on the quarter?

_____

7. Based on the illustration, in what year was Illinois admitted to the United States?

_____

8. What do the tall buildings show?

_____

9. What does the caption tell you that is not reflected in the image?

_____

10. How many stars appear on the coin? What do you think they signify?

_____

_____

 Home Activity Your child learned how illustrations and captions can help convey information about a story. Look at one of your child's favorite books and discuss how the illustrations in it help your child learn more about the story.

© Pearson Education, Inc., 5

Name _____

Final Syllables -*er*, -*ar*, -*or*

Proofread a Sign There are seven spelling errors and one capitalization error. Circle the errors and write the corrections on the lines.

> welcome to the Wildlife and Alligater Preserve
>
> • Admission is one dollar for an all-day parking pass.
> • You can rent an all-day locker for your convenience.
> • Helicoptor rides are available to see the harber from the air.
> • To preserve the ecology, stay on the path. Do not wandar off.
> • There is no dangor. Animals stay behind a motion senser fence.
> • Linger over lunch on our beautiful terrace.
> • Do not forget to surrendar your parking pass at the gate when leaving.

Spelling Words

danger
wander
tractor
dollar
harbor
eager
eraser
surrender
solar
sticker

locker
helicopter
pillar
refrigerator
caterpillar
rumor
glimmer
linger
sensor
alligator

1. _____ 2. _____
3. _____ 4. _____
5. _____ 6. _____
7. _____ 8. _____

Frequently Misspelled Words

another
we're

Proofread Words Circle the word that is spelled correctly.

9.	doller	dollar	dollor
10.	erasor	eraser	erasar
11.	stickar	sticker	stickor
12.	soler	solar	solor
13.	helicoptor	helicoptar	helicopter
14.	tracter	tractar	tractor
15.	rumer	rumor	rumar

Home Activity Your child identified misspelled words with the final syllables -*er*, -*ar*, and -*or*. Select three list words and ask your child to spell them.

© Pearson Education, Inc., 5

Subject-Verb Agreement

Directions Read the passage. Then read each question. Circle the letter of the correct answer.

Like Longfellow

     (1) My grandmother enjoy the poems of Longfellow. (2) Longfellow's poems uses both rhyme and rhythm. (3) "The Midnight Ride of Paul Revere" is called a narrative poem. (4) These poems tell a story. (5) My grandmother write poems too. (6) She entered a narrative poem in a poetry contest and won first prize. (7) Sometimes we recites the poem in a soft voice.

1 What change, if any, should be made in sentence 1?

- **A** Add -*s* to *enjoy*
- **B** Add -*s* to *grandmother*
- **C** Change *poems* to **poem**
- **D** Make no change

2 What change, if any, should be made in sentence 2?

- **A** Change *poems* to **poem**
- **B** Change *uses* to **use**
- **C** Change *Longfellow's* to **Longfellows**
- **D** Make no change

3 In sentence 3, how would you describe the subject?

- **A** Collective noun
- **B** Plural subject
- **C** Singular subject
- **D** None of the above

4 What change, if any, should be made in sentence 5?

- **A** Change *My* to **The**
- **B** Change *write* to **writes**
- **C** Change *poems* to **poem**
- **D** Make no change

5 What is true about sentence 7?

- **A** The subject is plural.
- **B** The verb is a linking verb.
- **C** The subject is a collective noun.
- **D** The subject and verb do not agree.

Home Activity Your child prepared for taking tests on subject-verb agreement. Have your child copy some subject and verb pairs from a favorite book and explain why the subjects and verbs agree.

Digraphs *th*, *sh*, *ch*, *ph*

Spelling Words				
shovel	hyphen	challenge	shatter	charity
southern	chosen	approach	ethnic	china
northern	establish	astonish	shiver	attach
chapter	although	python	pharmacy	ostrich

Alphabetize Write the ten list words below in alphabetical order.

ethnic	python
ostrich	charity
hyphen	although
chapter	establish
northern	southern

1. _____   6. _____

2. _____   7. _____

3. _____   8. _____

4. _____   9. _____

5. _____   10. _____

Synonyms Write the list word that has the same or nearly the same meaning.

11. surprise _____   16. drugstore _____

12. dare _____   17. break _____

13. shake _____   18. fasten _____

14. pottery _____   19. dig _____

15. picked _____   20. near _____

 Home Activity Your child learned to spell words with the digraphs *th*, *sh*, *ch*, and *ph*. Ask your child to give an example of a word with each digraph and spell it.

© Pearson Education, Inc., 5

Regular and Irregular Plural Nouns

Directions Write the plural form of each noun.

1. guess _____

2. cocoon _____

3. ax _____

4. branch _____

5. boy _____

6. story _____

7. life _____

8. mouse _____

9. foot _____

10. jacket _____

Directions Underline the plural nouns in each sentence.

11. There are many kinds of beaches in our fifty states.

12. Some shores are packed with shops, restaurants, and hotels.

13. Some are friendly spaces, popular among families with children.

14. In other areas, fishermen catch trout, salmon, and other fish.

15. People can swim in the waves or collect seashells at the beach.

Directions Cross out each incorrectly spelled plural noun. Write the correct spelling above the word you crossed out.

16. In autumn, bushes with red leafs and berrys grow near the sand dunes.

17. Foxs, deers, and wolves are spotted on the sand.

18. Several men and woman relax on benchs near the water.

Name _____

Irregular Plurals

Spelling Words				
staffs	ourselves	pants	scissors	loaves
volcanoes	chiefs	buffaloes	flamingos	beliefs
echoes	shelves	quizzes	sheriffs	dominoes
thieves	measles	avocados	chefs	pianos

Analogies Write the word that completes each comparison.

1. Doctors are to hospitals as _____ are to restaurants.

2. Arms are to shirts as legs are to _____.

3. Drawers are to chests as _____ are to closets.

4. Articles are to essays as tests are to _____.

5. Storm is to tornado as disease is to _____.

6. Knives are to meat as _____ are to paper.

7. Ants are to insects as _____ are to birds.

8. Strings are to violins as keys are to _____.

9. Potatoes are to stews as _____ are to salads.

10. Ice is to cubes as bread is to _____.

Word Clues Write the list word that fits each clue.

11. These animals roamed all over the West.   _____

12. These are often black rectangles with white dots.   _____

13. You might hear these in a huge canyon.   _____

14. These people enforce the law.   _____

15. These people may steal from you.   _____

16. You don't want to be close when these erupt.   _____

17. These are in charge of tribes or companies.   _____

18. People have these about topics such as politics.   _____

19. Organizations such as schools have these.   _____

20. We use this word to describe us.   _____

© Pearson Education, Inc., 5

School + Home

Home Activity Your child learned to spell words that are irregular plurals. Locate three irregular plurals in a newspaper. Say the singular forms of the words and ask your child to spell the plurals.

Possessive Nouns

Directions Write the possessive form of each underlined noun.

1. <u>mother</u> advice _____

2. <u>survivor</u> story _____

3. <u>child</u> toy _____

4. <u>man</u> overcoat _____

5. <u>monument</u> history _____

6. <u>mothers</u> lessons _____

7. <u>survivors</u> groups _____

8. <u>children</u> books _____

9. <u>men</u> clothing _____

10. <u>monuments</u> construction _____

Directions Rewrite each sentence. Write the possessive form of the underlined noun.

11. A box is tucked away in my <u>grandfather</u> closet.

_____

12. It contains a <u>soldier</u> memories of service.

_____

13. Several <u>pictures</u> edges are worn and crumpled.

_____

14. In those pictures, the young <u>men</u> faces are handsome and smiling.

_____

_____

15. Grandpa treasures his war <u>friends</u> letters and visits.

_____

_____

Name _____

Vowel Sounds with *r*

Spelling Words				
snore	tornado	spare	appear	career
square	report	prepare	pioneer	chair
beware	smear	repair	sword	ignore
order	engineer	resort	volunteer	declare

Word Search Circle ten hidden list words. Words are down, across, and diagonal.
Write the words on the lines.

```
F  V  W  P  P  R  R  E  S  O
S  W  O  R  D  E  E  N  N  R
M  L  A  L  E  S  P  G  P  E
E  Q  W  I  U  L  O  I  S  P
A  R  I  A  T  N  R  N  N  T
R  E  S  O  R  T  T  E  O  Y
A  T  E  P  O  R  D  E  R  B
W  O  H  S  Q  U  A  R  E  E
T  R  S  A  I  P  Z  E  N  R
Z  B  E  W  A  R  E  A  S  E
```

1. _____   6. _____

2. _____   7. _____

3. _____   8. _____

4. _____   9. _____

5. _____   10. _____

Synonyms Write the list word that has the same or nearly the same meaning.

11. twister   _____   16. fix   _____

12. ready   _____   17. overlook   _____

13. occupation   _____   18. seem   _____

14. announce   _____   19. extra   _____

15. seat   _____   20. pathfinder _____

Home Activity Your child learned to spell words that have vowel sounds with *r*. Select three words from your child's spelling list and make up a sentence with him or her. Ask your child to write the sentence.

Action and Linking Verbs

Directions Underline the verb in each sentence. Write *A* if it is an action verb. Write *L* if it is a linking verb.

1. Myths and tales often seem true. _____

2. They are important to each civilization. _____

3. Myths address basic human questions. _____

4. Myths are part of every culture. _____

5. Animals often play a role in myths and tales. _____

6. These animals speak like people. _____

7. Their actions are clever. _____

8. Early civilizations understood the value of myths. _____

9. They sought answers around them. _____

10. Myths and tales answered questions about the world. _____

Directions Write a verb from the box to complete each sentence. On the line after the sentence, write *A* if the verb is an action verb. Write *L* if it is a linking verb.

brought	tells	was	cause
seems	honored	frightened	were

11. Children _____ the adults. _____

12. Children who _____ respectful received praise. _____

13. The guardian _____ a gift for his niece. _____

14. The uncle's mask _____ his niece. _____

15. There _____ a big party for this special day. _____

16. It _____ that many people attend this special party. _____

17. The Chinese New Year _____ the cause of the festivities. _____

18. The uncle _____ a story about this special day. _____

Final Syllables *-en, -an, -el, -le, -il*

Spelling Words				
example	level	slogan	quarrel	scramble
evil	oxygen	wooden	double	travel
cancel	chuckle	fossil	toboggan	veteran
chisel	suburban	single	sudden	beagle

Words in Context Write the word to complete each sentence.

1. I _____ when I hear an amusing joke.

2. You must _____ your appointment if you can't make it.

3. Breathe deeply to get plenty of _____.

4. Sailing is a(n) _____ of a water sport.

5. Molly's _____ is a friendly, cheerful dog.

6. The boys went down the snowy hill on a(n) _____.

7. A sculptor uses a(n) _____ to shape marble.

8. The scientist found a(n) _____ of a dinosaur in the ground.

9. People can _____ in cars, trains, and planes.

10. Baseball players use a(n) _____ bat.

11. Shall we fry, poach, or _____ the eggs?

12. The company's _____ was easy to remember.

Antonyms Write the list word that has the opposite or nearly the opposite meaning.

13. newcomer   _____

14. agree   _____

15. rural   _____

16. married   _____

17. good   _____

18. uneven   _____

19. gradual   _____

20. single   _____

Home Activity Your child learned to spell words with the final syllables *-en, -an, -el, -le,* and *-il*. To practice at home, dictate a word with each final syllable. Ask your child to spell the word and provide a synonym or antonym for it.

Main and Helping Verbs

Directions Find the verb phrase in each sentence. Underline the helping verb. Circle the main verb.

1. I am studying the American Southwest.

2. The Navajo have lived there for generations.

3. Many are living on reservations.

4. The people can farm the land.

5. Rugs and jewelry are taken to market.

6. My parents are traveling to the Navajo market.

7. I will go with them next year.

8. Everyone should learn about native cultures.

9. My moccasins were sewn by a Navajo artist.

10. I would like a traditional painting.

Directions Underline the verb phrase in each sentence. Write *Present* or *Past* to tell the time of the action.

11. The boy is working at a trading post. _____

12. He has saved some money for a saddle. _____

13. People can buy baskets, jewelry, and rugs there. _____

14 His grandmother had sold her bracelet. _____

15. The boy was worrying about his grandmother. _____

16. He had spent his money at the store. _____

17. The boy was giving her back the bracelet. _____

18. His grandmother has gotten the saddle for him. _____

19. He can see the saddle in the truck. _____

20. The boy is smiling at his grandmother. _____

© Pearson Education, Inc., 5

Name _____

Final Syllables *-er*, *-ar*, *-or*

Spelling Words

danger	wander	tractor	dollar	harbor
eager	eraser	surrender	solar	sticker
locker	helicopter	pillar	refrigerator	caterpillar
rumor	glimmer	linger	sensor	alligator

Analogies Write the word that completes each comparison.

1. Hot is to oven as cold is to _____.

2. Page is to book as penny is to _____.

3. Flower is to bud as butterfly is to _____.

4. Moon is to lunar as sun is to _____.

5. Clothes are to closet as books are to _____.

6. Walk is to stroll as roam is to _____.

7. Patio is to yard as port is to _____.

8. Fingernail is to finger as _____ is to pencil.

9. Fact is to fiction as truth is to _____.

10. Sail is to ship as fly is to _____.

Hidden Words Each of these small words can be found inside one of the list words. Write the list word that contains the small word.

11. in _____

12. tick _____

13. act _____

14. me _____

15. all _____

16. end _____

17. ill _____

18. so _____

19. an _____

20. age _____

© Pearson Education, Inc., 5

Home Activity Your child learned to spell words with the final syllables *-er*, *-ar*, and *-or*. Choose a word with each final syllable from your child's spelling list. Ask your child to spell the word and use it in a sentence.

Subject-Verb Agreement

Directions Underline the verb in ( ) that agrees with the subject of each sentence.

1. Today horses (is, are) no longer needed for transportation.

2. We (use, uses) them to ride for pleasure.

3. Some horse lovers (buy, buys) horses of their own.

4. Food and equipment (become, becomes) expensive.

5. Martin (take, takes) riding lessons at a stable.

6. He (enjoy, enjoys) a horse without the responsibilities of ownership.

7. A saddle and bridle (cost, costs) quite a bit.

8. Our family (do, does) not have the land to keep a horse.

9. A dude ranch (offer, offers) accommodations with horse riding privileges.

10. Guests (stay, stays) in a bunkhouse.

Directions Add a verb to complete each sentence. Be sure the verb agrees with the subject.

11. Paul Revere's horse _____ the ground impatiently.

12. Redcoats _____ the river under cover of night.

13. Two lights _____ from the church tower.

14. The man and horse _____ away on their journey.

15. A little moonlight _____ through the clouds.

16. A warning cry _____ out in the night.

17. As the sun rises, farmers _____ their muskets.

18. They _____ for independence.

19. The fighting _____ fierce.

20. The colonial militia _____ the redcoats.

Comic Book/Graphic Novel Chart

Directions Fill in the chart with the characters, problem, settings, and events for your comic book or graphic novel. Make notes about possible illustrations for the events.

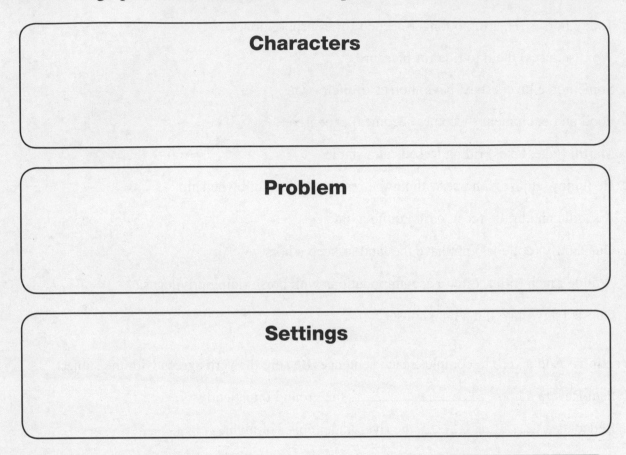

Events	Illustrations

Create Dialogue

Directions Write one or two sentences of dialogue for each part of your comic book or graphic novel. Be sure to indicate which character is speaking each piece of dialogue.

Beginning _____

_____

_____

_____

_____

Middle _____

_____

_____

_____

_____

End _____

_____

_____

_____

Adding, Deleting, or Rearranging Sentences

Directions Use the word in ( ) to combine the two sentences. Remember to capitalize the first word of the new sentence and to replace the first period with a comma.

(1) Rosa Parks was an African-American woman living in Montgomery, Alabama, in 1955. (2) At that time, African Americans were not allowed to sit in the front of public buses. (3) They also had to give up their seats to white people if the bus became overcrowded. (4) Parks knew these laws were unfair. (5) Rosa Parks later moved to Detroit. (6) One December day, Rosa Parks refused to give up her seat on a bus. (7) She was arrested and later found guilty of disorderly conduct. (8) The African-American community staged a boycott, refusing to ride on Montgomery buses for more than a year. (9) By taking one brave action, Rosa Parks did the right thing to help all African Americans achieve equal rights. (10) After this boycott, the unfair bus laws were changed.

1. Write the number of the sentence that should be deleted. Tell why you think it should be deleted.

   _____

   _____

2. Underline the two sentences that need to be rearranged. Write the sentences in the correct order.

   _____

   _____

   _____

   _____

3. Choose one fact below that could be added to improve the paragraph. Write the letter of the sentence. Tell where you would add the sentence. Explain why you think it would improve the paragraph.
   A. Rosa Parks worked as a seamstress.
   B. Rosa Parks had attended African-American political meetings.
   C. In the 1960s, Martin Luther King, Jr. led marches for racial equality.

   _____

   _____

   _____

Editing 2

Directions Edit these sentences. Look for errors in spelling, grammar, and mechanics. Use proofreading marks to show the corrections.

Proofreading Marks	
Delete (Take out)	⌐⌐⌐⌐ ∂
Add	∧
Spelling	⬭
Uppercase letter	≡
Lowercase letter	/

1. Lauren searched everywhere for Beth's book but she couldnt locate it.

2. Beth and her both liked books by that auther, so Beth generously let Lauren read her copy.

3. Lauren looked under her bed, in her closit and in her backpack.

4. Lauren was nervos about telling Beth about the book because everyone dislikes

   someone losing their things.

5. Finally, Lauren said, "Beth, unfortunately i have misplaced your book.

6. Beth was upset for a minute soon she said she had a grate idea.

7. Lauren and Beth agreed that Lauren would purchased a new book by they're favorite writer.

8. Giving both the opportunity to reed a new book.

Now you'll edit the draft of your personal narrative. Then you'll use your revised and edited draft to make a final copy of your narrative. Finally, you'll share your written work with your audience.

Sequence

- **Sequence** is the order in which events take place, from first to last.
- Clue words such as *first, next,* and *then* may show sequence in a story or article, but not always.
- Several events can occur at the same time. Words such as *meanwhile* and *during* give clues that two events are happening at the same time.

Directions Read the passage. Then use the diagram and the passage to answer the questions.

I went to an astronomy conference last week. Before attending any of the lectures I signed in and was given my free copy of *Earth: Its History and Future.* My favorite lecture was the very first one on the first day of the conference. The only speaker that I didn't enjoy was the person who spoke about Einstein's theories. It was great to be a part of the award ceremony at the close of the conference on the last day, but I have to admit that I was very tired at that point. Other than that, I learned a lot and would recommend the conference to anyone.

Astronomy Conference Lecture Schedule

	Mon.	**Tue.**	**Wed.**	**Thurs.**	**Fri.**
9:00 A.M.	Black Holes in our Galaxy	Einstein's Theories	Asteroids and the Earth	Jupiter's Moons	Supernovas
12:00 NOON	Lunch	Lunch	Lunch	Lunch	Lunch
1:00 P.M.	Life in Our Solar System	Space Travel in the 21st Century	Supernovas	The Expansion of the Universe	The Future of NASA

1. What is the first thing the author did? _____

2. What was topic of the first lecture on Wednesday? _____

3. Which lecture was given right after lunch on Monday? _____

4. On what day and time did the speaker discuss Einstein's Theories? _____

5. What was the last part of the conference? _____

Home Activity Your child read a passage including a schedule of lectures to determine sequence. Work with your child to have him or her produce a weekly schedule of extracurricular activities or chores. Then ask your child questions about the sequence of his or her activities.

© Pearson Education, Inc., 5

Writing · Short Play

Key Features of a Short Play

- includes a list of characters
- describes the setting, time, or place
- features characters who often think or act distinctly

Summer Dreams

CHARACTERS
SARAH, an 11-year-old girl
PATTY, a 12-year-old girl

SETTING AND TIME: a park on a sunny summer day

(Two girls sit on the grass eating ice cream cones.)

PATTY: *(Dreamily)* Wouldn't it be great if we could invent a 24-hour ice cream machine? All it would do is make ice cream all day, every day.

SARAH: Yeah! We could make the machine out of melted down old aluminum cans or something. What kind of flavors would we have it make?

PATTY: Everything. Chocolate, vanilla, strawberry, orange, raspberry—everything.

SARAH: *(Excitedly)* And we could have a "sprinkles" option and "fudge" and "whipped cream" options, too!

PATTY: And people could ask for whatever cone they wanted—sugar, waffle . . .

SARAH: And we could have a machine on every corner in the summer!

PATTY: And they'd be free for everyone!

SARAH: *(looking down as ice cream cone drops into her lap)* Um . . . how soon are we inventing this thing?

1. Tell where and when the play is taking place.

_____

2. Name two examples of stage directions included in the play.

_____

_____

Name_____

Vocabulary

Directions Choose the word from the box that best matches each definition.
Write the word on the line.

_____ 1. examining closely

_____ 2. claps hands in appreciation

_____ 3. especially good or unique

_____ 4. tasks planned and performed
to achieve a specific goal

_____ 5. viewing randomly or casually

Directions Choose the word from the box that best completes each sentence. Write the word on the line.

_____ 6. Building the scenery for the spring play was a _____, or plan,
that took us most of March to complete.

_____ 7. After carefully examining, or _____, the burned building, the
chief decided that the fire had been an accident.

_____ 8. _____ through the latest catalog, Shelly found just the right
hat to go with the jacket she'd bought last weekend.

_____ 9. If Dr. Omachi _____ after a performance, you know that the
orchestra was excellent.

_____ 10. I can't remember a more _____ warm, sunny summer day.

Write a Newspaper Article

On a separate piece of paper, write a newspaper article about an imaginary new invention. Describe
one or two failures the inventor experienced before he or she was successful. Use as many of the
vocabulary words as you can.

Home Activity Your child identified and used vocabulary words from *The Fabulous Perpetual Motion Machine*. Choose items in the room where you and your child are sitting. See if your child can guess what you are describing based on the clues you offer.

© Pearson Education, Inc., 5

Past, Present, and Future Tenses

The **tense** of a verb shows when something happens. Verbs in the **present tense** show action that happens now. Some present tense singular verbs end with *-s* or *-es*. Most present tense plural verbs do not end with *-s* or *-es*.

An inventor <u>creates</u> a new tool. Inventions <u>serve</u> us well.

Verbs in the **past tense** show action that has already happened. Most verbs in the past tense end in *-ed*.

Not long ago, electronics <u>changed</u> the world.

Verbs in the **future tense** show action that will happen. Add *will* (or *shall*) to most verbs to show the future tense.

Many more inventions <u>will appear</u>.

- Some regular verbs change spelling when *-ed* is added. For verbs ending in *e*, drop the *e* and add *-ed*: *used, celebrated*. For verbs ending in a consonant and *y*, change the *y* to *i* and add *-ed*: *spied, lied*.

- For most one-syllable verbs that end in one vowel followed by one consonant, double the consonant and add *-ed*: *wrapped, patted*.

- Irregular verbs change spelling to form the past tense: *are/were, bring/brought, eat/ate, find/found, fly/flew, go/went, have/had, is/was, make/made, see/saw, sit/sat, take/took, tell/told, think/thought, write/wrote*.

Directions Write the correct present, past, and future tense of each verb.

Verb	Present	Past	Future
1. jump	She _____.	She _____.	She _____.
2. sit	He _____.	He _____.	He _____.
3. worry	We _____.	We _____.	We _____.
4. stop	It _____.	It _____.	It _____.

Directions Rewrite each sentence. Change the underlined verb to the tense in ( ).

5. The Perez twins <u>dream</u> about a new invention. (present)

_____

6. They <u>study</u> the laws of motion. (past)

_____

Home Activity Your child learned about present, past, and future tenses. Have your child read a page in a story aloud, changing past tense verbs to present tense ones or present tense verbs to past tense ones.

© Pearson Education, Inc., 5

Words with Schwa

Spelling Words				
jewel	kingdom	gasoline	factory	garage
tropical	pajamas	estimate	tomorrow	humidity
Chicago	bulletin	carnival	illustrate	elegant
census	terrific	celebrate	operate	celery

Word Clues Write the list word that fits each clue.

1. This may have rides, contests, costumes, and parades.

2. This type of place has palm trees and year-round warm weather.

3. This is a type of board for special announcements.

4. This is what you do at birthdays, anniversaries, and holidays.

5. This is a time that is not yesterday or today.

6. This is where royalty lives and rules.

7. This green vegetable has long, crisp stalks.

8. This is anything with fancy, classic style.

9. This is what you do when you draw pictures.

10. This is a kind of nightwear.

1. _____

2. _____

3. _____

4. _____

5. _____

6. _____

7. _____

8. _____

9. _____

10. _____

Words in Context Write the list word that best completes each sentence.

11. The national ____ is a counting of everyone who lives in the U.S.

12. Can you ____ the number of students in your school?

13. Our car needs to be put in the ____ for the night.

14. We'll need to fill the tank with ____.

15. That ____ makes parts for lawnmowers.

16. Air conditioning is used in places with lots of heat and ____.

17. The doctor had to ____ on me to remove my appendix.

18. A diamond is a valuable and precious ____.

19. The largest city in Illinois is ____.

20. That was one ____ roller coaster ride!

11. _____

12. _____

13. _____

14. _____

15. _____

16. _____

17. _____

18. _____

19. _____

20. _____

© Pearson Education, Inc., 5

Home Activity Your child wrote words with the schwa sound. Ask your child to spell three list words, telling you where the schwa sound is in each word.

Story Sequence B

Title

Characters

Setting

Events

Vocabulary • Multiple-Meaning Words

- Some words have more than one meaning. They are called **multiple-meaning words.**
- When you see a word you don't know, you may find clues about the word's meaning in the words near the unknown word. These are called context clues.

Directions Read the following passage. Then answer the questions below. Use context clues to help you.

The two-wheeled vehicle known as the bicycle was invented in Europe in the nineteenth century. A French version, called a "boneshaker," ran on wooden wheels covered with iron. Its front wheel was slightly larger than the rear one. As indicated by its name, this was not a comfortable bike to ride.

In the 1880s, the English inventor John Kemp Starley took on the project of improving the bicycle. In 1885, he manufactured the Rover Safety Bicycle, a more stable bike. The air-filled tire and the "bicycle built for two," or tandem bicycle, contributed to the popularity of the bicycle in the 1890s.

Today, many cyclists still applaud the bicycle as a convenient and flexible way to get from place to place. Because bikes don't pollute, many people consider them a fabulous way to get around town.

1. What context clues helped you figure out the meaning of *stable*?

_____

_____

2. What is another meaning of *stable*?

_____

3. What are two meanings of the word *tire*?

_____

_____

4. How do you know which meaning of *tire* is used here?

_____

_____

Home Activity Your child read a passage containing multiple-meaning words and determined their definitions using context clues. Read a newspaper or magazine article with your child, and see who can find and define more multiple-meaning words.

© Pearson Education, Inc., 5

Advertisement

- An **advertisement** is meant to sell a product or service. Written advertisements may appear in newspapers or on the Internet. Advertisers use many techniques to persuade the reader.
- **Loaded words** affect the reader by creating emotions or making value judgments.
- A **slogan** is a short phrase that is easily remembered.
- A **generality** is vague. It lacks specific details and supporting evidence and facts.
- **Getting on the bandwagon** is another way of saying "everyone else does it."
- A **sweeping generalization** has inadequate evidence and speaks for a large group.

Directions Read this advertisement for a car dealership and answer the questions.

> **Best Deals Ever on Pre-Loved Cars!**
> If you've ever wanted a luxury sports car with all the extras, now's the time to buy. **Carz-for-U Sales** is having its biggest sale ever on many of its top-of-the-line sports cars. Most cars come equipped with many of the latest luxury features! Choose from the exciting new fluorescent colors that everyone's buying. These are orange, white, green, or pink. Have you had credit card problems? Don't worry. We always find a way for you to buy your dream car with a just small down payment. **Carz-for-U Sales**—the best deals on wheels!

1. Which technique is the advertisement's headline an example of? Why do you think the advertiser calls the cars "pre-loved" instead of "pre-owned" or "used"?

2. Which technique is being used in the third sentence?

3. Which sentence in the ad uses the getting-on-the-bandwagon technique?

4. The advertiser says that at Carz-for-U Sales, "We always find a way for you to buy your dream car with just a small down payment." What kind of technique is being used? What doesn't the advertiser tell the reader?

5. How might this advertisement be different if it were made for TV?

Directions Read this advertisement for a credit card and answer the questions.

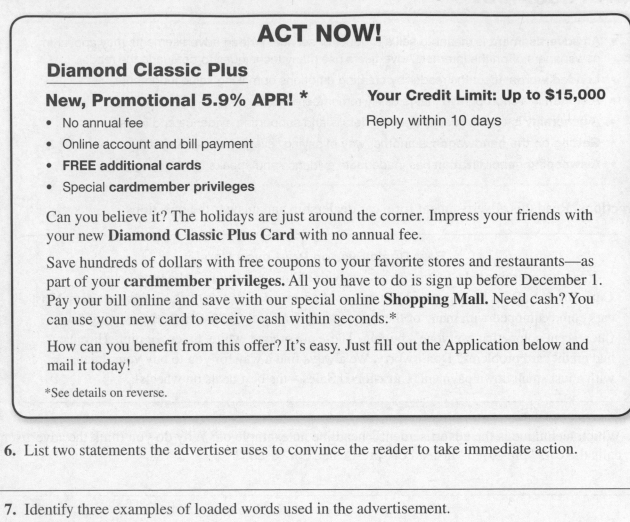

ACT NOW!

Diamond Classic Plus

New, Promotional 5.9% APR! *   **Your Credit Limit: Up to $15,000**

- No annual fee   Reply within 10 days
- Online account and bill payment
- **FREE additional cards**
- Special **cardmember privileges**

Can you believe it? The holidays are just around the corner. Impress your friends with your new **Diamond Classic Plus Card** with no annual fee.

Save hundreds of dollars with free coupons to your favorite stores and restaurants—as part of your **cardmember privileges.** All you have to do is sign up before December 1. Pay your bill online and save with our special online **Shopping Mall.** Need cash? You can use your new card to receive cash within seconds.*

How can you benefit from this offer? It's easy. Just fill out the Application below and mail it today!

*See details on reverse.

6. List two statements the advertiser uses to convince the reader to take immediate action.

_____

7. Identify three examples of loaded words used in the advertisement.

_____

8. The advertiser uses an asterisk twice to refer to the note at the bottom of the page. Why do you think the advertiser refers the reader to the other side of the letter?

_____

_____

9. List three services or extras the advertiser offers beyond being able to buy now and pay later.

_____

_____

10. Would this advertisement most likely appear on a billboard or in a letter mailed to a person's home? Why do you think so?

_____

 Home Activity Your child learned about advertisements. Write an advertisement for an imaginary product or service with your child using some of the advertising techniques your child has learned about. Discuss how the advertisement tries to persuade the reader.

186 **Research and Study Skills**

© Pearson Education, Inc., 5

Name _____

Words with Schwa

Proofread a Letter Laura wrote this letter to her aunt. Circle six spelling errors. Write the words correctly. Find one punctuation error. Write the sentence correctly.

> Dear Aunt Betty,
>   Next week we will celabrate at the carnaval. We've been decorating a float. Our theme will be the city of Chicago. The city has many eligant buildings. We want to illestrate this on our float. We were a little off on our estamate of how long it would take to complete it. It probly won't be easy, to get this beautiful, decorated platform out of the garage. Even so, we are looking forward to a terrific day!

1. _____   2. _____

3. _____   4. _____

5. _____   6. _____

7. _____

_____

Proofread Words Circle the correct spelling of the list word.

8. We moved to a _____ climate this winter.

    tropecal   tropical   troppicle

9. The _____ made people feel sticky when they went outside.

    humidity   humiduty   humidety

10. My favorite _____ have feet in them.

    pajammas   pajamers   pajamas

11. The _____ shows that the population of our town has doubled.

    sensus   census   censis

12. The weather _____ says that snow is on the way!

    bullatin   bulliten   bulletin

Spelling Words

jewel
kingdom
gasoline
factory
garage
tropical
pajamas
estimate
tomorrow
humidity

Chicago
bulletin
carnival
illustrate
elegant
census
terrific
celebrate
operate
celery

Frequently Misspelled Words

Christmas
beautiful
probably

Home Activity Your child identified misspelled words with schwa. Have your child tell you the three hardest words and then spell the words aloud.

Past, Present, and Future Tenses

Directions Read the passage. Then read each question. Circle the letter of the correct answer.

Science Fair

(1) Most schools in our county host an annual science fair. (2) In many cases, each grade hold its own competition. (3) Students from each grade compete against one another. (4) Students <u>perform</u> experiments and make displays to explain scientific ideas. (5) The most original projects will win the highest honors. (6) Winning projects _____ with winners from other schools. (7) Right now, avid competitors _____ daily on their projects for next year.

1 What is the verb tense in sentence 1?

   A   Past

   B   Present

   C   Future

   D   There is no verb.

2 What change, if any, should be made in sentence 2?

   A   Change *hold* to **holds**

   B   Change *cases* to **case**

   C   Change *its* to **it's**

   D   Make no change

3 In sentence 4, how would you change the underlined verb to future tense?

   A   has performed

   B   will perform

   C   performs

   D   performing

4 Choose the future tense form of *compete* to best complete sentence 6.

   A   were competing

   B   competed

   C   have competed

   D   will compete

5 Which form of *work* best completes sentence 7?

   A   worked

   B   works

   C   work

   D   working

© Pearson Education, Inc., 5

Home Activity Your child prepared for taking tests on present, past, and future tenses. Have your child explain the present, past, and future tenses of verbs and give examples of each.

Main Idea and Details

- The **main idea** is the most important idea about a paragraph, passage, or article.
- **Details** are small pieces of information that tell more about the main idea.

Directions Read the following passage and complete the diagram. State the main idea of the passage and three supporting details.

Artist Wesley Dennis (1903–1966) was an expert at painting horses. He had the ability to capture each horse's personality in his paintings. In 1945, writer Marguerite Henry asked him to illustrate her first book, *Justin Morgan Had a Horse.* He illustrated fifteen of Henry's horse books, including *King of the Wind* and *Misty of Chincoteague.* All three of these books were very popular with children and won awards for children's literature. Dennis is also known for his paintings in Anna Sewell's powerful story *Black Beauty.*

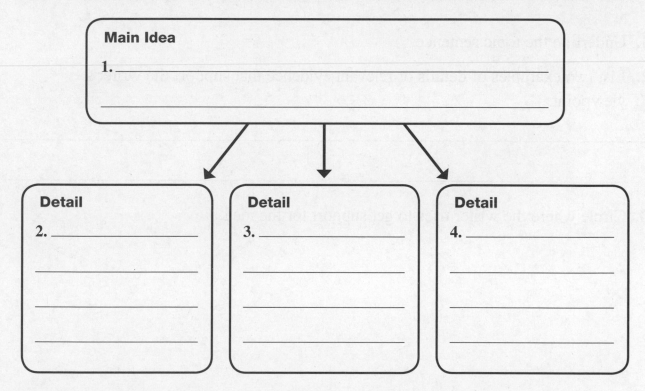

Main Idea

1._____

_____

Detail

2._____

_____

_____

Detail

3._____

_____

_____

Detail

4._____

_____

_____

5. Write a one-sentence summary of this passage.

_____

_____

Home Activity Your child identified the main idea and details of a brief passage. Work with your child to identify the main idea and details for individual paragraphs in a magazine or newspaper article. Challenge your child to write a summary of it.

© Pearson Education, Inc., 5

Name _____

Writing · Writing for Tests

How Cell Phones Changed Lives

The cell phone is the modern invention that has changed people's lives the most. Before cell phones were invented, people were unable to contact one another without being inside a house where there was a landline telephone. Now you use a cell phone to call people when you are just about anywhere! You can also use cell phones for more than just phone calls.

Cell phones now come in all shapes and sizes. You can keep them in your purse, pocket, or even attached to your ear. Cell phones are used to send e-mail,

surf the Internet, and play games. You can even take photos or make videos using your phone!

A cell phone can be a telephone, a computer, a camera, and a camcorder, a game player, and a music player all in one. Imagine if you had to carry around all of those things in your school bag at the same time. That would be too much! Don't you agree?

For these reasons, I think the cell phone is the most important invention of our times.

1. Underline the topic sentence.

2. List two examples of details or relevant evidence that support the writer's viewpoint.

_____

_____

3. Circle where the writer tries to get support for the idea.

Name_____

Vocabulary

Directions Choose the word from the box that best matches each definition. Write the word on the line.

_____ 1. a big gun mounted on a base or wheels

_____ 2. a person who designs and makes plans for buildings

_____ 3. made, shaped, or done

_____ 4. a person who studies the basic nature of knowledge and reality

_____ 5. a person who wants and tries to get the same thing as another or tries to do better than another

> ### Check the Words You Know
>
> ___achieved
> ___architect
> ___bronze
> ___cannon
> ___depressed
> ___fashioned
> ___midst
> ___philosopher
> ___rival

Directions Choose the word from the box that best fits in each sentence. Write the word on the line shown to the left.

_____ 6. The horse's yellow-brown coat was so rich and shiny it looked like it was made from ____.

_____ 7. Working together on their books about horses, Wesley Dennis and Marguerite Henry ____ great success.

_____ 8. Amelia was known as the best artist in school, but her ____ Lily was trying to outdo her with a new painting.

_____ 9. The wild pony did not like being fenced in. It was happier in the ____ of the wide open fields.

_____ 10. Julia felt sad, or ____, when she had to leave the ranch at the end of the summer.

Write a Journal Entry

On a separate sheet of paper write a journal entry describing an animal you have drawn. Use as many vocabulary words as you can. Include a drawing if possible.

Home Activity Your child identified and used vocabulary words from *Leonardo's Horse*. Read a story or nonfiction article with your child. Have your child point out unfamiliar words. Work together to figure out the meaning of each word by using other words that are near it.

Principal Parts of Regular Verbs

A verb's tenses are made from four basic forms. These basic forms are called the verb's **principal parts.**

Present	Present Participle	Past	Past Participle
watch	(am, is, are) watching	watched	(has, have, had) watched
study	(am, is, are) studying	studied	(has, have, had) studied

A **regular verb** forms its past and past participle by adding *-ed* or *-d* to the present form.

• The present and the past forms can be used by themselves as verbs.

• The present participle and the past participle are always used with a helping verb.

Directions Write the form of the underlined verb indicated in ( ).

1. For centuries, people <u>admire</u> the works of Leonardo da Vinci. (past participle)

   _____

2. Today he <u>enjoy</u> the title of greatest genius of the Renaissance. (present participle)

   _____

3. He <u>observe</u> everyday activities as a scientist. (past) _____

4. Leonardo <u>paint</u> with greater skill than any other artist of his time. (past)

   _____

5. He <u>fill</u> notebooks with his observations, illustrations, and original ideas. (past)

   _____

6. Scientists <u>create</u> working models from his instructions and drawings. (past participle)

   _____

7. Leonardo's life <u>inspire</u> me to be more observant. (past participle) _____

Directions Underline the verb in each sentence. Write *present, present participle, past,* or *past participle* to identify the principal part used to form the verb.

8. Leonardo lived in Vinci, Italy, as a boy. _____

9. Soon he had developed a keen eye and an observant nature. _____

10. Most people recognize the name Leonardo da Vinci. _____

Home Activity Your child learned about principal parts of regular verbs. Ask your child to write the principal parts of *love, live,* and *dream* and then use each part in a sentence about himself or herself.

© Pearson Education, Inc., 5

Name _____

Compound Words

Spelling Words				
waterproof	teaspoon	grasshopper	homesick	barefoot
courthouse	earthquake	rowboat	scrapbook	countryside
lightweight	fishhook	spotlight	blindfold	whirlpool
tablespoon	greenhouse	postcard	hummingbird	thumbtack

Complete the Sentence Write the list word that best completes the sentence.

1. Do you know that three teaspoons equal one ____?

2. The ____ is a place where justice is tested every day.

3. The ant stored food while the ____ played.

4. When you're away for a while, it is common to feel ____.

5. The hum from a ____ comes from its rapidly beating wings.

6. Some people wear a ____ to sleep on an airplane.

7. The ____ is full of exotic plants.

8. The circle of light on the stage was from the ____.

9. I like to walk ____ in the wet sand.

10. The ____ was full of old news clippings and photos.

1. _____
2. _____
3. _____
4. _____
5. _____
6. _____
7. _____
8. _____
9. _____
10. _____

Definitions Answer each clue with a list word. Write it on the line.

11. hills, trees, and lakes

12. not heavy at all

13. carries a message

14. hang something with it

15. stays dry

16. shaking ground

17. boat with oars

18. worm holder

19. one-third of a tablespoon

20. circling water

11. _____
12. _____
13. _____
14. _____
15. _____
16. _____
17. _____
18. _____
19. _____
20. _____

Home Activity Your child used the meanings of list words to write them in sentences and match them with synonyms. Ask your child to tell you what a compound word is and give three examples.

© Pearson Education, Inc., 5

Scoring Rubric: Persuasive Speech

	4	3	2	1
Focus/Ideas	Has a clear focus, position, or claim; uses reasons that support an opinion	Has a mostly clear focus, position, or claim; uses some reasons that support an opinion	Lacks a clear focus, position, or claim; lacks supporting reasons	Has no clear focus, position, or claim; has no supporting reasons
Organization	Has well-organized argument with strong evidence supported by facts and details	Includes an organized argument with some supporting facts and details	Lacks an organized argument or with few supporting facts and details	Has no argument or supporting facts and details
Voice	Uses clear persuasive language and an active voice	Uses mostly persuasive language and an active voice	Uses very little persuasive language; very little active voice	Uses no persuasive language or active voice
Word Choice	Strong persuasive language	Language persuasive	Language sometimes unpersuasive	Language unpersuasive
Sentences	Smooth, varied, rhythmic sentences	Some variety in sentences	Many sentences lacking variety	Choppy or rambling sentences
Conventions	Correct use of principal parts of regular verbs	Mostly correct use of principal parts of regular verbs	Little correct use of principal parts of regular verbs	No correct use of principal parts of regular verbs

Vocabulary • Greek and Latin Roots

- Many English words are based on **Greek or Latin roots,** which are often included in their definitions in a dictionary. Greek and Latin roots may help you understand the meanings of unfamiliar words.

- The root *bio-* means "life," *arch-* means "chief or ruler," and *philo-* means "loving."

Directions Read the following passage. Then answer the questions below.

The great Renaissance artist Raphael achieved fame during his lifetime. He was respected as an architect. He designed two churches in Rome, but he is known more for his painting than for his architecture. One of his most famous paintings is called *The School of Athens.* It shows the philosopher as a hero. The Greek philosophers Plato and Aristotle are at the center of the painting. They are standing in the midst of other great philosophers from ancient times.

Raphael had many students in his studio. They helped him complete his larger works. Raphael was a well-loved teacher, and some of the students thought of others students as rivals. After Raphael's death, however, his students worked together to complete many important works started by their teacher. The biographer Giorgio Vasari called Raphael "the prince of painters."

1. The Greek root *arch–* means "chief or ruler." The Greek word *tekton* means "builder." What do these tell you about the meaning of *architect*?

_____

2. The Greek root *philo–* means "loving." The Greek word *sophia* means "knowledge, learning." What do these tell you about the meaning of *philosopher*?

_____

3. The Greek root *bio–* means "life." The Greek word *graphia* means "record." What do these tell you about the meaning of *biographer*?

_____

4. The Latin word *studium* means "to study." What does this tell you about the meaning of *studio*?

_____

5. Write as many words as you can think of that use the roots *arch–, philo–,* and *bio–.* If you cannot think of any words on your own, use the dictionary for help.

_____

Home Activity Your child identified Greek and Latin roots to understand unfamiliar words in a passage. Read a passage with your child and see if you can find words with Greek and Latin roots. Use a dictionary for any words you are not sure of. Then think of other words with the same root to figure out their meanings.

Skim and Scan

- To **scan** is to move one's eyes quickly down the page, seeking specific words and phrases. Scanning is used to find out if a resource will answer a reader's questions. Once a reader has scanned a document, he or she might go back and skim it.

- To **skim** a document is to read the first and last paragraphs, as well as to use headings, summaries, and other organizers as you move down the page. Skimming is used to quickly identify the main idea. You might also read the first sentence of each paragraph.

Directions Scan the passage to answer the questions below.

Albrecht Dürer (1471–1528)
Early Life and Career. Dürer's training began as a draftsman in his father's workshop in Germany. By the age of thirteen, he had already made his first self-portrait. One year later, in 1485, he produced *Madonna with Musical Angels.* For four years, he studied painting and woodcutting with a master.

Travel and Artistic Growth. In 1490, Dürer began several years of travel and painting. His trips around Europe were very important to his artistic development.

His journeys to Italy, the Netherlands (Holland), France, and Switzerland especially influenced his art.

Important Works. By 1505, Dürer was famous. Eventually he became recognized as the greatest German Renaissance painter and printmaker. Some of Dürer's important works include *Self-Portrait* (1500), *Portrait of a Young Man* (1500), *The Feast of the Rose Garlands* (1506), *Adam and Eve* (1507), and *Four Apostles* (1526).

---

1. When you scan this passage, what helps you find specific information?

2. In which paragraph would you find the titles of Dürer's most famous paintings?

3. In which paragraph would you find out if Dürer painted as a youth?

4. In what part of the passage would you find when Dürer lived?

5. Can you find out about Dürer's printmaking methods by scanning this passage?

Name_____

Leonardo's Horse

Directions Skim the following passage to answer the questions below.

The Printing Press

The inventor of the printing press was a goldsmith named **Johannes Gutenberg**. The invention of the press occurred around 1450 in Germany, and it marked an important advance for Renaissance culture.

The use of the printing press spread rapidly throughout Europe. By the year 1500, as many as twenty million books had been printed. The discovery changed life during the Renaissance. For one thing, there was an increase in the number of people who learned to read. Secondly, printing spread knowledge and ideas. Some scholars believe that the invention of the printing press was nearly as important as the invention of writing itself.

6. What is a good way to skim this passage?

_____

_____

7. What is the topic of this passage?

_____

_____

8. Is the passage about silversmithing? How can you tell?

_____

_____

9. Is the writer of this passage conveying facts or opinions? How can you tell?

_____

_____

10. How would you express the main idea of this passage?

_____

_____

Home Activity Your child learned about skimming and scanning a text. Have your child quickly skim an encyclopedia entry and tell you what he or she learned.

© Pearson Education, Inc., 5

Compound Words

Proofread a Letter Halie wrote a letter home from camp. There are seven spelling errors and one capitalization error. Circle the errors and write the corrections on the lines.

Spelling Words

Dear Mom and Dad,

    I'm not crying or homsick. This paper got a little wet because I'm in a rowboat. I have a fish hook on the line. The countryside around camp is awesome. We run around bearfoot most days. My Counselor is the nature teacher. Yesterday, everybody saw a hummbird. The camp has a greenhouse where all the vegetables we eat are grown. Thanks for the waterproff slicker. It's litewait and will keep me dry. You sent a really beautiful postcard of the Grand Canyon. I used a thumtack to hang it on my bunk wall!

                Write soon,
                Halie

Spelling Words

waterproof
teaspoon
grasshopper
homesick
barefoot
courthouse
earthquake
rowboat
scrapbook
countryside

lightweight
fishhook
spotlight
blindfold
whirlpool
tablespoon
greenhouse
postcard
hummingbird
thumbtack

1. _____ 2. _____

3. _____ 4. _____

5. _____ 6. _____

7. _____

8. _____

Proofread Words Correct the spellings of the list words. Write the words correctly on the lines.

Frequently Misspelled Words

something
everybody
everyone

9. Meet me on the steps of the <u>corthouse</u>.   9. _____

10. My <u>scapebook</u> is full of pictures and mementos.   10. _____

11. Performers love to be in the <u>spotelite</u>.   11. _____

12. The bathwater went down the drain in a little <u>wirlpool</u>.   12. _____

13. Pictures fell off the wall during the <u>erthkwake</u>.   13. _____

14. I folded my scarf into a <u>blindefold</u>.   14. _____

15. A <u>grasshoper</u> has long, strong legs.   15. _____

Home Activity Your child identified misspelled compound words. Ask your child to spell three of the compound words for you.

© Pearson Education, Inc., 5

Principal Parts of Regular Verbs

Directions Read the passage. Then read each question. Circle the letter of the correct answer.

Leonardo's Journals

(1) Leonardo da Vinci <u>pursued</u> a wide range of interests. (2) He had so many ideas that new ones <u>distracted</u> him from other projects. (3) Some <u>have observed</u> that he <u>possessed</u> too many abilities. (4) One lifetime contains too few hours for such a man. (5) Leonardo's journals (preserve) many of his plans and ideas. (6) In them, he recorded plans for many inventions. (7) This is how we learn of his great genius today.

1 Which describes the principal part of the underlined verb in sentence 1?

  A Past

  B Present

  C Past participle

  D Present participle

2 What is the present form of the underlined verb in sentence 2?

  A distract

  B am distracting

  C is distracting

  D are distracting

3 Which describes the principal parts of the two underlined verbs in sentence 3?

  A Past/Past

  B Present participle/Past

  C Past participle/Past

  D Present participle/Past participle

4 Which two present tense verbs are found in this passage?

  A preserved, learn

  B have, learn

  C recorded, learn

  D contains, learn

5 Which form of the verb in parentheses best completes sentence 5?

  A has preserved

  B have preserved

  C are preserved

  D is preserving

© Pearson Education, Inc., 5

Home Activity Your child prepared for taking tests on principal parts of verbs. Ask your child to name the principal parts of the verbs *paint* and *invent* and then use each part in a sentence.

Fact and Opinion

- You can prove a **statement of fact** true or false. You can do this by using your own knowledge, asking an expert, or checking a reference source such as an encyclopedia or a nonfiction text.
- A **statement of opinion** gives ideas or feelings, not facts. It cannot be proved true or false.
- A sentence may contain both a statement of fact and a statement of opinion.

Directions Read the following passage. Then complete the diagram below by following its instructions, and answer the questions.

In 1861, the fossil remains of an *Archaeopteryx* (Ahr-key-OP-ter-iks) were discovered in Germany. They are about 150 million years old. Many scientists believe *Archaeopteryx* is the earliest known bird. When I saw it in a museum, I thought it looked like it was part dinosaur and part bird. It had feathers and wings like birds. It also had teeth and three claws on each wing. According to many scientists, *Archaeopteryx* could fly, but I'm not so sure. I think it might have flapped its wings, but I can't imagine it ever got off the ground.

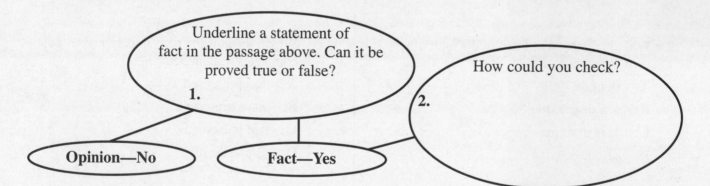

Underline a statement of fact in the passage above. Can it be proved true or false?

1.

How could you check?

2.

Opinion—No

Fact—Yes

3. Write a statement of opinion from the passage. How do you know it is a statement of opinion?

_____

_____

4. Which sentence contains both a fact and an opinion?

_____

_____

5. In the last sentence, the author expresses an opinion that *Archaeopteryx* couldn't have flown. What kind of details would support this opinion?

_____

 Home Activity Your child read a short passage and identified facts and opinions. Read an article together. Ask your child to identify statements of fact and ask how they can be proven.

© Pearson Education, Inc., 5

Name _____

Writing · Advertising Brochure

Key Features of an Advertising Brochure

- persuades readers to do something, such as buy a product or attend an event
- lists reasons why reader should do something
- may appeal to a specific audience, such as teens, women, fathers

---

Come Visit the Oak Lake Music Festival!

The Oak Lake Music Festival offers pleasing sounds for the whole family. Come and hear something new!

When and Where
The Festival takes place at the Main Pavilion, Oak Lake Park.
It runs daily from Thursday, March 6 through Sunday, March 9.

What is the Festival?
The Oak Lake Music Festival began in 1973. It has brought a wide variety of musical performers to the Oak Lake region. Features of the festival include:

- National acts playing a variety of musical styles; lineup includes Shanita, the Stockton Boys, and Avery Taylor
- Workshops on playing both traditional and contemporary music
- A refreshment tent offering delicious and affordable food
- Fireworks on Saturday!

Mariana Ciwiec, who attended last year's festival, writes, "I'm definitely coming back to Oak Lake with my husband and kids. Last year we all had a blast!"

What better way to celebrate the beginning of spring than listening to music in the beautiful environs of the lake? Make your reservation today: you can call or e–mail us.

---

1. Why does the author include the quote by Mariana Ciwiec?

_____

_____

2. Put a box around the list of reasons for attending. How did the author decide to order the list?

_____

_____

Vocabulary

Directions Draw a line to connect each word on the left to the matching definition on the right.

1. proportion   a special event

2. foundations   put up; built

3. erected   space or building where work is done

4. workshop   a proper relation among parts

5. occasion   parts on which other parts rest for support

> ## Check the Words You Know
>
> ___erected
> ___foundations
> ___mold
> ___occasion
> ___proportion
> ___tidy
> ___workshop

Directions Choose the word from the box that best completes each sentence. Write the word on the line to the left.

_____ 6. Julia poured plaster into a _____ shaped like a bird.

_____ 7. She was creating a statue for a special event, or _____.

_____ 8. We _____, or built, a statue in front of the new library.

_____ 9. When she finished making the bird, her _____ was a mess.

_____ 10. She likes to wipe up the dust made by the plaster and _____ her workbench before she goes home.

Write a News Report

On a separate sheet of paper, write a news report about an important discovery, like the discovery of the *Archaeopteryx* fossil remains. Use as many vocabulary words as you can.

Home Activity Your child identified and used vocabulary words from *The Dinosaurs of Waterhouse Hawkins*. Read a story or nonfiction article with your child about dinosaurs or animals. Have him or her describe the dinosaur or animal and then explain whether the description is a statement of fact or of opinion.

Name _____

Principal Parts of Irregular Verbs

Usually you add *-ed* to a verb to show past tense. **Irregular verbs** do not follow this rule. Instead of having *-ed* forms to show past tense, irregular verbs usually change to other words.

Present Tense	The king <u>sees</u> the Crystal Palace.
Present Participle	The king <u>is seeing</u> the Crystal Palace.
Past Tense	The king <u>saw</u> the Crystal Palace.
Past Participle	The king <u>has seen</u> the Crystal Palace.

Present Tense	Present Participle	Past Tense	Past Participle
bring	(am, is, are) bringing	brought	(*has, have, had*) brought
build	(am, is, are) building	built	(*has, have, had*) built
choose	(am, is, are) choosing	chose	(*has, have, had*) chosen
come	(am, is, are) coming	came	(*has, have, had*) come
draw	(am, is, are) drawing	drew	(*has, have, had*) drawn
eat	(am, is, are) eating	ate	(*has, have, had*) eaten
find	(am, is, are) finding	found	(*has, have, had*) found
grow	(am, is, are) growing	grew	(*has, have, had*) grown
run	(am, is, are) running	ran	(*has, have, had*) run
set	(am, is, are) setting	set	(*has, have, had*) set
speak	(am, is, are) speaking	spoke	(*has, have, had*) spoken
tell	(am, is, are) telling	told	(*has, have, had*) told

Directions Underline the verb in each sentence. Write *present, present participle, past,* or *past participle* to identify the principal part of the verb.

1. He built a studio in Manhattan. _____

2. Hawkins had chosen Central Park for his display. _____

Directions Write the sentence using the principal part of the underlined verb indicated in ( ).

3. Archaeologists <u>find</u> many more dinosaur bones. (past participle)

_____

4. Today dinosaur exhibits <u>draw</u> huge crowds. (present participle)

_____

© Pearson Education, Inc., 5

Home Activity Your child learned about principal parts of irregular verbs. Ask your child to write the principal parts of *tell* and *write* and then use each part in a sentence telling what he or she could communicate about dinosaurs.

Consonant Sounds /j/, /ks/, /sk/, and /s/

Spelling Words				
excuse	scene	muscle	explore	pledge
journal	science	schedule	gigantic	scheme
Japan	excellent	exclaim	fascinate	ginger
scholar	scent	dodge	smudge	schooner

Classify Write the list word that best completes the group.

1. plan, plot, ____

2. avoid, elude, sidestep, ____

3. diary, log, magazine, ____

4. setting, landscape, ____

5. aroma, perfume, odor, ____

6. captivate, interest, ____

7. bone, skin, ____

8. yacht, kayak, ____

9. outstanding, brilliant, ____

10. basil, oregano, ____

1. _____

2. _____

3. _____

4. _____

5. _____

6. _____

7. _____

8. _____

9. _____

10. _____

Words in Context Write the list word that completes each sentence.

11. Tokyo is the largest city in ____.

12. Cry out and ____ mean the same thing.

13. A ____ enjoys learning and studying.

14. The bad weather is my ____ for being late today.

15. Astronauts ____ outer space.

16. I'll add the meeting to my ____.

17. I made a donation ____ to the local charity.

18. My ____ book contains many experiments.

19. The ____ on the wall is from finger paint.

20. The redwood trees in California are ____.

11. _____

12. _____

13. _____

14. _____

15. _____

16. _____

17. _____

18. _____

19. _____

20. _____

Home Activity Your child wrote words with special spellings for certain consonant sounds. Have your child pick the five most difficult words for him or her. Go over the spellings of these words with your child.

© Pearson Education, Inc., 5

Name _____

Web A

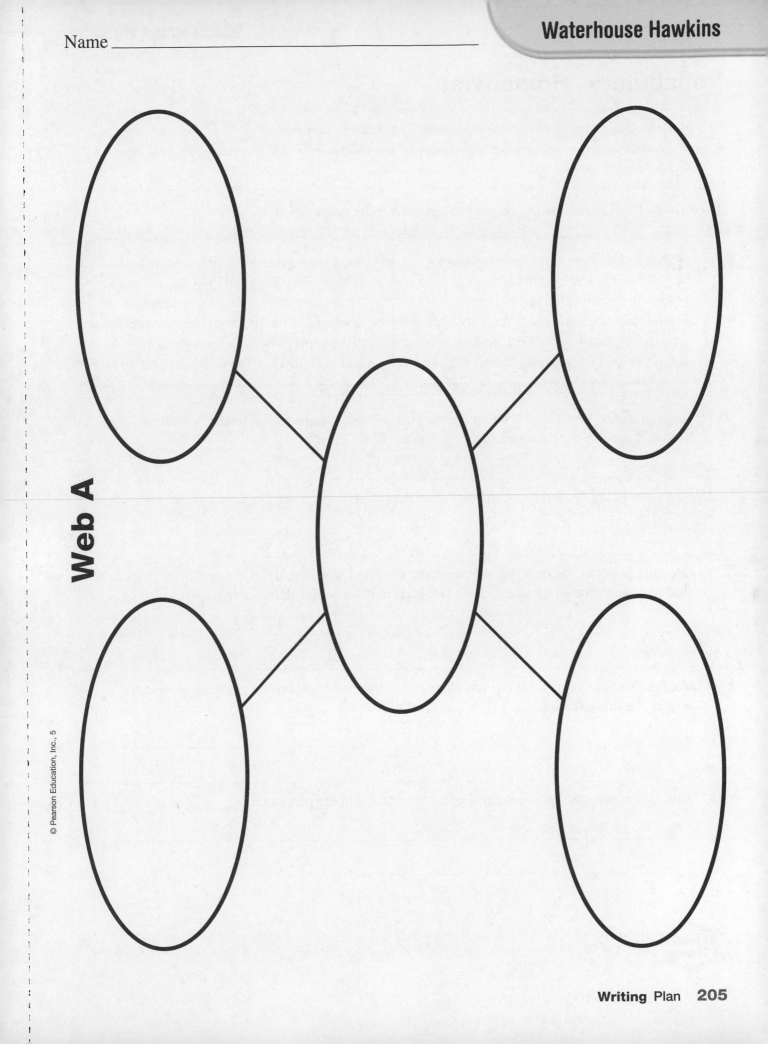

Vocabulary • Homonyms

- **Homonyms** are words with the same spelling but different meanings.
- Sometimes an unfamiliar word is a homonym. The words around the homonym can offer clues to its meaning.

Directions Read the following passage. Then answer the questions below.

Fossil collectors know that they are not allowed to remove fossils from most places. It is against the law to remove fossils from someone else's property and from public lands. In order to collect fossils, collectors meet at a "fossil fair" to buy fossils from other collectors. It's also possible they might add to their collection by keeping a file with photographs and drawings of fossils. Sometimes collectors make copies of fossils by pouring plaster into a mold. They can look very realistic.

1. *Fair* can mean "not favoring one more than others" or "a gathering of buyers or sellers." How is it used in the passage? How can you tell?

_____

2. *Might* can mean "possibly would" or "great power." How is it used in the passage? How can you tell?

_____

3. *File* can mean "a container, drawer, or folder for keeping papers in order" or "a steel tool used to smooth rough surfaces." How is it used in the passage? How can you tell?

_____

_____

4. *Mold* can mean "a furry, fungus growth" or "a shape in which anything is formed or cast." How is it used in the passage? How can you tell?

_____

_____

5. Write a sentence using the meaning of *mold* not used in the passage.

_____

_____

 Home Activity Your child read a short passage and used context clues to understand new homonyms in a passage. Read an article with your child. Identify homonyms in that article. Write sentences that use each meaning of the homonyms.

Name_____

Schedule

A **schedule** is a kind of table with **rows** and **columns**. The rows and columns meet at boxes that are called **cells**. Schedules show times, dates, and locations for airplanes, trains, buses, activities, and sporting events.

Directions Use this train schedule to answer the questions.

Departure Schedule for Trains to Chicago

		A.M.	A.M.	A.M.	P.M.	P.M.	P.M.
Waukekee		5:01	7:30	11:30	1:00	3:30	5:00
Hampton		5:45	8:15	12:15	1:45	4:15	5:45
Rainville	*	6:15	8:45	12:45	2:15	4:45	6:15
Harbor Park	*	7:00	9:30	1:30	3:00	5:00	7:00
Arrive in Chicago		**8:00**	**10:30**	**2:30**	**4:00**	**6:00**	**8:00**

* **Indicates food service.**

1. How many trains go to Chicago every day? Which train leaves Waukekee in the morning and arrives in Chicago in the afternoon?

_____

2. Counting Waukekee, how many stops does the train make? What is the fourth stop?

_____

3. You live in Rainville. You want to meet your friends in Chicago at 10:30 A.M. What time do you have to catch the train in Rainville to be on time? How much extra time will you have when you arrive in Chicago?

_____

4. You live in Harbor Park and have to take the train that leaves at 7:00 A.M. for Chicago. You don't have time to fix yourself breakfast. Will you be able to get something to eat on the train? How do you know?

_____

5. You live in Hampton. Every Monday at 5:00 P.M., you have violin lessons in Rainville. To be on time, which train do you have to catch? Will you have time to spare?

_____

Directions Use this camp schedule to answer the questions.

Camp Want-To-Get-Away Schedule

	Monday	Tuesday	Wednesday	Thursday	Friday	Saturday	Sunday
8 A.M.	Breakfast in Olson Hall	Breakfast in Olson Hall	Breakfast in Olson Hall	Breakfast in Olson Hall	Breakfast in Olson Hall	Breakfast in Olson Hall	Breakfast in Olson Hall
10 A.M.	Swimming at Lake Beluga	Play Rehearsal	Archery	Swimming at Lake Beluga	Band Practice	You Choose	Play Rehearsal
1 P.M.	Crafts	Crafts	Horseback Riding	Letters Home	Horseback Riding	You Choose	Parents Visit
4 P.M.	Group Games	Archery	Water Sports	Group Games	Hiking	Group Games	Swimming at Lake Beluga
8 P.M.	Lights Out	Lights Out	Lights Out	Lights Out	MOVIE	Campfire Stories	Lights Out

6. How many time slots for each day are listed on this schedule? How many days are listed?

_____

7. You want to sharpen your swimming skills. What days and times can you go swimming?

_____

_____

8. You want your parents to come for a visit. What day and time is best?

_____

9. What time can you eat breakfast every day? Where is breakfast held?

_____

10. You love to act. What is a good activity to take part in? When is this activity available?

_____

© Pearson Education, Inc., 5

Home Activity Your child learned about reading schedules. Look at the schedule of a sports team your child likes. Find out when the next game is and whether or not it takes place during school hours.

Name _____

Consonant Sounds /j/, /ks/, /sk/, and /s/

Proofread a Travel Poster There are seven spelling errors and one punctuation error. Circle the errors and write the corrections on the lines.

> Exsplore Japan
>
> This trip will facinate the scolar or the casual traveler.
>
> Exsellent first-class hotels are available.
>
> Experience the exotic taste of ginger and other spices.
>
> Visit a typical school full of excited children.
>
> Enjoy the sent of lotus flower in your own private spa.
>
> Enjoy the peaceful cene of a
> Japanese garden and teahouse.
>
> The skedule is made to meet your needs

1. _____   2. _____

3. _____   4. _____

5. _____   6. _____

7. _____

8. _____

Proofread Words Circle the correct spelling of the list word.

9.	plege	pleje	pledge
10.	sceme	scheme	skeme
11.	smudge	smuge	smuje
12.	mussle	muscel	muscle
13.	dodje	dodge	dogde
14.	journal	journle	jurnal
15.	jigantic	gidgantic	gigantic
16.	skooner	schooner	scooner

Spelling Words

excuse
scene
muscle
explore
pledge
journal
science
schedule
gigantic
scheme

Japan
excellent
exclaim
fascinate
ginger
scholar
scent
dodge
smudge
schooner

Frequently Misspelled Words

except
excited
school

School + Home **Home Activity** Your child identified misspelled list words. Review the *sch* and *sc* words and their pronunciations with your child.

Principal Parts of Irregular Verbs

Directions Read the passage. Then read each question. Circle the letter of the correct answer.

If These Bones Could Talk

(1) Scientists <u>have sought</u> dinosaur skeletons for many years. (2) They study the bones to learn about the behavior and appearance of prehistoric animals. (3) The dinosaur's skull <u>has been</u> especially important to scientists. (4) The skull helps the scientist tell what type of animal it was. (5) Also, it (speak) volumes about the dinosaur's vision, hearing, and sense of smell. (6) We (build) many skeletons from skulls and bones. (7) There is a lot to learn from these ancient bones!

1 Which describes the principal part of the underlined verb in sentence 1?

A   Past

B   Present

C   Past participle

D   Present participle

2 What is the present form of the underlined verb in sentence 1?

A   seek

B   is seeking

C   am seeking

D   sought

3 Which describes the principal part of the underlined verb in sentence 3?

A   Past

B   Present

C   Past participle

D   Present participle

4 Which form of the verb in parentheses best completes sentence 5?

A   has spoken

B   have spoken

C   is speaking

D   speak

5 Which form of the verb in parentheses best completes sentence 6?

A   are building

B   is building

C   has built

D   have built

Home Activity Your child prepared for taking tests on principal parts of irregular verbs. Ask your child to name the principal parts of the verbs *choose* and *find* and then use each part in a sentence.

210   **Conventions** Principal Parts of Irregular Verbs

© Pearson Education, Inc., 5

Main Idea and Details

- The **main idea** is the most important idea about the topic.
- **Details** are small pieces of information that tell more about the main idea.

Directions Read the following passage. Then complete the diagram below.

> Who earned the title *Mother of the Blues*? That would be Ma Rainey (1886–1939), the first great African American blues singer. Her career began when she was fourteen years old in a local talent show in Georgia. Just four years later, she married "Pa" Rainey, and they formed a song-and-dance act that included blues songs. They traveled and performed throughout the South.
>
> In 1923, she made her first recording. She recorded about 100 songs. She performed with many notable jazz musicians during her career, which lasted until the 1930s. Her singing influenced many younger blues singers.

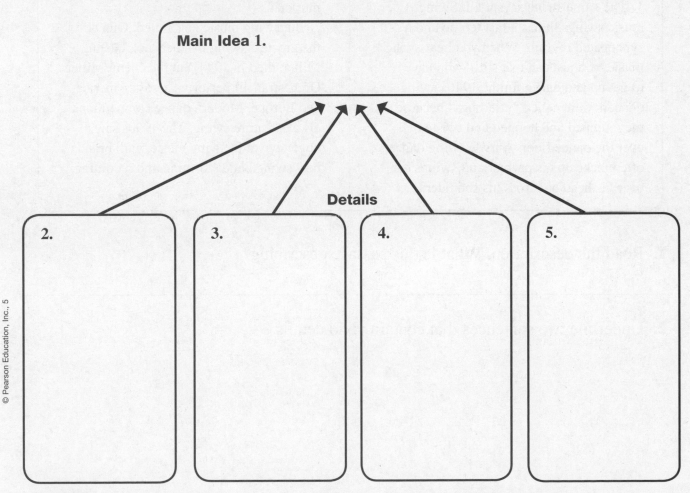

Main Idea 1.

Details

2.

3.

4.

5.

© Pearson Education, Inc., 5

School + Home **Home Activity** Your child read a short passage and used a graphic organizer to identify the main idea and details. Work with your child to identify the main idea and details of individual paragraphs in a magazine article about music.

Writing · Description

Key Features of a Description

- creates a vivid mental picture
- imagery may appeal to the five senses
- uses precise words and vivid adjectives

Swing Music

Swing grew out of jazz music, and in the 1930s and 1940s it was as popular as could be. A top-flight swing band might have twenty or twenty-five musicians in it, playing trumpets, trombones, clarinets, saxophones, a piano, and drums. Just imagine the sound!

The name *swing* says it all. Swing music swings. It has a fast tempo and a syncopated rhythm. When you hear swing music, you just can't sit still—you have to get up and dance. In the 1940s swing dancers were called "jitterbugs" because they jumped and hopped and twisted all over the dance floor. A male swing dancer often picks up his partner and swings her over his head or across his shoulders.

Swing music is still around. Its popularity faded during World War II because most musicians were men, and most men joined the military. The types of popular music that came later, such as bebop and rock and roll, were made by smaller bands—often just three or four musicians.

But swing music never died. One of the greatest swing bandleaders, Glenn Miller, died in 1944, but the Glenn Miller Orchestra still performs across America and Europe. Modern dance competitions always feature swing. The 1990s saw a huge revival in swing music, with brand new swing bands forming and recording.

1. Read the description. What is this passage describing?

_____

2. Underline two sentences that contain vivid details.

Vocabulary

Directions Choose the word from the box that best matches each definition below.

_____ 1. to think highly of

_____ 2. the condition of being owned by another person and being made to work without wages

_____ 3. devoted to religion

_____ 4. a group of singers who sing together often in a church service

_____ 5. a person in his or her teens

Directions Match each word on the left with the word that has a similar meaning on the right. Write the correct letter on the line.

_____ 6. released   **a.** spiritual

_____ 7. barber   **b.** singers

_____ 8. appreciate   **c.** haircutter

_____ 9. choir   **d.** published

_____ 10. religious   **e.** value

Write a Journal Entry

On a separate sheet of paper, write a journal entry describing your favorite kind of music and why you like it. Use as many vocabulary words as you can.

Home Activity Your child identified and used vocabulary words from *Mahalia Jackson.* Make up a song using the vocabulary words from the story to help your child remember their meanings.

Troublesome Verbs

Some pairs of verbs are confusing because they have similar meanings or because they look alike.

	Present	Past	Past Participle
Lay means "put" or "place."	lay	laid	(*has, have, had*) laid
Lie means "rest" or "recline."	lie	lay	(*has, have, had*) lain
Set means "put something somewhere."	set	set	(*has, have, had*) set
Sit means "sit down."	sit	sat	(*has, have, had*) sat
Let means "allow."	let	let	(*has, have, had*) let
Leave means "go away."	leave	left	(*has, have, had*) left

Directions Write the form of the underlined verb indicated in ( ).

1. A teenage girl <u>sit</u> with the choir. (past) _____

2. She has <u>lay</u> her hand over her heart. (past participle) _____

3. The choir director <u>let</u> her join. (past) _____

4. The music never <u>leave</u> her head. (past) _____

5. When she <u>set</u> her suitcases down in Chicago, Mahalia knew she was home. (past) _____

6. Mahalia's father had <u>let</u> her follow her dream. (past participle) _____

Directions Use context to help you decide which verb is needed. Then find the principal part needed on the chart. Underline the verb that correctly completes the sentence.

7. I (set, sit) a CD on the counter.

8. Will you (leave, let) me pay for it?

9. My parents have already (left, let) the store.

10. After dinner we (sat, set) down and listened to the CD.

11. Tom has (laid, lain) down on the floor.

12. Fiona (laid, lied) a log on the fire.

Home Activity Your child learned about troublesome verbs. Ask your child to explain the difference in meaning between *sit/set, lie/lay,* and *leave/let* and then act out the meanings of the verbs in each pair to demonstrate the difference.

One Consonant or Two

Spelling Words				
address	collar	mirror	recess	committee
collect	Mississippi	immediate	command	appreciate
announce	possess	Tennessee	gallop	opponent
barricade	broccoli	accomplish	allowance	zucchini

Words in Context Write the list word that best completes the sentence.

1. The vegetable ____ looks like little trees.

2. It was hard to cross the street because of the police ____.

3. The capital of ____ is Nashville.

4. Don't forget to button your ____.

5. "Faster, faster," he urged the horse as it began to ____.

6. He looked in the ____ to comb his hair.

7. The ____ River is the second-longest river in the United States.

8. Our class has ____ after lunch.

9. Do you get a weekly ____ for doing chores?

10. I need your telephone number and ____ for our records.

1. _____

2. _____

3. _____

4. _____

5. _____

6. _____

7. _____

8. _____

9. _____

10. _____

Antonyms Write the list word that has the opposite or nearly the opposite meaning.

11. scatter

12. delayed

13. obey

14. disregard

15. remove

11. _____

12. _____

13. _____

14. _____

15. _____

Synonyms Write the list word that has the same or almost the same meaning.

16. declare

17. group

18. foe

19. summer squash

20. succeed

16. _____

17. _____

18. _____

19. _____

20. _____

Home Activity Your child wrote words with double consonants. Take turns saying and spelling the list words aloud.

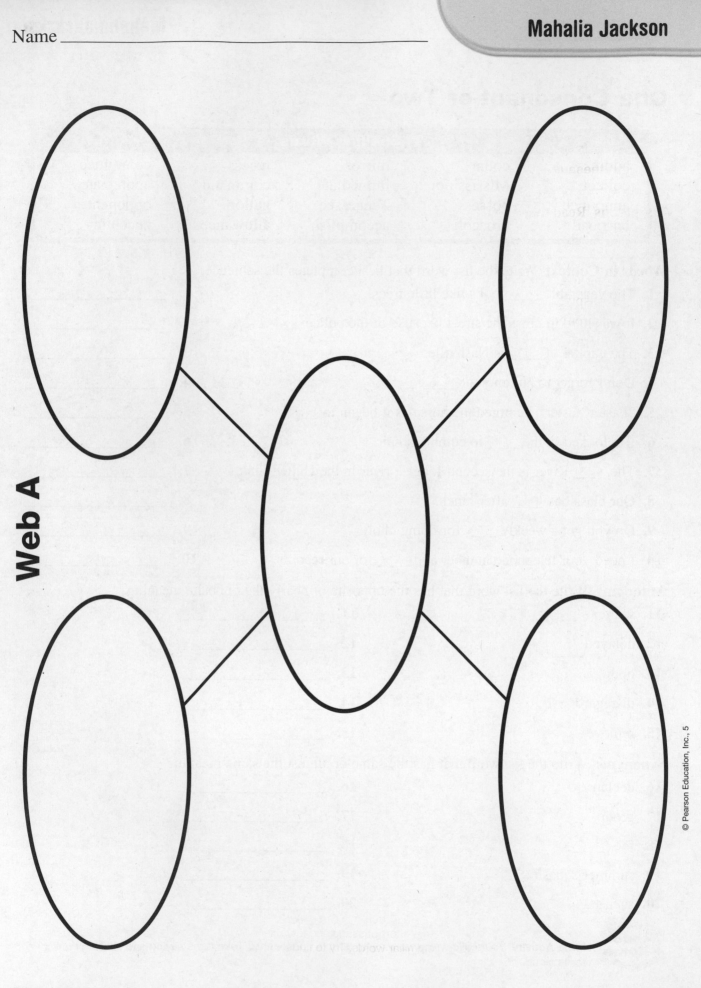

Web A

Vocabulary • Antonyms

- An **antonym** is a word that means the opposite of another word.
- Words such as *unlike, but,* and *instead* may indicate the presence of antonyms.
- A **thesaurus** is a book that lists words and their antonyms and synonyms.

Directions Read the following passage. Then answer the questions below. You may use a thesaurus.

The songs called spirituals were inspired by the lives of the people who wrote them: slaves living in the southern United States. By singing spirituals, slaves expressed their hope of being released and not enslaved, either in this life or the next. After slavery ended, spirituals were neglected because they reminded people of something they wanted to forget. But time passed, and spirituals came to be appreciated for their message and music. Spirituals are closely related to the gospel music, blues, and jazz that we hear today.

1. Find the antonym in the passage for *released*. How does this antonym help to define *released*?

_____

2. Find the antonym for *appreciated*. How does this antonym help to define *appreciated*?

_____

3. In this passage, the word *spiritual* means "a religious song." *Spiritual* also means "interested in the belief and worship of God or gods." What is an antonym for the second meaning?

_____

4. In this passage, the word *slavery* means "the condition of being owned by another person and being made to work without wages." What is an antonym for *slavery*?

_____

5. Write down a word from the passage and its antonym. Write a sentence or sentences using the original word and its antonym.

_____

_____

Home Activity Your child read a short passage and identified words and their antonyms. Read an article with your child and identify unfamiliar words. Try to find their meanings by identifying their antonyms in the article.

Card Catalog/Library Database

- You can use a **card catalog** or **library database** to find books, magazines, audiotapes, videotapes, CD-ROMS, and other materials in the library. You can search for materials by author, title, or subject. A card catalog is a box of drawers filled with cards containing detailed information about books and other library materials. A library database is an electronic version of a card catalog.

- If you don't know exactly what you are searching for in the library database, you can use "keywords." Be sure to type and spell words carefully. If you use more than one keyword in your search, put the word "AND" between the keywords.

- Both card catalog and library databases contain certain types of basic information. For instance, call numbers are used by libraries to identify and organize the items in their collections. Nonfiction books, videos, and recordings are arranged on library shelves by call number. Fiction books are arranged in alphabetical order by the author's last name.

Directions Look at the starting search screen for a library database below. For each of the numbered items, tell which of the six categories you would choose for each search. Then write the information you would enter into the library database.

Search Summerville Elementary Library
- ○ Title (exact search)
- ○ Title (keywords)
- ○ Author (last name, first name)
- ○ Author (keywords)
- ○ Subject (exact search)
- ○ Subject (keywords)

Search

1. Ray Charles's autobiography

2. a Louis Armstrong recording on CD, audiotape, or vinyl LP

3. a biography of Louis Armstrong

4. *Mahalia: A Life in Gospel Music*

5. a critical history of Motown Records

Directions Use the following sample card from a library card catalog to answer the questions below.

L424.7 RE

Roots of Blues Music

Parker, Mark, 1959-

Blues has influenced many different types of music today. It changed the way many people felt about music, as well. Blues emerged after slavery was abolished and changed the way singers approached music. Blues is still a popular form of music played today.

Publisher: Wilson Musical Reference

Pub date: c2001.

Pages: 313 p.

ISBN: 0534212311

6. Who is the author of this reference book?

_____

7. What is the book's call number?

_____

8. What is the title of the book?

_____

9. How many pages does this book have? When was it published, and by whom?

_____

10. What do you learn about the book from the card's summary?

_____

_____

_____

Home Activity Your child learned about using a library database and a card catalog. Visit the library with your child. Take turns searching for subjects that interest one or both of you.

One Consonant or Two

Proofread a Newspaper Article Circle six misspelled words. Write the words correctly. Find one capitalization error. Write the sentence correctly.

> Something odd hapenned in the students' dining room. Some students wanted brocoli at every meal. Their oponents wanted zuchinni. A commitee was formed. They decided to take a vote. No one expected an immediat result. The committee had something surprising to announce. most of the students preferred carrots!

1. _____   2. _____

3. _____   4. _____

5. _____   6. _____

7. _____

Proofread Words Circle the correct spelling of the list words.

8. Memphis and Nashville are cities in _____.

   Tenessee   Tennese   Tennessee

9. Most students love _____ after being inside.

   recess   reccess   recces

10. I _____ a collection of old comic books.

    posess   possess   posses

11. The settlers used a wooden plank to _____ the door.

    barricade   barricad   bariccade

12. I am hoping to _____ a lot this school year.

    acomplish   accomplish   accommplish

13. The bathroom _____ was foggy because of the steam from the shower.

    mirrer   miror   mirror

14. I will _____ the winner at the end of the game.

    announce   anounce   anounnce

© Pearson Education, Inc., 5

Spelling Words

address
collar
mirror
recess
committee
collect
Mississippi
immediate
command
appreciate

announce
possess
Tennessee
gallop
opponent
barricade
broccoli
accomplish
allowance
zucchini

Frequently Misspelled Words

different
happened

Home Activity Your child identified misspelled list words. Have your child tell you the three most difficult list words and then spell them to you.

Troublesome Verbs

Directions Read the passage. Then read each question. Circle the letter of the correct answer.

The Missing Book

(1) My father had let me borrow his book about Bessie Smith, the great blues singer. (2) Last night, I (lay) on my bed, reading. (3) My mother called for dinner, so I (set) my book on the bed. (4) After dinner, I went back to my room to lie down with my book. (5) To my surprise, my book was not where I leaved it! (6) How would I learn what happened to Bessie when she left Chattanooga? (7) I (sit) down to consider where the book might have gone. (8) Later, I learned that my father had picked up the book and had set it down on the bookshelf.

1 Which form of the verb in parentheses best completes sentence 2?

   A   lay

   B   laid

   C   lie

   D   lain

2 Which form of the verb in parentheses best completes sentence 3?

   A   sit

   B   sat

   C   have set

   D   set

3 What change, if any, should be made in sentence 4?

   A   Change *lie* to **laid**

   B   Change *lie* to **let**

   C   Change *lie* to **lay**

   D   Make no change

4 What change, if any, should be made in sentence 5?

   A   Change *leaved* to **leave**

   B   Change *leaved* to **left**

   C   Change *leaved* to **have left**

   D   Make no change

5 Which form of the verb in parentheses best completes sentence 7?

   A   sat

   B   sit

   C   set

   D   have sat

Home Activity Your child prepared for taking tests on principal parts of troublesome verbs. Ask your child to name the principal parts of the verbs *lie, lay, sit, set, leave,* and *let* and then use each part in a sentence.

Graphic Sources

- Some graphic sources are maps, time lines, charts, diagrams, and pictures with captions.
- A graphic source makes information easy to see and understand.

Directions Study the circle graph below. Then answer the following questions.

Small Films Company Annual Budget for Special Effects

21% Sound   17% Props

10% Make-up

22% Costumes

30% Lighting

1. What do the percentages show?

_____

2. On what special effect did the company spend the most money?

_____

3. How much more of the budget went toward costumes than make-up?

_____

4. In what kind of article might you see a circle graph?

_____

_____

5. What prior knowledge did you use to help you understand the graphic source?

_____

_____

Home Activity Your child learned how to interpret a graphic source. Together, imagine you are both writing an article about a favorite subject. Draw a graphic source that could be included in the article.

Writing • Expository Text

Key Features of Expository Text

- gives information about a topic
- is often written in the present tense
- includes main ideas and supporting details
- has an introduction, body, and conclusion

Movies vs. Television: The Showdown

I enjoy watching movies and television. I love exciting stories, interesting characters, and crazy plot twists. But I prefer watching movies to watching television. Let me tell you why.

First of all, movies are on a bigger screen (if you watch them in the theater, of course). Big screens make things a lot more exciting. Television screens, even big ones, are a lot smaller than theater screens. Nothing is as big or as fancy on television screens.

Second, the special effects are better in movies. Television shows have better effects than they did a long time ago. But they're nothing compared to what you see in movies like *Transformers* and *Spider-Man*.

Finally, movies have better actors than television shows do. I like movies that star people like Brad Pitt, Shia LaBeouf, and Harrison Ford. Actors like these bring a story to life. Television actors are good, but they don't seem as realistic as movie actors.

In conclusion, I definitely like watching movies more than television. But I still enjoy television. After all, who doesn't love *Hannah Montana*?

1. What is the main idea in each paragraph?

_____

_____

_____

2. Transitional words are words that link ideas, details, or paragraphs together. What transitional words does the author use in the text?

_____

Vocabulary

Directions Choose the word from the box that best matches each definition. Write the word on the line.

_____ 1. of or belonging to periods before recorded history

_____ 2. put back together again

_____ 3. view of scenery on land

_____ 4. done or made on an extremely small scale

_____ 5. the part of a picture or scene toward the back

> **Check the Words You Know**
>
> ___background
> ___landscape
> ___miniature
> ___prehistoric
> ___reassembled

Directions Choose the word from the box that best completes the sentence. Write the word on the line shown to the left.

_____ 6. Three hours after the storm, the set for the movie had already been put together again, or_____.

_____ 7. In preparing for the movie, the crew created a _____ village.

_____ 8. The film crew built a ruined temple to appear in the _____ of the scene.

_____ 9. The dinosaur film used models of huge, _____ creatures to show what some animals may have looked like before history was recorded.

_____ 10. The park provided a perfect _____ for the film.

Write a Movie Review

On a separate sheet of paper write a review of a movie that had lots of special effects. Describe the special effects and how they worked. Use as many vocabulary words as you can.

Home Activity Your child identified and used vocabulary words from *Special Effects in Film and Television*. Read the review of a movie with your child. Have him or her point out unfamiliar words. Work together to try to figure out the meaning of each word.

© Pearson Education, Inc., 5

Prepositions and Prepositional Phrases

A **preposition** begins a group of words called a **prepositional phrase**. The noun or pronoun that follows the preposition is called the **object of the preposition**. Prepositional phrases convey location, time, or direction or provide details.

People have watched animated movies <u>for</u> a long time. (preposition)
People have watched animated movies <u>for a long time</u>. (prepositional phrase)
People have watched animated movies for a long <u>time</u>. (object of the preposition)

Common Prepositions

about	around	by	into	over	until
above	at	down	near	through	up
across	before	for	of	to	with
after	below	from	on	toward	
against	between	in	onto	under	

Directions Underline the prepositional phrase in each sentence. Write *P* above the preposition. Write *O* above the object of the preposition.

1. The characters in animated films often seem quite real.

2. Young viewers may identify with the superheroes.

3. Ariel was a mermaid who lived under the sea.

4. She wanted a life on dry land.

Directions Underline the prepositional phrases. The number in ( ) tells how many prepositional phrases are in that sentence.

5. Many fairy tales have been made into animated movies for children. (2)

6. Their stories take youngsters from childhood into adulthood. (2)

7. The hero of the tale must pass through trials and adventures. (2)

8. At the end, he or she has shown great strength of character. (2)

Home Activity Your child learned about prepositions and prepositional phrases. Read a favorite story with your child. Ask him or her to point out prepositional phrases and identify the preposition and object of the preposition in each.

Prefixes *un-*, *de-*, *dis-*

Spelling Words				
uncover	defrost	uncomfortable	discourage	disadvantage
unfortunate	unfamiliar	disability	discomfort	deodorant
unemployed	deflate	disbelief	unpredictable	disapprove
disappoint	unpleasant	dehydrated	disqualify	undecided

Definitions in Context Write the list word that has the same or almost the same meaning as the underlined word or words.

1. Moisture is removed from <u>dried out</u> food.

2. I need to <u>melt</u> the turkey.

3. It was <u>unlucky</u> that I broke my leg.

4. My mother has been <u>out of work</u> since the factory closed.

5. The outcome of the contest was <u>in doubt</u> for months.

6. The player's tardiness was a <u>difficulty</u> for the team.

7. I took a route home from school that was <u>new</u> to me.

8. The roller coaster ride was <u>disagreeable</u> to me.

9. It was <u>painful</u> to sleep on the old, lumpy mattress.

10. The team decided to <u>ban</u> a player for cheating.

1. _____

2. _____

3. _____

4. _____

5. _____

6. _____

7. _____

8. _____

9. _____

10. _____

Antonyms Write the list word that has the opposite or nearly the opposite meaning.

11. ability

12. with odor

13. belief

14. expected

15. please

16. inflate

17. conceal

18. support

19. encourage

20. comfortable

11. _____

12. _____

13. _____

14. _____

15. _____

16. _____

17. _____

18. _____

19. _____

20. _____

© Pearson Education, Inc., 5

Home Activity Your child wrote words with prefixes. Say a prefix and have your child respond with one word from the list that has that prefix.

Name

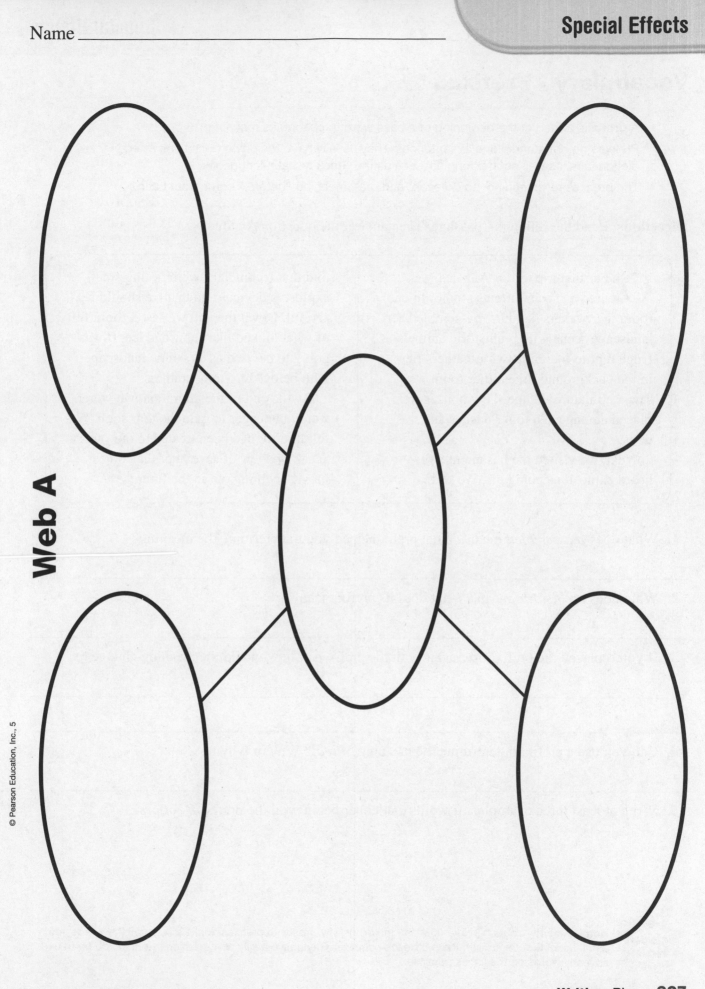

Web A

Vocabulary • Prefixes

- A **prefix** is added at the beginning of a base word to change its meaning.
- Prefixes do not stand alone in sentences. They usually have their own definitions listed in dictionaries, as well as their origins, such as the Greek or Latin languages.
- The prefixes *re-,* meaning "to do over," and *pre-,* meaning "before," come from Latin.

Directions Read the following passage. Then answer the questions below.

On our first trip to Los Angeles, we toured a special-effects studio. In one room the workers had just reassembled a landscape scene with prehistoric animals. Huge reptile-like birds with feathers flew in the background. In another room we saw a miniature village. Tiny houses were placed among even tinier bushes and trees.

Next, we visited the basement. We heard explosions going off. We were told that technicians were testing small explosive devices and that we should be careful. Down the hall we saw a room full of what looked like snow and ice. It was going to be used as an Arctic landscape with below-zero temperatures.

By the end of the afternoon, we were weary but eager to redo the tour soon. We felt like we had been treated to our own sneak preview of several of the coolest movies coming out in the future.

1. What does *reassembled* mean? What prefix helped you to determine the meaning?

_____

2. What does *prehistoric* mean? What does its prefix mean?

_____

3. If you replaced the prefix in *preview* with the prefix *re–,* how would the meaning change?

_____

_____

4. Can you use a prefix to determine the meaning of *real*? Why or why not?

_____

5. Write at least three examples of words that either begin with the prefix *re–* or *pre–*.

Home Activity Your child identified the meanings of words with prefixes. Make a list of all the words you can think of that begin with the prefixes *re–* or *pre–*. Then, have a silly conversation in which you try to use as many words on the list as possible.

Name_____

Graphics/Symbols

- **Graphics** aid in the use of instructions and communication. They identify and summarize information.
- **Graphics** have an effect on the user's understanding of material and provide additional meaning to the text that they accompany.
- **Symbols** and icons can be used to represent ideas, concepts, and information.

Directions Study the Web page below.

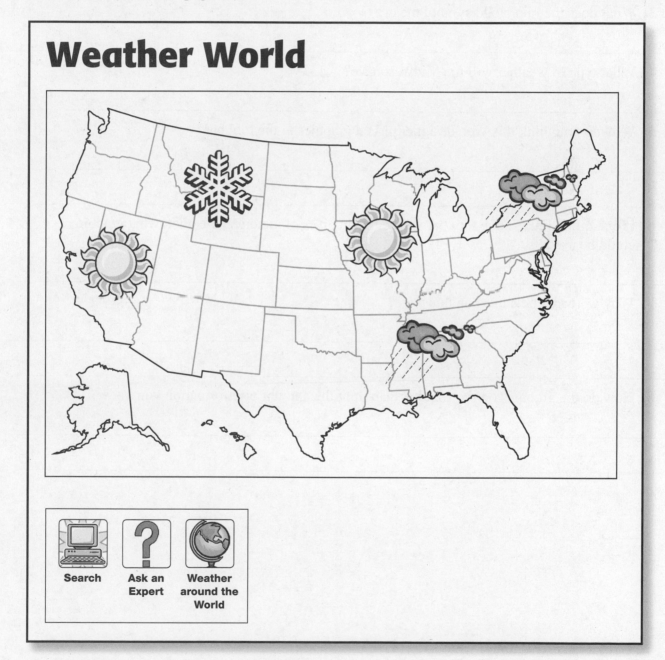

Name_____

1. What is the name of this Web page? How do you know?

_____

_____

2. What do the symbols on the weather map tell you?

_____

3. What does the rain cloud symbol mean?

_____

4. What type of weather will the Midwest have?

_____

5. Why do you think this Web designer placed graphics in the tool bar?

_____

_____

6. If one of the links in the tool bar was to the archives of historical weather, what graphic could be used?

_____

_____

7. Why were symbols used on this page?

_____

_____

8. How do the graphics on the weather map limit the amount of information you know?

_____

_____

 Home Activity Your child learned about the use of graphics and symbols as visual representations of information. Look at a Web page or book that uses graphics and symbols. Challenge your child to explain what the graphics and symbols mean.

Name_____

Prefixes *un-*, *de-*, *dis-*

Proofread an Article There are seven spelling errors and one capitalization error. Circle the errors and write the corrections on the lines.

Spelling Words

uncover
defrost
uncomfortable
discourage
disadvantage
unfortunate
unfamiliar
disability
discomfort
deodorant

unemployed
deflate
disbelief
unpredictable
disapprove
disappoint
unpleasant
dehydrated
disqualify
undecided

> ### A Very Long Race
>
> Many look upon marathon runners with disbeleaf. These athletes run 26 miles in unfamilar cities. They deal with unpredictible and sometimes unplesant weather. Many run with discomfort and some with a disbility. Many runners become dehidrated. Spectators do not disapoint the runners. They give cups of water to all Runners.

1. _____   2. _____

3. _____   4. _____

5. _____   6. _____

7. _____

8. _____

Frequently Misspelled Words

until
before

Proofread Words Circle the correct spelling of the list word.

9. deordorent   deodorant   deoderant

10. disqualify   disqualyfie   dequalify

11. uncomfortible   unconfortable   uncomfortable

12. deflate   deflait   defleat

13. deapprove   disapprove   disaprove

14. disadvantadge   disadvantige   disadvantage

15. undecided   indecided   undecide

16. discomfrt   discomfort   discomefrt

Home Activity Your child identified misspelled list words. Ask your child to name one word for each prefix studied and spell the word.

© Pearson Education, Inc., 5

Prepositions and Prepositional Phrases

Directions Read the passage. Then read each question. Circle the letter of the correct answer.

Pinocchio's Journey

(1) The film *Pinocchio* is a tale _____ a puppet who wants to be a real boy.
(2) Pinocchio was carved _____ Gepetto and turned _____ a wooden boy.
(3) He is lured away by a con artist named Honest John and sold over a puppeteer.
(4) In time, Pinocchio winds up on Pleasure Island, where wild boys are turned into donkeys! (5) Next, the poor puppet is swallowed _____ Monstro the whale.
(6) Finally, father and son are reunited. (7) Pinocchio becomes a real boy in the end.

1 Which preposition best completes sentence 1?

A on

B from

C about

D for

2 Which pair of prepositions best completes sentence 2?

A by/into

B by/about

C for/from

D with/into

3 What change, if any, should be made in sentence 3?

A Change *by* to **until**

B Change *over* to **to**

C Change *over* to **into**

D Remove both prepositions

4 How many prepositional phrases does sentence 4 have?

A 0

B 1

C 2

D 3

5 Which preposition best completes sentence 5?

A by

B down

C up

D through

Home Activity Your child prepared for taking tests on prepositions and prepositional phrases. Ask your child to make flash cards for prepositions he or she has learned. Show each card and have your child use the preposition in a sentence.

Words with Schwa

Spelling Words				
jewel	kingdom	gasoline	factory	garage
tropical	pajamas	estimate	tomorrow	humidity
Chicago	bulletin	carnival	illustrate	elegant
census	terrific	celebrate	operate	celery

Synonyms Write the list word that has the same or nearly the same meaning.

1. great   _____
2. festival   _____
3. count   _____
4. carport   _____
5. tasteful   _____

6. gem   _____
7. rejoice   _____
8. nightclothes   _____
9. moisture   _____
10. guess   _____

Scramble Unscramble the list words and write them on the lines.

11. seloaing   _____
12. slurtileat   _____
13. tublelin   _____
14. wormorto   _____
15. plorcita   _____

16. troycaf   _____
17. torapee   _____
18. coaCgih   _____
19. midkong   _____
20. rylcee   _____

Home Activity Your child learned to spell words with the schwa sound. Ask your child to name three words with this sound and spell them.

Name _____

Past, Present, and Future Tenses

Directions Write the correct present, past, and future tense of each verb.

Verb	Present	Past	Future
1. spy	He _____.	He _____.	He _____.
2. have	I _____.	I _____.	I _____.
3. trap	You _____.	You _____.	You _____.
4. think	She _____.	She _____.	She _____.
5. eat	They _____.	They _____.	They _____.

Directions Identify the tense of each underlined verb. Write *present, past,* or *future.*

6. Many people <u>dreamed</u> of a perpetual motion machine. _____

7. This machine <u>runs</u> forever. _____

8. It <u>will make</u> its own energy. _____

9. The machine <u>will save</u> tons of money! _____

10. The Perez twins <u>created</u> a version of the machine. _____

11. But the machine <u>borrows</u> energy from other machines. _____

12. Sadly, the perpetual motion machine <u>will remain</u> a dream. _____

Directions Rewrite each sentence. Change the underlined verb to the tense in ( ).

13. Once, the idea of a computer <u>seems</u> impossible. (past)

_____

14. Now, people constantly <u>use</u> computers for work and enjoyment. (present)

_____

_____

15. Someday, perhaps a perpetual motion machine <u>is</u> a reality. (future)

_____

_____

Name _____

Compound Words

Spelling Words				
waterproof	teaspoon	grasshopper	homesick	barefoot
courthouse	earthquake	rowboat	scrapbook	countryside
lightweight	fishhook	spotlight	blindfold	whirlpool
tablespoon	greenhouse	postcard	hummingbird	thumbtack

Analogies Write the word that completes each comparison.

1. Urban is to city as rural is to _____.

2. Short is to tall as heavy is to _____.

3. Librarian is to library as judge is to _____.

4. Animal is to zoo as plant is to _____.

5. Snake is to reptile as _____ is to insect.

6. Glue is to tape as nail is to _____.

7. Pedal is to bicycle as oar is to _____.

8. Scarf is to neck as _____ is to eyes.

9. Cup is to china as _____ is to silverware.

10. E-mail is to computer as _____ is to mailbox.

Word Clues Write the list word that fits each clue.

11. This might describe a raincoat and boots. _____

12. Cooks use this to measure ingredients. _____

13. Make this to remember a special trip. _____

14. Don't become an actor if you don't like this. _____

15. You can feed this in your backyard. _____

16. A big one might cause buildings to fall. _____

17. Beware of this when swimming in a big lake or river. _____

18. Going away to summer camp might make you feel like this. _____

19. Walk this way at the beach if you like sand between your toes. _____

20. Put this on the end of your line. _____

Home Activity Your child learned to spell compound words. Find four compound words in a magazine. Write all the words in the compounds in random order. Ask your child to put the correct words together to make the compound words.

Name _____

Principal Parts of Regular Verbs

Directions Write *present, present participle, past,* or *past participle* to identity the principal part of the underlined verb.

1. What <u>defines</u> genius? _____

2. A genius <u>offers</u> a fresh view. _____

3. Often, the public <u>has rejected</u> ideas of genius at first. _____

4. After time <u>has passed</u>, we understand what was offered. _____

5. People <u>recognized</u> Leonardo's genius at once. _____

6. He <u>concealed</u> many of his ideas in journals. _____

7. Today we <u>are studying</u> them. _____

8. Many of his ideas <u>have appeared</u> as inventions. _____

9. His ideas <u>waited</u> for the right time and place. _____

10. We <u>acknowledge</u> his genius gratefully. _____

Directions Write the sentence using the principal part of the underlined verb indicated in ( ).

11. Brilliant ideas <u>change</u> the world. (present participle)

_____

12. Sir Isaac Newton <u>discover</u> universal laws of motion. (past)

_____

13. An object in motion <u>tend</u> to stay in motion. (present)

_____

14. This concept <u>form</u> the basis for the first of his laws of motion. (present)

_____

15. Newton's laws <u>help</u> us understand how the world works. (past participle)

_____

© Pearson Education, Inc., 5

Consonant Sounds /j/, /ks/, /sk/, and /s/

Spelling Words

excuse	scene	muscle	explore	pledge
journal	science	schedule	gigantic	scheme
Japan	excellent	exclaim	fascinate	ginger
scholar	scent	dodge	smudge	schooner

Word Search Circle ten hidden list words. Words are down, across, and diagonal. Write the words on the lines.

```
F  V  S  C  H  E  D  U  L  E
E  X  C  L  A  I  M  N  N  R
C  D  H  M  G  I  N  G  E  R
K  Q  O  I  U  L  O  I  S  S
E  R  L  D  T  S  S  N  M  C
D  E  A  O  G  T  C  E  U  I
U  X  R  P  O  E  E  L  R  E
L  C  H  E  O  U  N  R  E  N
S  C  H  O  O  N  E  R  N  C
Z  F  A  S  C  I  N  A  T  E
```

1. _____   6. _____
2. _____   7. _____
3. _____   8. _____
4. _____   9. _____
5. _____   10. _____

Hidden Words Each of these small words can be found inside one of the list words. Write the list word that contains the small word.

11. ant _____   16. our _____
12. cell _____   17. aim _____
13. mud _____   18. edge _____
14. use _____   19. hem _____
15. pan _____   20. cent _____

School + Home **Home Activity** Your child learned to spell words with various consonant sounds. Ask your child to write two words in which the *sk* sound is spelled in different ways.

Principal Parts of Irregular Verbs

Directions Write *present, present participle, past,* or *past participle* to identify the principal part used to form the underlined verb.

1. Dinosaurs <u>have been</u> extinct for millions of years. _____

2. The iguanodon <u>was</u> a plant eater. _____

3. An iguanodon <u>stood</u> about 16 feet tall. _____

4. It <u>ran</u> on two legs or walked on four. _____

5. Gideon Mantell <u>had found</u> a few bones in 1822. _____

6. He <u>had seen</u> the similarity to an iguana. _____

7. Mantell <u>gave</u> the dinosaur its name. _____

8. Even today, archaeologists <u>are finding</u> dinosaur bones. _____

9. Bones and fossils <u>tell</u> us much about extinct animals. _____

10. We <u>draw</u> conclusions about their size and shape. _____

Directions Write the sentence using the principal part of the underlined verb indicated in ( ).

11. Once all of Earth's land <u>be</u> one big mass. (past)

_____

12. Over time, it <u>break</u> into pieces. (past)

_____

13. We now <u>know</u> these pieces moved. (present)

_____

14. They <u>become</u> the seven continents. (past participle)

_____

15. Forces inside the Earth <u>make</u> the landmasses move. (past)

_____

© Pearson Education, Inc., 5

One Consonant or Two

Spelling Words				
address	collar	mirror	recess	committee
collect	Mississippi	immediate	command	appreciate
announce	possess	Tennessee	gallop	opponent
barricade	broccoli	accomplish	allowance	zucchini

Analogies Write the word that completes each comparison.

1. Jog is to run as trot is to _____.

2. Pecan is to nut as _____ is to squash.

3. Speak is to talk as own is to _____.

4. Friend is to enemy as teammate is to _____.

5. Car is to tire as shirt is to _____.

6. President is to company as chairman is to _____.

7. Open is to close as discard is to _____.

8. Car is to automobile as obstacle is to _____.

9. Cut is to scissors as reflect is to _____.

10. Yell is to shout as proclaim is to _____.

Word Clues Write the list word that fits each clue.

11. a break in the school day   _____

12. the second-longest river in the United States   _____

13. to make an effort and succeed   _____

14. your street number and name and city   _____

15. a green vegetable with stalks and florets   _____

16. a general's job in the army   _____

17. money received each week   _____

18. a state that borders Kentucky   _____

19. to value and treasure   _____

20. happening right now   _____

Home Activity Your child learned to spell words with double consonants. To practice at home, dictate three words with double consonants. Have your child write them.

Name _____

Troublesome Verbs

Directions Write the form of the underlined verb indicated in ( ).

1. Mahalia <u>leave</u> listeners dazzled by her talent. (past) _____

2. They <u>lay</u> down their troubles for a while. (past) _____

3. Her success <u>lets</u> other women dream of a career in music. (past) _____

4. Young Aretha Franklin <u>sit</u> with Mahalia's fans. (past participle) _____

5. Aretha <u>set</u> goals and achieved them. (past) _____

Directions Underline the verb that correctly completes the sentence.

6. They have (sat, set) in this pew for years.

7. The choir (sat, set) their hymnals on the bench.

8. A bell (lays, lies) on its side.

9. Someone (lay, laid) it there.

10. She has (left, let) a cup of water on the stand.

11. (Leave, Let) us ask for her autograph.

12. The piano (sets, sits) on a platform.

Directions Complete each sentence with the correct form of the verb in ( ).

13. Please _____ with us at the concert. (sit)

14. The singers have _____ their music down. (set)

15. Yesterday we _____ our friends at school. (leave)

16. Did you _____ your guitar at home? (leave)

17. Ms. Guthrie _____ me pick my recital piece. (let)

18. Yesterday afternoon he _____ the horn on the table. (lay)

19. The horn has _____ there ever since. (lay)

20. She will _____ down and rest before the performance. (lie)

Prefixes *un-*, *de-*, *dis-*

Spelling Words				
uncover	defrost	uncomfortable	discourage	disadvantage
unfortunate	unfamiliar	disability	discomfort	deodorant
unemployed	deflate	disbelief	unpredictable	disapprove
disappoint	unpleasant	dehydrated	disqualify	undecided

Synonyms Write the list word that has the same or nearly the same meaning.

1. jobless _____

2. strange _____

3. handicap _____

4. reject _____

5. uneasiness _____

6. expose _____

7. doubt _____

8. bar _____

9. dried _____

10. changeable _____

Analogies Write the word that completes each comparison.

11. Fix is to break as freeze is to _____.

12. Easy is to difficult as lucky is to _____.

13. Happy is to sad as relaxed is to _____.

14. Soap is to cleanser as antiperspirant is to _____.

15. Mad is to angry as uncertain is to _____.

16. Drain is to pool as _____ is to balloon.

17. Freedom is to liberty as weakness is to _____.

18. Beautiful is to ugly as charming is to _____.

19. Help is to support as frustrate is to _____.

20. Please is to annoy as encourage is to _____.

School + Home **Home Activity** Your child learned to spell words with the prefixes *un-*, *de-*, and *dis-*. Find three words with these prefixes in a newspaper. Ask your child to spell each word and name a word that means the opposite.

Prepositions and Prepositional Phrases

Directions Underline the prepositional phrase in each sentence. Circle the preposition.

1. Over the holidays, we had a movie marathon.

2. The family watched a series of animated films.

3. We have quite a few in our film library.

4. I have watched *Dumbo* about 20 times.

5. Dumbo is a baby elephant with enormous ears.

6. Dumbo stays near his mother.

7. She feels protective toward her baby.

8. Dumbo finds a great use for his ears.

9. Dumbo can fly through the sky.

10. He is the biggest hit at the circus.

Directions Write *P* if the underlined word is a preposition. Write *O* if it is the object of the preposition.

11. Heckle and Jeckle are two crows <u>in</u> *Dumbo*.   _____

12. They make fun <u>of</u> the baby elephant.   _____

13. They are amazed when Dumbo soars into the <u>air</u>.   _____

14. Some encouragement <u>from</u> a little mouse helps Dumbo.   _____

15. I think the moral is "Believe in <u>yourself</u>."   _____

Directions Underline the prepositional phrases. The number in ( ) tells how many prepositional phrases are in that sentence.

16. The theater is down this street and around a corner. (2)

17. Buy four tickets at the booth and two bags of popcorn from the concession stand. (3)

18. We always sit toward the back under the balcony. (2)

19. At the beginning, it seems very dark in the theater. (2)

20. The ads before the show make me hungry for a snack. (2)

Name _____

Venn Diagram

Directions Fill in the Venn diagram with similarities and differences about the two things you are comparing.

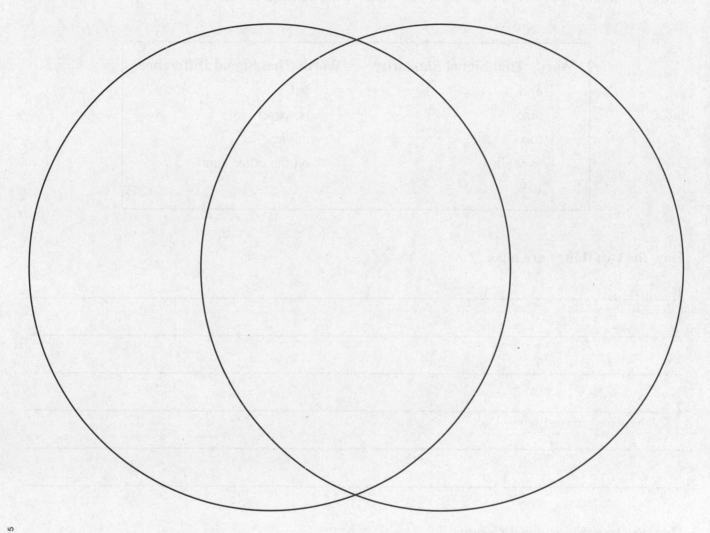

Words That Compare and Contrast

Directions The words in the box signal that two things are alike or different. Write two sentences that explain how your two inventions are alike, using words from the box. Then write two sentences that explain how your two inventions are different, using words from the box.

Words That Signal Similarity	Words That Signal Difference
and	but
also	however
too	unlike
as well	on the other hand
like	

How the two things are alike

1. _____

_____

_____

2. _____

_____

_____

How the two things are different

1. _____

_____

_____

2. _____

_____

_____

Adding and Deleting Sentences

One part of revising your writing is deciding whether you need to add or delete sentences.

Add a sentence if you need another supporting detail in a paragraph or a smoother transition between paragraphs

Delete a sentence if it does not support the main idea of the paragraph or the topic of the writing

Directions Read the paragraphs. Answer each question by circling the letter or writing on the lines.

The Starry Night and *Self-Portrait 1889* are paintings by Vincent van Gogh. Both paintings feature the swirling backgrounds and heavy, visible brushstrokes Van Gogh used in many of his paintings at that time.

However, *The Starry Night* shows a night sky filled with clouds, glowing stars, and a yellow moon above houses with brightly colored windows and a church with a steeple. Viewers find many things to look at in the painting. The mood of *The Starry Night* is serene and hopeful.

Self-Portrait 1889, on the other hand, shows a person, the artist himself. Van Gogh painted many self-portraits during his career. The mood of *Self-Portrait 1889* is more somber because Van Gogh looks so sad and worn. His deep eyes stare directly at viewers, holding their attention in one place.

1. Which sentence should be deleted?

    A Viewers find many things to look at in the painting.

    B The mood of *The Starry Night* is serene and hopeful.

    C Van Gogh painted many self-portraits during his career.

    D His deep eyes stare directly at viewers, holding their attention in one place.

2. Why should it be deleted? _____

_____

3. Which sentence is the best one to add?

    A A dark unknown shape looms on the left in *The Starry Night*.

    B Van Gogh sold only one painting while he was alive.

    C *The Starry Night* is probably Van Gogh's best-known painting.

    D Van Gogh painted both paintings in Saint-Rémy in 1889.

Peer and Teacher Conferencing Compare-and-Contrast Essay

Directions After exchanging drafts, read your partner's essay. Refer to the Revising Checklist as you make notes about your partner's essay. Write your comments or questions on the lines. Offer compliments as well as suggestions for revisions. Take turns talking about each other's draft using your notes. Give your partner your notes.

Revising Checklist

Focus/Ideas

☐ Is the compare and contrast essay focused and informative?

☐ Do all sentences tell about similarities and differences? Should any sentences be deleted? Should more detail sentences be added?

Organization

☐ Are words that compare and contrast used to signal similarities and differences?

☐ Are there smooth transitions between paragraphs?

Voice

☐ Is the writer engaged with the topic?

Word Choice

☐ Are specific words used to tell about similarities and differences?

Sentences

☐ Are sentences written in a variety of types and lengths?

Things I Thought Were Good _____

_____

Things I Thought Could Be Improved _____

_____

Teacher's Comments _____

_____

Draw Conclusions

- A **conclusion** is a decision you make after thinking about the details in what you read.
- Often your prior knowledge can help you draw, or make, a conclusion.
- When you draw a conclusion, be sure it makes sense and is supported by what you have read.

Directions Read the following passage. Then complete the diagram.

Several factors led to the formation of cities. First, small agricultural groups grew larger when farmers and hunters were able to provide a steady supply of food for more people. Also, settlers started keeping herds of animals for food and other purposes. Because of these developments there was enough food for everyone, so settlers had time to learn new skills. They started making better tools and finding new uses for them. Better tools led to improvements in living conditions. Workers built structures to protect the community and to store food. They traded with other groups for items they needed. As more people lived together, members of the community started having different responsibilities and social relationships changed. Eventually, these communities developed a system to govern themselves. They also created a written language.

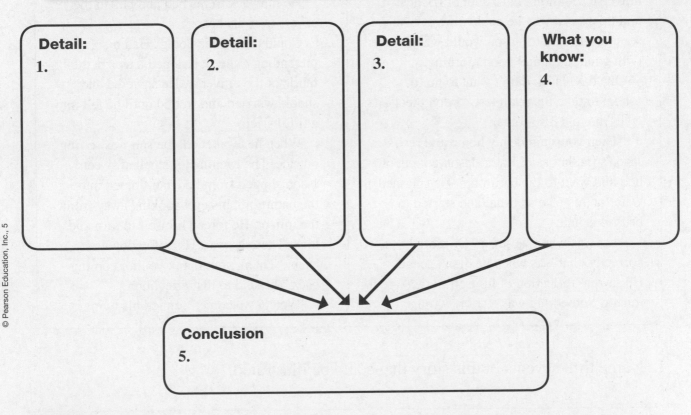

| Detail: 1. | Detail: 2. | Detail: 3. | What you know: 4. |

Conclusion
5.

Home Activity Your child drew a conclusion from facts or details found in a reading passage. Tell him or her a short story about an event that happened in your life. Have your child single out two or three details from the story and form a conclusion about it.

Writing • Fictional Narrative

Key Features of a Fictional Narrative

- may tell a story or describe a true event
- often contains dialogue
- includes illustrations or art

The Boy in the Mirror

The last face Jason saw at night and the first he saw in the morning was his own. He saw himself in the mirror at night when he brushed his teeth before bed. He saw himself again in the mornings as he washed his face and brushed his hair before breakfast.

Jason liked to pretend that the boy that he saw in the mirror was not a reflection of himself, but a twin who lived in a parallel universe. He didn't have a lot of friends, and this was a way he could always have someone to talk to. Jason would wish his twin good night and good morning.

One day, Jason didn't want to go to school to take his math test. "I don't feel well," he told his mother.

"Then you should stay home and rest," Jason's mother said. Later, Jason got out of bed and went to the bathroom. He splashed water on his face as usual and started to brush his hair.

That was when he saw it. Or more correctly, that was when he didn't see it. He saw no reflection of himself in the mirror. Something was terribly wrong.

Jason drew close to the glass, peering into the bottom, the sides, and even the corners. His reflection wasn't there. "Where are you?" he asked.

Jason looked at his hands and body and feet. He felt his arms, his chest, his face, and his hair. He certainly could feel himself. He stared at the mirror. But he could not see himself there. "Oh, no," he cried. "What have I done?"

He ran back to his bed and pulled the covers over his head.

Could this be his doing? Had his pretending to be sick ripped a tear in the fabric of the universe? He shivered and shook, worried and fretted until he fell into a fitful sleep.

When he awakened, the sun was setting outside. The evening air smelled sweet. Jason slipped from bed and tiptoed into the bathroom, his eyes looking away from the mirror. He forced himself to turn and look. There he was. His reflection was back. "Thank you, thank you for coming back," he said to his reflection.

"You're welcome," replied his twin.

1. Name three events in this story that could be illustrated.

_____

2. Circle the first key sentence that tells this narrative is fiction.

Name_____

Vocabulary

Directions Choose the word from the box that best matches each definition below. Write the word on the line.

_____ 1. the ways of living of a people or nation

_____ 2. the skillful planning and management of anything

_____ 3. causing a light, soft sound of things gently rubbing together

_____ 4. stupid mistakes

Directions Choose the word from the box that best fits in the sentence. Write the word on the line shown to the left.

_____ 5. In his dreams, dragons were after him and he was _____, or running away.

_____ 6. Cities are more _____ than tiny villages.

_____ 7. The people who created the earliest forms of writing were motivated, or _____, by a need to communicate ideas.

_____ 8. _____ arises when someone else gets something we wanted.

_____ 9. To play a game or sport well, you need to form a _____.

_____ 10. As they hiked through the woods, they could hear the fallen leaves _____.

Write a Description

On a separate sheet of paper, describe a sport you like to play, like soccer or chess. What are the rules? What are the best strategies?

Home Activity Your child identified and used vocabulary words from *Weslandia*. Read a short story with your child. Have him or her point out unfamiliar words. Work together to figure out the meaning of each word by using words that appear near it.

© Pearson Education, Inc., 5

Name _____

Subject and Object Pronouns

A **subject pronoun** is used in the subject of a sentence. Singular subject pronouns are *I, you, he, she,* and *it.* Plural subject pronouns are *we, you,* and *they.* When you use a person's name and a pronoun in a compound subject, be sure to use a subject pronoun.
    He has many original ideas. They are exciting and unusual.
    Mom and I made bird feeders.

An **object pronoun** is used in the predicate of a sentence after an action verb or with a preposition, such as *for, at, into, with,* or *to.* Singular object pronouns are *me, you, him, her,* and *it.* Plural object pronouns are *us, you,* and *them.* When you use a person's name and a pronoun in a compound object, be sure to use an object pronoun.
    The teacher asked him about his project. It seemed brilliant to me.
    This project was fun for James and me.

Directions Write *S* if the underlined word is a subject pronoun. Write *O* if the word is an object pronoun.

1. Some kids don't know what to think about him. _____

2. They can't understand someone who is different from them. _____

3. She praised his project for its originality. _____

4. Rainelle and I invited him to sit with us. _____

5. We were fascinated by his ideas. _____

6. He has become a valued friend to her and me. _____

Directions Underline the correct pronoun in ( ) to complete each sentence.

7. Most people choose friends who are like (them, they).

8. (Them, They) feel comfortable with people who agree with them.

9. You and (I, me) have different points of view.

10. A friend with original ideas always surprises (I, me).

11. (Us, We) need to think about what we do and say.

12. (I, Me) prefer independent thinkers.

13. José and (her, she) agree with me.

14. We have many exciting conversations with (he, him) and (she, her).

© Pearson Education, Inc., 5

Name_____

Words from Many Cultures

Spelling Words				
khaki	hula	banana	ballet	waltz
tomato	vanilla	canyon	yogurt	banquet
macaroni	polka	cobra	koala	barbecue
safari	buffet	stampede	karate	kiosk

Word Histories Write a list word for each description.

1. This is French for a table full of different foods.   1. _____

2. Many students practice this Japanese form of self-defense.   2. _____

3. Native Americans introduced this fruit to the settlers.   3. _____

4. This is a Turkish treat made from milk.   4. _____

5. This Polynesian dance is usually performed in a grass skirt.   5. _____

6. This is a Spanish word for a large group of running buffaloes or horses.   6. _____

7. Although it has a French name, this dance form started in Russia.   7. _____

8. This furry animal has kept its Australian name.   8. _____

9. Soldiers wear this yellowish brown fabric named by the Persians   9. _____
   and Hindus so they can't be easily seen.

10. This partner dance means "to turn" in German.   10. _____

11. This is an Italian name for a well-known pasta.   11. _____

12. The Spanish and Portuguese used the same name for this yellow fruit.   12. _____

13. A Native American word is used to name this kind of outside cooking.   13. _____

14. This Polish dance is very lively.   14. _____

15. Although this word is Arabic, this type of journey is done in Africa.   15. _____

16. The Spanish named this flavorful type of bean long before there was   16. _____
    ice cream.

17. This word for a feast or a formal dinner comes from French.   17. _____

18. This is a Spanish word for a very deep valley carved out by a river.   18. _____

19. The name for this hooded, poisonous snake comes from the Portuguese.   19. _____

20. This is a Turkish word for a newsstand.   20. _____

Home Activity Your child wrote words from other cultures. Go over the pronunciation of the French words *buffet* and *ballet*. Remind your child that in French *-et* in these words is pronounced as long *a*.

Story Sequence C

Title_____

Characters

Setting

Problem

Events

_____
_____
_____
_____
_____
_____
_____
_____
_____

Solution

Name_____

Vocabulary • Endings

- **Endings** are a letter or letters added to the end of a base word.
- Recognizing an ending will help you figure out the word's meaning.
- The endings *-s* and *-es* can be added to singular nouns to make them plural. The endings *-s*, *-ed*, and *-ing* can be added to verbs to change the tense. The endings *-er* and *-est* can be added to adjectives to use them to compare.
- The definition of endings can be found in dictionaries, books that list words and their meanings.

Directions Read the following passage. Then answer the questions below.

Lisa enjoyed camping with her brother and parents every autumn. In a way she felt they were fleeing civilization and their complex city life. She had noticed that life in the city often makes people anxious. She always felt happier while hiking through the woods and sleeping under the stars. There was no one to envy because the beauty of nature surrounded them. Even the blunders they made turned into games to play. Once they hiked down the wrong trail and got lost. Instead of worrying, they worked together to find the quickest way back. When she returned to the city, Lisa felt inspired by the beauty she had enjoyed.

1. In the word *fleeing*, how does the *-ing* change the meaning of the base word?

_____

2. What is the difference between the *-s* in *blunders* and the *-s* in *makes*?

_____

_____

3. How does the *-er* change the meaning of the endings in *happier*?

_____

_____

4. What does the *-ed* in *hiked* do to the meaning of the base word?

_____

5. Change some of the endings in this sentence to put the verbs in the past tense: "Lisa calls out to her family and then walks down the trail to meet them."

_____

 Home Activity Your child identified and used endings added to base words, such as *-s*, *-ed*, *-ing*, and *-est*. Read a newspaper or magazine article with your child. Change the endings of some of the words and discuss with him or her how the sentences' meanings change.

Instruction Manual

- **Following directions** involves doing or making something.
- Directions are usually numbered.
- Read all the directions before starting to act on the first direction given.
- Read the first direction, do what it says to do, and then proceed to the next step.
- Try to visualize the purpose or result of the process.

Directions Read these directions. Then answer the questions.

> **How to Make Crystals**
> 1. Gather the materials you will need. They are: a small amount of Epsom salts, water, a sponge, and a shallow dish.
> 2. Boil water. Remove from heat. Add about 1/4 cup of Epsom salts to about 1/2 cup of boiling water. Stir until the salts dissolve.
>
> 3. Put a sponge in a shallow dish. Pour the liquid over the sponge. (The crystals will be easier to see on a sponge.) Only pour in enough of the mixture to cover the bottom of the dish.
> 4. Put the glass dish in a secure spot in the sun. Soon the water will evaporate and crystals will grow.

1. You and a friend have decided to make crystals. What would you do first? Explain.

_____

_____

2. What would you do next?

_____

3. How are the directions organized to make them easier to follow?

_____

4. Which word told you when to look for crystals?

_____

5. What do you think would have happened if you hadn't heated the water before you added the Epsom salts?

_____

_____

_____

Name_____

Directions Read this recipe. Then answer the questions below.

How to Make Pizza Dough

1. Assemble ingredients: 3 cups flour, 1 package active dry yeast, 2 tablespoons butter, 1 teaspoon salt, and water.
2. In a small mixer bowl combine 1 cup of flour and yeast.
3. In a saucepan, heat water, butter, and salt until warm, stirring constantly to melt butter. (Always work with an adult when using the stove.)
4. Add liquid ingredients to dry mixture in mixer bowl. Beat at low speed with electric mixer for 1 minute.
5. Beat 3 minutes at high speed. Then turn the dough out on a flat surface and add enough of the remaining flour to make a soft dough.
6. Cover and let rise about 45 to 60 minutes until it doubles its size.
7. Spread dough evenly on a greased pizza pan. Add toppings and cook in oven for 30 minutes to an hour.

---

6. How much time do you think you will need to prepare the dough? Explain.

_____

_____

7. How much time do you think you will need from step #2 until your pizza is ready to eat? Explain.

_____

_____

8. Describe what you will have created at the end of step #3.

_____

_____

9. Go through the sequence of steps in making pizza. Do you think any of the steps could be rearranged? Why or why not?

_____

_____

10. How can you find out what equipment you will need before you start?

_____

_____

Home Activity Your child learned about following directions and the concept of steps in a process. Go over an instruction manual together. Ask your child questions about the sequence of tasks and how long the project will take.

Words from Many Cultures

Proofread a Poster Circle the seven spelling errors in the school poster.
Write the words correctly. Write the last sentence, using correct punctuation.

Spelling Words

khaki
hula
banana
ballet
waltz
tomato
vanilla
canyon
yogurt
banquet

macaroni
polka
cobra
koala
barbecue
safari
buffet
stampede
karate
kiosk

Our New After-School Programs

Learn to Dance
- poka and Texas two-step
- ballet (with tutus and toe shoes)
- walts and other ballroom dances
- hula and dances of the Pacific

Learn Martial Arts
- karatie
- judo
- kung fu

Learn How to Cook
- barbecue sauces
- tomatoe salads
- homemade yogurt
- macaronie and cheese and other pastas
- bananana cream pie and other desserts

Sign up at the kyosk outside the office.
Bring a permission form from your parents?

---

1. _____
2. _____
3. _____
4. _____
5. _____
6. _____
7. _____
8. _____

Frequently Misspelled Words

our
again

Proofread Words Circle the correct spelling of the list word.
Write the word.

9. The frightened cattle started to ____.

   stamped   stampede   stampeed

9. _____

10. I love the assortment of foods on the restaurant ____.

   buffet   buffay   buffee

10. _____

Home Activity Your child identified misspelled list words. Say a list word and spell it incorrectly. Ask
your child to spell the word correctly.

Subject and Object Pronouns

Directions Read the passage. Then read each question. Circle the letter of the correct answer.

Wild Foods

(1) My mother is a nature enthusiast. (2) _____ and my father know where to find foods in the wild. (3) _____ and Uncle Dick locate and use different wild plants for food. (4) <u>We</u> have made entire meals out of wild plants! (5) In the fall, my grandfather will harvest cattails. (6) Mom and <u>I</u> grind the roots to make flour for <u>him</u>. (7) She and my father hunt for mushrooms in the woods. (8) Wild foods are a lot of work, but it is fun to hunt for _____.

1 Which pronoun best completes sentence 2?

   A Her

   B She

   C Them

   D Him

2 Which pronoun best completes sentence 3?

   A Him

   B Them

   C Her

   D They

3 Which best describes the underlined word in sentence 4?

   A Object pronoun

   B Subject pronoun

   C Predicate

   D None of the above

4 Which pair describes the two underlined words in sentence 6?

   A Subject pronoun/object pronoun

   B Subject pronoun/subject pronoun

   C Object pronoun/predicate

   D Object pronoun/object pronoun

5 Which is the correct pronoun/type of pronoun for sentence 8?

   A they/object pronoun

   B them/subject pronoun

   C them/object pronoun

   D it/object pronoun

Home Activity Your child prepared for taking tests on subject and object pronouns. Have your child write subject pronouns and object pronouns on index cards. Then mix the cards and sort them into subject pronoun and object pronoun piles.

Generalize

- An author may write similar details about different things or people. You can use these similar details to make a general statement that covers all the things or people. This statement is called a **generalization.**
- A **valid** generalization can be supported by facts or details. A **faulty** generalization cannot.
- Sometimes an author makes a generalization and uses a clue word such as *all, many,* or *generally* to signal it.

Directions Read the following passage. Then complete the diagram below.

John heard a program on the radio about diabetes. One woman described how she found out she had the disease. She always felt thirsty even though she drank a lot of water. She was also really hungry all the time, even though she ate a lot. She went to see her doctor, who said that she should be tested for diabetes because unusual thirst and hunger are generally symptoms. The test showed that she had diabetes.

A young boy spoke next. He too was always thirsty and hungry. He thought he was just growing, but one day he passed out at school. As the boy finished speaking, John realized that he was really hungry and thirsty. He was pouring some juice when he remembered he had eaten just a half-hour ago. He thought about the program, and he asked his mom to make a doctor's appointment.

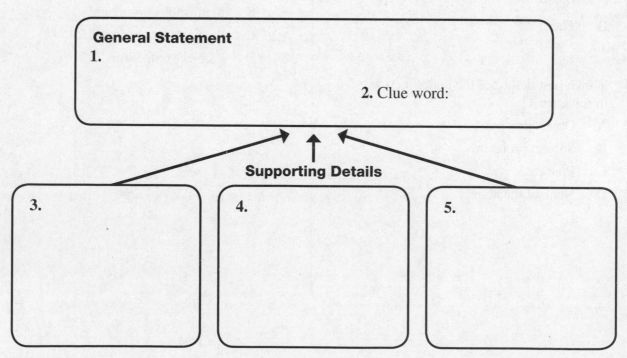

General Statement

1.

2. Clue word:

Supporting Details

3.

4.

5.

Home Activity Your child read a short passage and recognized a generalization. Read a newspaper or magazine article together and ask your child to find a generalization along with details that support it.

Writing · Friendly Letter

Key Features of a Friendly Letter

- is written to a friend or someone you know well
- uses informal language to communicate ideas
- has a casual tone
- contains a date, salutation, and closing

May 12, 20__

Dear Jinx,

    I hope this letter finds you healthy and free from injury. I am writing to tell you that I miss you, and I have decided I want to write another story about you. If it's okay with you, I will give you a new sport to try.

    What do you think about badminton? A lot of families like to play badminton outside in their yards. All you need is a net, some rackets, and this ball-like thing called a shuttle. I imagine Mr. Deimeister has a badminton set stored somewhere at the school.

    I've tried to think of ways that you could get hurt playing badminton. It is a quick sport. I suppose you could run into another player or get hit in the head with a racket somehow. I wonder, though, would you rather turn out to be a good badminton player?

    I think I'll start writing the story. We'll just see how it turns out. After all, you are the person you are. Why mess up a good thing?

    Fondly,
    Angela Johnson

---

1. How does Angela Johnson's use of questions affect the tone of the letter?

_____

_____

2. Make a list of other salutations and closings that Angela Johnson might have used.

Openings _____

Closings _____

Vocabulary

Directions Choose the word from the box that best matches each definition. Write the word on the line.

_____ 1. injured tissue at a joint caused by a sudden twist or wrench

_____ 2. full of ruffles

_____ 3. a large, short-haired dog, usually white with black spots

_____ 4. walking for pleasure or for show

_____ 5. something that is used instead of something else

> **Check the Words You Know**
>
> ___ Dalmatian
> ___ frilly
> ___ promenading
> ___ sprained
> ___ substitute

Directions Choose the word from the box that best completes each sentence. Write the word on the line to the left.

_____ 6. Many firehouses have a _____ as their adopted pet.

_____ 7. Mrs. Green was sick today, so we had a _____ teacher.

_____ 8. Becky _____ her ankle during basketball practice.

_____ 9. Mom had a _____ dress for parties.

_____ 10. While my sister and I played in our cabin, Mom and Dad spent time _____ around the deck.

Write a Newspaper Article

On a separate sheet of paper, write an imaginary newspaper article about a group of local square dancers who try for First Prize at the National Square Dancing Championship. Use as many of the vocabulary words as you can.

Home Activity Your child identified and used vocabulary words from *Tripping Over the Lunch Lady.* Together, look through newspapers or magazines for stories about people who adapt to face physical, emotional, or mental challenges. Discuss what gives people the motivation to succeed.

© Pearson Education, Inc., 5

Pronouns and Antecedents

A **pronoun** takes the place of a noun or nouns. An **antecedent,** or referent, is the noun or nouns to which the pronoun refers. A pronoun and its antecedent must agree in number and gender.

Before you use a pronoun, ask yourself whether the antecedent is singular or plural. If the antecedent is singular, decide whether it is masculine, feminine, or neutral. Then choose a pronoun that agrees. In the following sentences, the antecedents are underlined once and the pronouns are underlined twice.

Victoria went with Jinx to practice square dancing. She helped her practice.

Directions Circle the correct pronoun or pronouns in ( ) to complete each sentence. The antecedent of each pronoun is underlined to help you.

1. The girl was nicknamed Jinx because (she, her) was clumsy.

2. The square dancers were very good, and (them, they) smiled for the camera.

3. The girl talks with the gym teacher and becomes friends with (him, he).

4. Victoria helped Jinx practice, but (she, they) broke her foot.

5. People can practice sports but may never be good at (they, them).

6. The girl kept a journal, and (it, they) tells of her experiences.

Directions Underline the antecedent once and the pronoun twice in each sentence.

7. Nate went to tryouts with the new football he had gotten.

8. Juwon could not play because a sore knee bothered him.

9. The sky grew cloudy, and it threatened rain.

10. When Mrs. Panizzi jogged by, Nate waved to her.

11. Nate made a great catch, and it impressed the coach.

12. The coach thanked his new players, and they shook hands.

Home Activity Your child learned about pronouns and antecedents. Read a magazine article together and have your child find pronouns that have antecedents and identify both.

© Pearson Education, Inc., 5

Prefixes *over-*, *under-*, *sub-*, *super-*, *out-*

Spelling Words				
overlook	underline	subway	subset	supermarket
outlet	underground	overboard	undercurrent	superstar
overtime	supersonic	submarine	undercover	overcast
outfield	output	supernatural	subdivision	subhead

Classifying Write the list word that belongs in each group.

1. city, trains, underground, ____

2. sky, clouds, gray, ____

3. diamond, mound, infield, ____

4. police officer, disguise, ____

5. grocery, bakery, butcher, ____

6. daydream, forget, omit, ____

7. highlight, line, ____

8. plane, jet engine, speed of sound, ____

9. work, extra hours, ____

10. performer, actor, singer, ____

1. _____

2. _____

3. _____

4. _____

5. _____

6. _____

7. _____

8. _____

9. _____

10. _____

Definitions Write the list word that fits each definition.

11. This is part of a community.

12. This is the result of production.

13. This means eerie and ghostly.

14. This is a small part of a larger group.

15. This means beneath the earth.

16. This is a vessel that travels underwater.

17. This comes under a heading.

18. This is a pull under the waves.

19. This means falling off a ship.

20. This can be a store that offers discounts.

11. _____

12. _____

13. _____

14. _____

15. _____

16. _____

17. _____

18. _____

19. _____

20. _____

© Pearson Education, Inc., 5

School + Home

Home Activity Your child wrote words with prefixes. Ask your child to name four words and tell you how the prefixes in each word affect its meaning.

Name _____

T-Chart

Vocabulary · Context Clues

- When you find an **unfamiliar word** in a text, look for context clues to its meaning.
- You can find context clues among the words around the unfamiliar word.

Directions Read the following passage about overcoming obstacles. Then use context clues to answer the questions below.

Anita's friend Jessica asked her a hard question. "Anita, what is it like to live with your disability? Is it hard for you to be in a wheelchair?"

Anita thought carefully about how she would answer. "I don't mind using a wheelchair. I get around in it very well. But because I have cerebral palsy, it's difficult for people to understand what I'm saying. Sometimes my words can sound very confusing. Sometimes my speech sounds muddled, like I have something in my mouth."

Jessica said, "But I can understand you just fine."

"You are used to me," said Anita. "I go to a speech therapist every week to help me learn how to speak more clearly. I want people to better understand what I'm saying."

1. What does *wheelchair* mean? What context clues helped you to determine the meaning?

_____

_____

2. What does *disability* mean? What context clues helped you to determine the meaning?

_____

3. What does *muddled* mean? What context clues help you to determine the meaning?

_____

4. How would using context clues help you determine the meaning of *speech therapist*?

_____

_____

5. What context clues helped you understand what *cerebral palsy* means?

_____

_____

Home Activity Your child identified and used context clues to understand new words of a passage. Have a discussion with your child in which you use context clues to give clues to the meanings of new words.

Telephone Directory

A **telephone directory** is an alphabetical index of names and telephone numbers for a selected geographical area. The **white pages** list entries for individual people and businesses. The **yellow pages** list entries and ads for businesses. Entries are grouped by category or type of business, such as *restaurants.* This information is available in reference books or on the Internet. You can search online to find phone numbers for people and businesses in other cities, states, and even countries.

Directions The computer screen shows you how to search a directory of online white pages. Use the computer screen to answer the questions that follow.

Enter the first and last name of the person and click *Find!*

For better results, enter the city and state also.

Last Name (required) [   ]

First Name [   ]

City [   ]   **State** [   ]

Country [   ]

(**Find!**)   If you need help, click here.

---

1. What entries will you get if you type "Reyes" in the field for Last Name, "Philadelphia" in the City field, and "PA" (for Pennsylvania) in the State field?

_____

_____

2. You know Sue Costello lives in Florida. Tell how to find her phone number and address.

_____

_____

3. Would typing "Julia" in the First Name field and "Texas" in the State field give you good search results? Explain.

_____

_____

4. How does using an online telephone directory rather than a telephone book increase the information you can get?

_____

_____

Directions The computer screen shows you how to search a directory of online yellow pages. Use the computer screen to answer the questions that follow.

Enter a business category or name. Then click *Find!*

City [   ]   State [   ]

Find!   If you need help, click here.

---

5. What will you get if you enter the category "state park" and "FL" for State?

_____

_____

6. If you want information on Nancy & Beth's Catering Services in St. Louis, Missouri, what should you enter?

_____

_____

7. If you want to find a bike rental in Phoenix, Arizona, what should you enter?

_____

_____

8. If you enter "toy store" in the category field, will this produce good search results? Explain.

_____

_____

9. Which of the three fields could you leave blank? Explain how filling in this field would narrow your search.

_____

_____

10. Can you use an online telephone directory if you don't know how to spell the name of a business? Explain.

_____

_____

© Pearson Education, Inc., 5

Home Activity Your child learned about using telephone directories. Look at an online telephone directory together. Ask your child to locate emergency phone numbers, maps, and phone numbers of local businesses and residences.

Prefixes *over-*, *under-*, *sub-*, *super-*, *out-*

Proofread a Paragraph Circle six spelling errors. Write the words correctly. Find one punctuation error and write the sentence using the correct punctuation.

If you had a choice, would you want to break the sound barrier in a super sonic jet? Is cruising beneath the surface of the sea in a sub marine more your style? What about riding underground on a large sub way system? Would you rather stay all night in a deserted house waiting for something super natural to happen? Do you like sports. Perhaps you'd really rather be playing ball in the out field? Fortunately, one doesn't have to be a super star to do any of these things.

1. _____   2. _____

3. _____   4. _____

5. _____   6. _____

7. _____

© Pearson Education, Inc., 5

Spelling Words

overlook
underline
subway
subset
supermarket
outlet
underground
overboard
undercurrent
superstar

overtime
supersonic
submarine
undercover
overcast
outfield
output
supernatural
subdivision
subhead

Frequently Misspelled Words

outside
because

Proofread Words Circle the word that is spelled correctly.

8. submarine	submareen	submarein
9. subdivsion	subdivison	subdivision
10. subersonic	supersonic	supresonic
11. underline	undeline	undrline
12. outfeild	outfeeld	outfield
13. overcast	overcas	ovrcast
14. overlok	overlook	ovarlock
15. suparmarkit	suprmarkat	supermarket
16. overboard	overbored	ovarboard

School + Home **Home Activity** Your child identified misspelled list words. Ask your child to tell you which three words are most difficult and then have your child spell them with you.

Name _____

Lunch Lady

Pronouns and Antecedents

Directions Read the passage. Then read each question. Circle the letter of the correct answer.

Team Works

(1) People admired Ben and Sasha when _____ went to the gymnastics event. (2) The tournament was long, and _____ would not be easy. (3) Ben was strong, and he was a hard worker. (4) Sasha was team captain, and her was a great gymnast. (5) <u>Sasha</u> hurt her knee, and the team had to help <u>her</u>. (6) Jenny and I were there, and we cheered for the team. (7) Ben and Sasha led the way, but they got much help from the others.

1 Which pronoun best completes sentence 1?

  A her

  B she

  C they

  D he

2 Which pronoun best completes sentence 2?

  A him

  B it

  C her

  D they

3 What change, if any, should be made in sentence 4?

  A Change *was* to **were**

  B Remove the comma after *captain*

  C Change *her* to **she**

  D Make no change

4 In sentence 5, what is the relationship between the underlined words?

  A Antecedent-pronoun

  B Pronoun-pronoun

  C Pronoun-antecedent

  D Antecedent-antecedent

5 In sentence 6, which is the antecedent for the pronoun *we*?

  A Jenny

  B Jenny and I

  C the team

  D Jenny and I were there

© Pearson Education, Inc., 5

Home Activity Your child prepared for taking tests on pronouns and antecedents. Have your child rewrite a paragraph from a story, replacing each pronoun with its antecedent. Ask him or her to explain why pronouns make the story sound better.

268 Conventions Pronouns and Antecedents

Graphic Sources

- A **graphic source,** such as a picture, diagram, or chart, organizes information visually.
- Preview the graphic sources to help you predict what you will be reading about.

Directions Study the following diagram. Then answer the questions below.

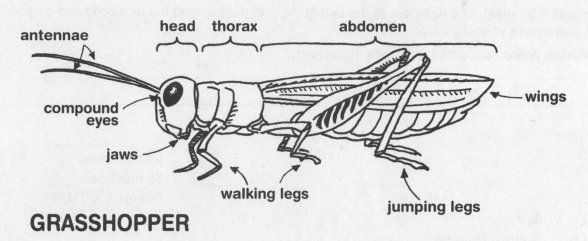

GRASSHOPPER

1. What is the purpose of this diagram?

_____

_____

2. What are the three main sections of the grasshopper's body?

_____

3. What do grasshoppers use to hop, walk, and fly?

_____

4. How many legs does the grasshopper have? How does the diagram show you this?

_____

5. What is the location of the grasshopper's two front legs? What other job might the front legs perform in addition to walking?

_____

_____

Home Activity Your child used a graphic source to answer questions. Together, read a newspaper or magazine article that includes a graphic source. Ask your child to answer questions about the article based on the information shown in the graphic source.

Writing • Formal Letter

Key Features of a Formal Letter

- has a purpose, such as asking for information
- includes a *heading* with your address, the address of the person you are writing to, and the date you are writing the letter
- has a greeting, or *salutation*, at the beginning and a *closing* at the end, followed by your name and your signature
- uses polite, respectful language in the body

Laura Moleen
86 Elm Street
Oxbow, TX 73333

Dr. Willa Ayers
Oxbow Animal Hospital
222 State Road 202
Oxbow, TX 73330

August 11, 20__

Dear Dr. Ayers,

I asked my mother for a dog or a cat as a pet, but she has allergies to dogs and cats. She thought that I might like a Bearded Dragon and wants me to research this kind of lizard. Could you help me decide whether a Bearded Dragon would be a good pet by answering some questions or sending me information about where I can find out more about Bearded Dragons?

I would like to know whether a Bearded Dragon lizard likes to be petted. What kind of home does it need? What do I have to do to properly care for a Bearded Dragon? How big will it get? How long will it live? Is it friendly? Does it like to play? What toys should I get for it?

Thank you taking the time to answer my questions about Bearded Dragons. If you have information about Bearded Dragons, could you send it to me?

Yours sincerely,

Laura Moleen

© Pearson Education, Inc., 5

1. What are the salutation and the closing in this letter?

_____

2. Which sentence tells the purpose of this letter? Underline that sentence.

Vocabulary

Directions Choose the word from the box that best matches each definition. Write the word on the line.

_____   1. a slimy substance produced in the nose and throat to moisten and protect them

_____   2. free from germs

_____   3. gives ability, power, or means to; makes able

_____   4. to develop in a special way

_____   5. being important to the outcome of a situation

> **Check the Words You Know**
>
> ___critical
> ___enables
> ___mucus
> ___scarce
> ___specialize
> ___sterile

Directions Circle the word or group of words that has the same or nearly the same meaning as the first word.

Example: **melody**	words	(tune)	ringing
6. scarce	plenty	many	rare
7. critical	important	useful	relaxed
8. sterile	dirty	germ-free	bacteria
9. enables	teaches	makes empty	allows
10. specialize	stretch	adapt	organize

Write a Description

On a separate sheet of paper, write a description of a grasshopper or another insect with which you are familiar. Your description should include as many details as possible. Use as many vocabulary words as you can.

© Pearson Education, Inc., 5

Home Activity Your child identified and used vocabulary words from _Exploding Ants_. Pretend each of you is a research scientist. Use the vocabulary words to discuss a new species of insect you have discovered together.

Possessive Pronouns

Possessive pronouns show who or what owns, or possesses, something. *My, mine, your, yours, her, hers, his, its, our, ours, their,* and *theirs* are possessive pronouns.

- Use *my, your, her, our,* and *their* before nouns.
  Is that <u>your</u> cat? It was <u>her</u> gerbil. They pet <u>our</u> dog.
- Use *mine, yours, hers, ours,* and *theirs* alone.
  The cat is <u>yours</u>. That gerbil is <u>hers</u>. The dog is <u>ours</u>.
- *His* and *its* can be used both before nouns and alone.
  He lost <u>his</u> ferret. The ferret is <u>his</u>.
  The dog lost <u>its</u> collar. The collar is <u>its</u>.
- Do not use an apostrophe with a possessive pronoun.

Directions Replace the underlined words or phrases with possessive pronouns. Rewrite the sentences.

1. An ant colony relies on <u>the ant colony's</u> queen.

   _____

   _____

2. Both males and females have wings on <u>the males' and females'</u> bodies.

   _____

   _____

3. The queen ant flies to a new location to start a colony and then sheds <u>the queen's</u> wings.

   _____

   _____

4. Ants are very strong for <u>ants'</u> size and can carry 25 times <u>ants'</u> weight.

   _____

   _____

5. Most of us think that ants are pests to be swept out of <u>most of us's</u> way.

   _____

   _____

 Home Activity Your child learned about possessive pronouns. Ask your child to make up sentences about objects at home that belong to him or her, to the family, and to others. Have your child identify the possessive pronouns he or she uses.

© Pearson Education, Inc., 5

Name _____

Homophones

Spelling Words				
cent	sent	scent	threw	through
weather	whether	their	there	they're
chili	chilly	tide	tied	pale
pail	aloud	allowed	course	coarse

Words in Context Write homophones to complete the sentences.

On a (1)____ day, hot, spicy (2)____ with cheese really tastes good.

1. _____ 2. _____

We made sure the boats were (3)____ down securely against the rising (4)____.

3. _____ 4. _____

The (5)____ will determine (6)____ or not we play the game.

5. _____ 6. _____

I (7)____ away for that special one- (8)____ offer for my favorite perfume (9)____.

7. _____ 8. _____ 9. _____

Speaking (10)____ is not (11)____ in the library.

10. _____ 11. _____

You (12)____ the ball so far that it went (13)____ the window!

12. _____ 13. _____

(14)____ starting (15)____ lemonade business over (16)____ near the bakery.

14. _____ 15. _____ 16. _____

The golf (17)____ is designed to be challenging. It has sand, water traps, woods, and smooth and (18)____ grass.

17. _____ 18. _____

The (19)____ child carried the (20)____ onto the beach.

19. _____ 20. _____

School + Home **Home Activity** Your child learned to use homophones in context. Ask your child to make up other sentences using list words.

Writing • Formal Letter

Sender's Name _____

Address _____

City, ST Zip _____

Date _____

Recipient's Name _____ , [Title]

Address _____

City, ST Zip _____

Salutation_____

Opening: Statement of Purpose:

_____

_____

Supporting Details:

_____

_____

_____

Desired Action:

_____

_____

_____

Thank you in advance for:

_____

Closing _____

Signature _____

Vocabulary • Synonyms

- A **thesaurus** is a book that lists words, their **synonyms,** and their **antonyms.**
- **Synonyms** are different words that mean the same or almost the same thing, while **antonyms** are words that have the opposite meaning of each other.
- Sometimes authors write synonyms next to difficult words to help readers understand the word. To find synonyms, look for the words *or, such as,* and *like,* or a phrase set off by commas.

Directions Read the following passage about insects. Then answer the questions below. You may use a thesaurus.

> To some people, insects such as mosquitoes are simply pests. But many insects are useful. Honeybees, for example, make honey. They also pollinate plants by carrying pollen from one plant to another. This enables, or allows, the plant to grow and develop. Pollination is essential, or critical, for many things we eat. Growers use honeybees in apple orchards, for example. Beekeepers raise colonies, or communities, of bees.
>
> Some insects eat garbage. Others specialize in or focus on eating harmful insects. Caterpillars eat lots of plants but don't usually do permanent damage. Butterflies eat very little.

1. What word in the passage is a synonym for *enables*? How do you know it is a synonym?

_____

2. What suggests that *essential* and *critical* are synonyms?

_____

_____

3. The word *mosquitoes* follows the words *such as.* How do you know it is not a synonym for *insects*?

_____

_____

4. What is another word for *colonies*? What context clue helps you to identify the synonym?

_____

5. Rewrite the last sentence to provide a synonym for the word *scarce.*

_____

_____

Home Activity Your child identified and used synonyms to help him or her understand other words. Together, read an article about a scientific subject in a newspaper or magazine, noting any challenging vocabulary. Try to use synonyms and other context clues to clarify the meanings of these words.

Magazine/Periodical

- **Magazines** and **periodicals** are excellent sources of current information. They contain news articles, opinion columns, reports, reviews, letters, cartoons, advertisements, and other features.
- A table of contents helps readers locate particular stories and other information.
- Many magazine and periodical articles follow the "5 Ws and H" format. That is, they tell you *Who? What? When? Where? Why?* and *How?* in the first few paragraphs.

Directions Read this table of contents for an issue of a magazine. Then answer the questions that follow.

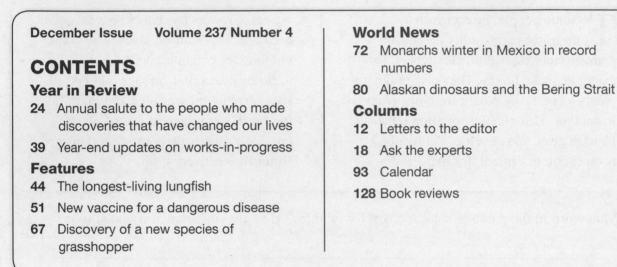

December Issue   Volume 237 Number 4

CONTENTS

Year in Review

24 Annual salute to the people who made discoveries that have changed our lives

39 Year-end updates on works-in-progress

Features

44 The longest-living lungfish

51 New vaccine for a dangerous disease

67 Discovery of a new species of grasshopper

World News

72 Monarchs winter in Mexico in record numbers

80 Alaskan dinosaurs and the Bering Strait

Columns

12 Letters to the editor

18 Ask the experts

93 Calendar

128 Book reviews

1. How would you describe the subject of this magazine?

_____

_____

2. On what page could you find information about lungfish?

_____

3. Where could you read what people think about a new book?

_____

4. Do you think this is a new magazine or one that has been published for some time? How do you know?

_____

_____

5. If you wrote to the magazine, where might you find your comments published in the next issue?

_____

Directions Read this passage from a magazine and answer the questions below.

Who's Got the Longest-Living Lungfish?

Two cities are competing for the honor of possessing the nation's longest-living lungfish. On Monday, the city of Will announced that its aquarium is celebrating the 67th birthday of its Australian lungfish on April 9. On Tuesday, one day later and fifty miles east, the city of Franklyn declared its plans to celebrate the 70th birthday of its lungfish on April 9. However, neither aquarium can prove the exact age of its lungfish.

Why the interest in elderly lungfish? Perhaps because it is a most unusual creature. It has both gills and lungs, leading scientists to believe that it is the missing link between fish and amphibians. The lungfish has the ability to be, as the saying goes, "a fish out of water." In other words, it can survive on land as well as in water. This adaptation is a big reason why the lungfish has survived for ages. Fossils show that it existed some 400 million years ago. Today the lungfish is an endangered species.

6. What part of the passage gives you a first impression of the article's subject?

_____

7. What would you identify as the *Who* of this article?

_____

_____

8. What would you say is the *What* of the article?

_____

9. What is the *When* of the article?

_____

_____

10. When might you use the information in this article?

_____

_____

© Pearson Education, Inc., 5

Home Activity Your child learned about reading tables of contents and articles in magazines. Look at a current issue of a magazine together and discuss the *Who, What, When, Where, Why,* and *How* of one of the articles.

Homophones

Proofread an Ad Circle six spelling errors. Write the words correctly. Find one capitalization error. Write the sentence correctly.

> On a chilly day, shout allowed for our delicious chilly! It will warm you through and threw! Ask about our ninety-nine sent special. If the whether is bad, call us. We Deliver for free! Of course, their is no finer tasting treat!

1. _____   2. _____

3. _____   4. _____

5. _____   6. _____

7. _____

Proofread Words Circle the correct spelling of the list word. Write the word.

8. Burlap is a ____ fabric.

   corse   cuarse   coarse

8. _____

9. I think ____ going on a class trip tomorrow.

   they're   their   they'ar

9. _____

10. Sky blue is a ____ color.

   pail   pale   paile

10. _____

11. Your perfume has a lovely ____.

   scent   cent   sent

11. _____

12. I am not sure ____ I can go.

   wheather   whether   weather

12. _____

13. The sailor ____ down the ship's hatch.

   tide   teid   tied

13. _____

14. The candy cost one ____.

   scent   cent   sent

14. _____

15. The score was even and the game was ____.

   tide   teid   tied

15. _____

Spelling Words

cent
sent
scent
threw
through
weather
whether
their
there
they're

chili
chilly
tide
tied
pale
pail
aloud
allowed
course
coarse

Frequently Misspelled Words

their
there
they're

© Pearson Education, Inc., 5

Home Activity Your child identified misspelled and misused homophones. Say a homophone in a sentence and have your child spell it.

Possessive Pronouns

Directions Read the passage. Then read each question. Circle the letter of the correct answer.

Our Owls

(1) When I was young, my brother and I heard a haunting sound outside their window. (2) We ran into our yard to see what it was. (3) "It's just a screech owl," Rich said, but _____ hoot still made me nervous. (4) After that, owls became a hobby of ours. (5) Did you know that owls can turn <u>owls'</u> heads almost completely around? (6) This is an adaptation of theirs that allows them to turn their heads to follow a moving object. (7) Now biologists, my brother and I spend our time studying these birds of prey.

1 What change, if any, should be made in sentence 1?

   A   Change *my brother and I* to **my brother and me**

   B   Change *was young* to **were young**

   C   Change *their* to **our**

   D   Make no change

2 Which possessive pronoun best completes sentence 3?

   A   its

   B   my

   C   our

   D   their

3 What change, if any, should be made in sentence 4?

   A   Change *became* to **have become**

   B   Change *ours* to **our**

   C   Change *ours* to **yours**

   D   Make no change

4 Which possessive pronoun replaces the underlined word in sentence 5?

   A   their

   B   our

   C   theirs

   D   its

5 How many possessive pronouns are in sentence 6?

   A   0

   B   1

   C   2

   D   3

Home Activity Your child prepared for taking tests on possessive pronouns. Have your child choose a magazine article and find possessive pronouns in it. Ask him or her to name the person or thing each possessive pronoun stands for.

Name_____

Generalize

- To **generalize** is to make a broad statement or rule that applies to several examples.
- Active readers pay close attention to what authors tell them about story characters and make generalizations about those characters as they read.

Directions Read the following passage.

Matt and his family moved to a new town where he went to a new school. He disliked the school a lot. When Matt wasn't complaining, he just stayed quiet and kept to himself. He played soccer and found classmates to sit with at lunch, but longed to see his old friends. He begged to go back to his old hometown for a visit, and his parents finally agreed. As they neared his old school, Matt was excited. He raced into the school and walked around. Everything seemed strange. Even his old friends didn't seem as familiar. On the way home he found himself looking forward to soccer practice.

Directions Complete the diagram by making a generalization about Matt.

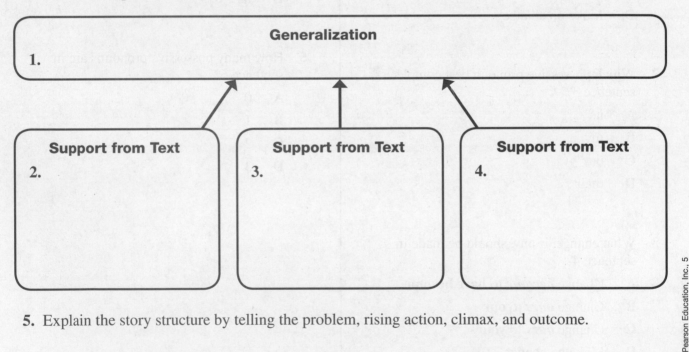

Generalization

1.

Support from Text

2.

Support from Text

3.

Support from Text

4.

5. Explain the story structure by telling the problem, rising action, climax, and outcome.

_____

_____

_____

Home Activity Your child made a generalization about a character in a story. Read a short story about friendship together. Ask your child to generalize about one of the characters. Ask your child to analyze the story structure also—the problem, rising action, climax, and outcome.

Writing · Narration Poetry

Key Features of Narrative Poetry

- tells a story
- uses sensory details
- may include graphic elements

The First Day

The worst day is always the first day.
I try to stay out of everyone's way.
I talk only to myself in the noisy hall,
Maybe I could blend in to the cold wall.

Everyone stares but nobody cares.
Then I see a girl in the bathroom mirror.
WAIT—
          is that a SMILE I see?
Is she smiling at herself or at me?

I was sure this day would make me blue,
But I guess life can surprise you.
Today I made a FRIEND to stay,
So the first day isn't always the worst day!

1. Summarize the story that the poem tells.

_____

_____

2. Underline two examples of sensory details in the poem.

3. Circle two examples of graphic elements, such as capital letters and varying line lengths, in the poem.

Name_____

Vocabulary

Directions Choose the word from the box that best matches each definition below. Write the word on the line.

_____ 1. hollow places in teeth caused by decay

_____ 2. shows how a thing is done

_____ 3. very careful in following a rule or making others follow it

_____ 4. one part of a story that is published or broadcast in several parts

_____ 5. attitude or position

Directions Choose the word from the box that best matches each clue below. Write the word on the line.

_____ 6. This is one in a series.

_____ 7. This opens some locks.

_____ 8. Some teachers act this way.

_____ 9. A movie star would have a high one of these.

_____ 10. If you don't brush your teeth, you might get these.

Write a Friendly Letter

On a separate sheet of paper, write a friendly letter that you might send to a relative telling about the beginning of a new school year. Use as many vocabulary words as you can.

Home Activity Your child identified and used vocabulary words from *The Stormi Giovanni Club*. Read a story or nonfiction article with your child. Have him or her point out unfamiliar words. Together try to figure out the meaning of each word by using the words that appear near it.

© Pearson Education, Inc., 5

Indefinite and Reflexive Pronouns

Indefinite pronouns may not refer to specific words. They do not have definite antecedents. Someone called and left a message.

Some common indefinite pronouns are listed below.

Singular Indefinite Pronouns
someone, somebody, anyone, anybody, everyone, everybody, something, no one, either, each

Plural Indefinite Pronouns
few, several, both, others, many all, some

• Use singular verb forms with singular indefinite pronouns and plural verb forms with plural indefinite pronouns: Everyone feels lonely at times. Others offer them friendship.

Reflexive pronouns reflect the action of the verb back on the subject. Reflexive pronouns end in -*self* or -*selves*: Vic wrote a note to himself.

Singular Reflexive Pronouns
himself, herself, myself, itself, yourself

Plural Reflexive Pronouns
ourselves, yourselves, themselves

• There are no such words as *hisself, theirself, theirselves,* or *ourself.*

Directions Underline the correct pronoun in ( ) to complete each sentence.

1. (Anyone, Many) benefits by making new friends.

2. (Many, Anyone) treasure old friends too.

3. My friends and I taught (ourself, ourselves) chess.

4. We play in the cafeteria, but (few, no one) know this.

5. (Everyone, Others) is welcome to join us.

6. A new student introduced (himself, hisself).

7. (Some, Someone) calls him Dylan.

8. (Something, Many) tells me Dylan has learned chess from a master.

9. We know the moves, but he knows the game (itself, themselves).

10. (Someone, Others) tell me I'm good at chess, but Dylan beat me.

11. I hope Dylan enjoyed (herself, himself) today.

12. You should learn chess (ourself, yourself).

Home Activity Your child learned about indefinite and reflexive pronouns. Ask your child to make up several statements about making friends using pronouns such as *everybody, no one, many, few,* and *myself.*

Suffixes *-ible*, *-able*

Spelling Words				
sensible	washable	available	agreeable	fashionable
valuable	flexible	reasonable	favorable	breakable
convertible	forgettable	laughable	sociable	allowable
divisible	hospitable	reversible	responsible	tolerable

Synonyms Write the list word that has the same or nearly the same meaning.

1. in style
2. bendable
3. welcoming
4. ridiculous
5. car with top down
6. positive
7. permissible
8. able to turn inside out
9. can be cleaned
10. accountable

1. _____
2. _____
3. _____
4. _____
5. _____
6. _____
7. _____
8. _____
9. _____
10. _____

Antonyms Write the list word that has the opposite or nearly the opposite meaning.

11. memorable
12. unfriendly
13. disagreeable
14. unreasonable
15. unbreakable
16. unavailable
17. intolerable
18. can't be divided
19. foolish
20. worthless

11. _____
12. _____
13. _____
14. _____
15. _____
16. _____
17. _____
18. _____
19. _____
20. _____

© Pearson Education, Inc., 5

Home Activity Your child used meanings to select list words that were synonyms and antonyms. Have your child tell you the meaning of three list words and spell the words.

Story Sequence B

Title

Characters

Setting

Events

Vocabulary • Unfamiliar Words

- Sometimes when you are reading, you see an unfamiliar word. Use the **context**, or words around the unfamiliar word, to find clues to its meaning.
- Context clues include synonyms, examples, and explanations.

Directions Read the following passage. Then answer the questions below.

In class, Meg's teacher demonstrated, or showed, how to open the new lockers. "Dial the combination and then pull the handle," she said. Instead of paying attention, however, Meg talked to her friend about an episode of her favorite TV show, the last one of the series. "Meg, you are not supposed to talk while I am talking. I am very strict about following this rule. Please stay in class during recess," her teacher said sternly. Meg was very embarrassed, but she was glad she didn't have to stay after school. She had to go to the dentist to have her cavities filled after school.

1. What does *demonstrated* mean? What clue helps you to determine the meaning?

_____

_____

2. What does *combination* mean? How does the context help you to determine the meaning?

_____

_____

3. What is an *episode*? What clue helps you to determine this?

_____

_____

4. How do context clues help you determine the meaning of *strict*?

_____

_____

5. What does *cavities* mean? How can you use context clues to determine the meaning?

_____

_____

Home Activity Your child read a short passage and used context clues to understand new words. Work with your child to identify unfamiliar words in an article. Ask your child to find context clues to help with the understanding of the new words. Confirm the meanings with your child.

© Pearson Education, Inc., 5

Thesaurus

A **thesaurus** is a kind of dictionary in which synonyms (words that have the same or similar meanings), antonyms (words that have the opposite meanings), and other related words are classified under headings. You can use a thesaurus to help you find new and interesting words when writing.

Directions Use this thesaurus entry to answer the questions that follow.

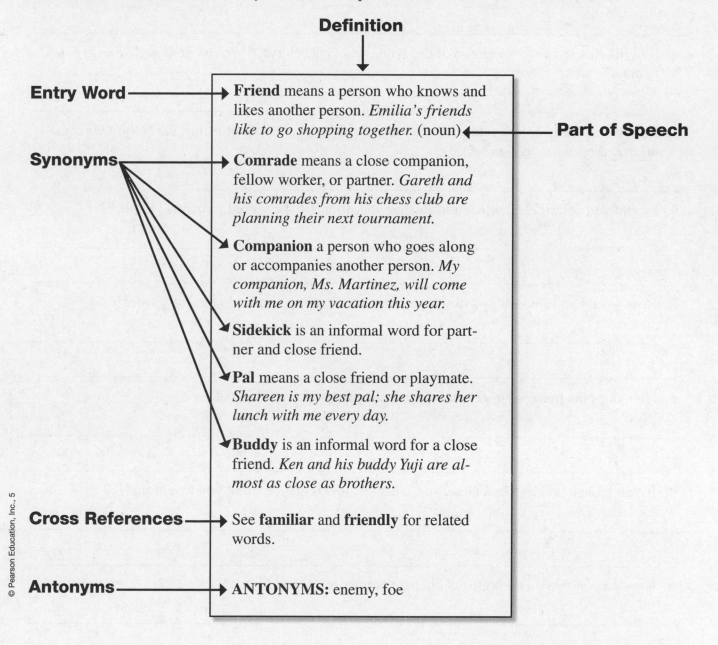

Definition

Entry Word

Part of Speech

Synonyms

Friend means a person who knows and likes another person. *Emilia's friends like to go shopping together.* (noun)

Comrade means a close companion, fellow worker, or partner. *Gareth and his comrades from his chess club are planning their next tournament.*

Companion a person who goes along or accompanies another person. *My companion, Ms. Martinez, will come with me on my vacation this year.*

Sidekick is an informal word for partner and close friend.

Pal means a close friend or playmate. *Shareen is my best pal; she shares her lunch with me every day.*

Buddy is an informal word for a close friend. *Ken and his buddy Yuji are almost as close as brothers.*

Cross References

See **familiar** and **friendly** for related words.

Antonyms

ANTONYMS: enemy, foe

1. What entry word is shown?

_____

2. Name the part of speech of the entry word.

_____

3. What synonyms are given for the entry word?

_____

4. Rewrite this sentence using one of the synonyms in the entry: *My friend May and I like to listen to music.*

_____

5. Rewrite this sentence by replacing the underlined words with a word from the entry: *Our cat is no friend of our neighbor's dog.*

_____

6. Would you use *sidekick* when introducing your friend to the school principal? Explain.

_____

_____

7. How would you find additional words that have meanings similar to the entry word?

_____

_____

8. How does the meaning of *friend* help you understand the meaning of *foe?*

_____

_____

9. If you looked up *large* in a thesaurus, what synonyms do you think you would find?

_____

_____

10. How do you think a thesaurus could help you write a report?

_____

_____

Home Activity Your child answered questions about a thesaurus entry. Look at a thesaurus together. Ask your child to locate several entries using entry words you tell him or her. Discuss the synonyms for different shades of meaning.

© Pearson Education, Inc., 5

Suffixes *-ible, -able*

Proofread an Article Find five spelling errors and one capitalization error in the article. Circle the errors and write the corrections on the lines.

Fashion Sense

Store buyers are responsible for ordering fashionible clothing customers will like. Last year, mrs. Clark, the store buyer, ordered dozens of reversible sweaters. The sweaters were washible, availible in a variety of colors, and sold at a reasonible price. When the sweaters sold out quickly, the buyer knew she had made a sensable choice.

1. _____   2. _____

3. _____   4. _____

5. _____   6. _____

Proofread Words Circle the correct spelling of the list word.

7. The gymnast is as ____ as a rubber band.

   flexable   flexibel   flexible

8. Porcelain china is delicate and ____.

   breakable   brakeable   breakible

9. Be ____ to your guests when they visit.

   hospital   hospitable   hospitible

10. I'd love to have a car with a ____ top.

   convertible   convertable   convertibel

11. Sixty-three is ____ by seven.

   dividable   divisable   divisible

12. Eat three ____ and balanced meals every day.

   sensible   sensable   senseable

Spelling Words

sensible
washable
available
agreeable
fashionable
valuable
flexible
reasonable
favorable
breakable

convertible
forgettable
laughable
sociable
allowable
divisible
hospitable
reversible
responsible
tolerable

Frequently Misspelled Words

when
then
went

Home Activity Your child identified misspelled list words. Ask your child to spell three list words that end in *-ible* and three list words that end in *-able*.

Indefinite and Reflexive Pronouns

Directions Read the passage. Then read each question. Circle the letter of the correct answer.

The New Kid

(1) "Someone new is starting today" was the buzz at school. (2) _____ likes it when a new student comes to class. (3) However, no one really likes to be the new kid. (4) Efrain, the new kid, clearly preferred to spend those first few days by himself. (5) Some tried to talk to him, but Efrain was shy. (6) Lara noticed Efrain liked to draw and told him she was an artist himself. (7) They became good friends and spent many afternoons by themselves.

1 What is the indefinite pronoun in sentence 1?

   A school

   B buzz

   C new

   D Someone

2 Which pronoun would **not** best complete sentence 2?

   A Everybody

   B Everyone

   C Either

   D Anyone

3 Which describes the underlined word in sentence 4?

   A Singular indefinite pronoun

   B Singular reflexive pronoun

   C Plural indefinite pronoun

   D Plural reflexive pronoun

4 Which describes the underlined word in sentence 5?

   A Singular indefinite pronoun

   B Singular reflexive pronoun

   C Plural indefinite pronoun

   D Plural reflexive pronoun

5 What change, if any, should be made to sentence 6?

   A Change *himself* to **herself**

   B Change *him* to **her**

   C Change *she* to **he**

   D Make no change

School + Home

Home Activity Your child prepared for taking tests on indefinite and reflexive pronouns. Have your child write each indefinite and reflexive pronoun on an index card. Mix the cards and have your child sort them by type and number.

Draw Conclusions

- A **conclusion** is a sensible decision you make after you think about facts or details that you read.
- Drawing conclusions may also be called making inferences.
- Use your prior knowledge to help you draw conclusions.

Directions Read the following passage. Then complete the diagram below.

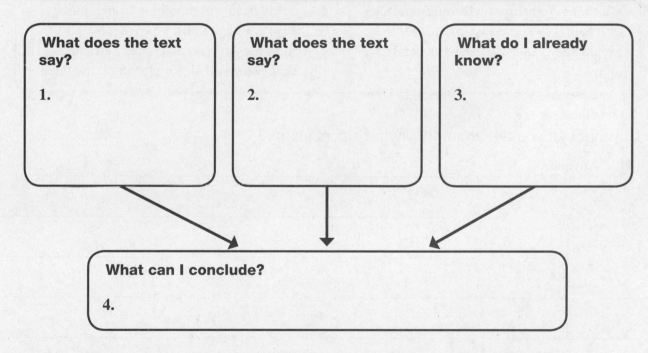

Enrique is a young gymnast who is training for the Olympics. He goes to live at the Olympic Training Center in Colorado Springs. There he trains twelve hours a day with other athletes. In addition, he regularly takes part in competitions to test his skills. Enrique sets goals for himself. He wants to improve in gymnastics skills and to learn routines that are more difficult. His training schedule is so demanding, he does not have time to go to a regular school. He studies all of his school subjects with a tutor. After more years of training, Enrique hopes to make the Olympic team.

What does the text say?

1.

What does the text say?

2.

What do I already know?

3.

What can I conclude?

4.

5. Visualize Enrique studying with his tutor. What conclusion can you draw about the advantages or disadvantages of studying with a tutor rather than studying at a regular school?

_____

Home Activity Your child read a short passage and drew a conclusion based on the details in it. Tell your child a story about an athlete you know about. Ask your child to visualize the details as you describe them. Ask your child to draw a conclusion based on the details you provide.

Writing • Writing for Tests

The Runner

One evening my grandfather said to me, "Come watch television with me. The show is about Jesse Owens."

"Who is he?" I asked with hesitation. My grandfather loves history, but I don't.

My grandfather turned to me with an amazed face to tell me that Jesse was the athlete whom the whole world saw as the fastest and best track star. I snuggled in next to my grandfather to watch the television show about Jesse.

After I watched the show, I wanted to be the fastest track star like Jesse. The next day, I ran to school and skidded in early! Since then, I have run home every afternoon, sometimes wincing from lack of breath. I have run fast errands for my grandfather, doing cartwheels when I arrived.

I have run so much that my brother has asked me, "Who do you think you are?" My father and teacher have asked me, "For whom do you hurry?" My grandfather has said simply, "Thank you."

I told everyone that I love running, and that I am practicing to be a track star like Jesse. However, my brother said that I have to eat more vegetables and fewer potato chips. My father said that track and field also includes long jumps and hurdles. My grandfather said, "World records come from people who are not only the fastest in short and long runs, but also the best at jumping."

My head was throbbing from all their advice. But now that I have a record of short runs to class and speedy errands, next year I will sign up for track and field!

1. What can you tell about the author's personality?

   _____

   _____

   _____

   _____

2. What details does the author give about his or her feelings? Underline sentences that tell about feelings.

Vocabulary

Directions Choose the word from the box that best matches each definition below. Write the word on the line.

_____ **1.** to run or jump, turning the heels over the head

_____ **2.** a sport in which very difficult exercises are performed

_____ **3.** act of failing to act promptly

_____ **4.** somewhat blue

_____ **5.** sideways handsprings with the legs and arms kept straight

> ### Check the Words You Know
>
> ___bluish
> ___cartwheels
> ___gymnastics
> ___hesitation
> ___limelight
> ___skidded
> ___somersault
> ___throbbing
> ___wincing

Directions Choose the word from the box that matches the clues and complete the crossword puzzle.

DOWN

6. the pain I felt when I broke my toe
7. the color of a pale sky
8. the place the star wants to be

ACROSS

9. what my bicycle did when I slammed on the brakes
10. what I am doing when I eat food I don't like

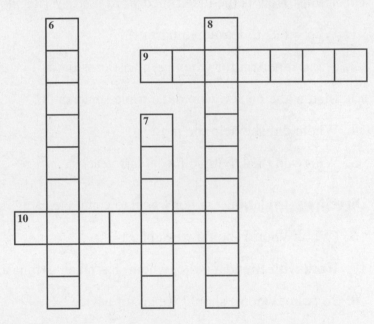

Write a News Report

Imagine you're a sports reporter covering a gymnastics meet. On a separate sheet of paper write a news report. Use as many vocabulary words as you can.

Home Activity Your child identified and used vocabulary words from *The Gymnast*. Skim the articles about a single sport in the sports section of a newspaper. Point out and define the vocabulary word that is used to describe each type of sport.

Using *Who* and *Whom*

People sometimes confuse the pronouns *who* and *whom* when they write. *Who* is a subject form. It is used as a subject of a sentence or a clause.

Who made this mess?

I saw a performer *who* could do four back flips. [*Who* is the subject in the dependent clause *who could do four back flips.*]

Whom is an object form. It is used as the object of a preposition or as a direct object.

To *whom* did you send a letter?

Whom will you ask?

In the first example, *whom* is the object of the preposition *to*. In the second example, *whom* is a direct object.

• To understand why *whom* is used in the second sentence, change the word order so that the subject comes first. (*Whom will you ask?* becomes *You will ask whom?*) This makes it easier to see that *whom* is a direct object.

Directions How is the underlined word used? Write *subject*, *object of preposition*, or *direct object*.

1. <u>Who</u> wants to learn gymnastics? _____

2. She is a person for <u>whom</u> gymnastics is hard. _____

3. Matt is the person <u>who</u> did a triple somersault. _____

4. <u>Whom</u> did she help the most? _____

5. <u>Who</u> won the Olympic medal last year? _____

Directions Underline *who* or *whom* to complete each sentence correctly.

6. (Who, Whom) should we support?

7. Work with Brenda, (who, whom) has taken gymnastics for years.

8. To (who, whom) should we go for advice?

9. (Who, Whom) remembers the order of events?

10. The gymnast (who, whom) stumbled on the dismount still won a medal.

© Pearson Education, Inc., 5

School + Home

Home Activity Your child learned about using *who* and *whom*. Ask your child to write sentences about a sport using *whom* as an object and *who* as a subject.

Name _____

Negative Prefixes

Spelling Words				
invisible	illiterate	irregular	irresistible	impossible
informal	illegal	impatient	independent	incorrect
inactive	imperfect	impolite	immature	illogical
indefinite	inappropriate	immobile	irresponsible	inexpensive

Missing Words Write the missing list word.

1. If you learn to read, you are not ____.

2. If you have good manners, you'll rarely be ____.

3. If you earn a living, you can be ____.

4. If you have a "can do" attitude, little is ____.

5. If you're always trustworthy, you are never ____.

6. If you always follow the law, then you never do anything ____.

7. If you're always right, then you're never ____.

8. If you always act responsibly, then you are not ____.

9. If you set an exact time to meet, it is not ____.

10. If something always makes sense, it is not ____.

1. _____
2. _____
3. _____
4. _____
5. _____
6. _____
7. _____
8. _____
9. _____
10. _____

Classifying Write the list word that completes the group.

11. cheap, reasonable, low-cost, ____

12. flawed, faulty, defective, ____

13. restless, fidgety, ____

14. unseen, faint, ____

15. casual, relaxed, ____

16. idle, quiet, immobile, ____

17. out of place, unsuitable, ____

18. stationary, motionless, ____

19. tempting, appealing, enticing, ____

20. uneven, lopsided, ____

11. _____
12. _____
13. _____
14. _____
15. _____
16. _____
17. _____
18. _____
19. _____
20. _____

Home Activity Your child wrote words with prefixes. Ask your child to spell one word for each of the four negative prefixes.

© Pearson Education, Inc., 5

Scoring Rubric: Writing for Tests: Autobiographical Sketch

	4	3	2	1
Focus/Ideas	Auto-biographical sketch clearly focused on an important event in writer's life	Auto-biographical sketch fairly clear; somewhat focused on an event in writer's life	Auto-biographical sketch with some details about an event in writer's life	Auto-biographical sketch with no focus on writer's life
Organization	Clear events in chronological order	Events largely in chronological order	Events somewhat disorganized	Little or no organization
Voice	Clearly shows writer's personality and feelings about the subject	Gives some indication of writer's personality and feelings about the subject	Gives little indication of writer's personality and feelings about the subject	No indication of writer's personality or feelings about the subject
Word Choice	First-person used appropriately throughout	First-person used correctly, but not consistently	First-person pronouns used incorrectly	First-person pronouns used incorrectly, if at all
Sentences	Sentences clear and interesting	Sentences mostly clear and interesting	Choppy sentences	Fragments or run-ons
Conventions	Excellent control and accuracy; *who* and *whom* used consistently and correctly	Good control; *who* and *whom* used correctly but not consistently	Errors may prevent understanding; *who* and *whom* used or spelled incorrectly	Frequent errors that interfere with meaning; *who* and *whom* used incorrectly, if at all

Name_____

Vocabulary · Suffixes

- A **suffix** is a syllable added to the end of a base word to change its meaning or the way it is used in a sentence. For example, the Old English suffix -*ish* means "somewhat," as in *childish*. The Latin suffix -*ion* means "the act or state of being _____," as in *determination*. The suffix -*ics* means "study or system," as in *athletics*. The suffix -*ist* means "a member of a profession" as in *dentist*. You can use suffixes to help you figure out the meanings of words.

- In dictionaries, the definition of a base word with the suffix added is usually found near that of the base word. The base word's definition is helpful in understanding a word's meaning.

Directions Read the following passage. Notice the words with suffixes as you read. Then answer the questions below.

> The gymnastics meet started with a spectacular balance beam routine by Amy's main competitor. Then Amy hopped onto the beam and started her routine with no hesitation. She did fine on her somersaults and cartwheels, but on one backflip she had a bad landing. Her ankle felt like a knife had ripped through it, and she saw bluish stars in front of her eyes. As she finished her routine, Amy thought, "There goes my chance to be a finalist." But when the numbers came up, she scored the highest! Although her ankle was throbbing, she stepped to the judges' table and accepted her medal.

1. What is the suffix in *gymnastics*? How does the suffix change the meaning of the base word?

_____

_____

2. What is the suffix in *hesitation*? How does the suffix change the meaning of the base word?

_____

_____

3. What is the suffix in *bluish*? How does the suffix change the meaning of the base word?

_____

4. Change the suffix of *competitor* from -*or* to -*ion*. What is the meaning of the new word?

_____

5. Which word in the passage has a suffix like *dentist*? Write its definition.

_____

_____

Home Activity Your child read a short passage and identified and used suffixes to understand new words. Work with your child to identify unfamiliar words with suffixes. Then ask your child how the suffixes help him or her to understand the meanings of the new words. Confirm the meanings by looking them up in a dictionary.

Graphs

Graphs show information visually. You can use graphs to compare different pieces of information. Look at the title of a graph to see what is being compared. There are many types of graphs, but two types of graphs are bar graphs and circle graphs. A **bar graph** uses horizontal and vertical lines. Words or numbers along each line explain what is being compared. A **circle graph**, which is also called a pie chart, compares the parts of a whole.

Directions Use this graph to answer the questions below.

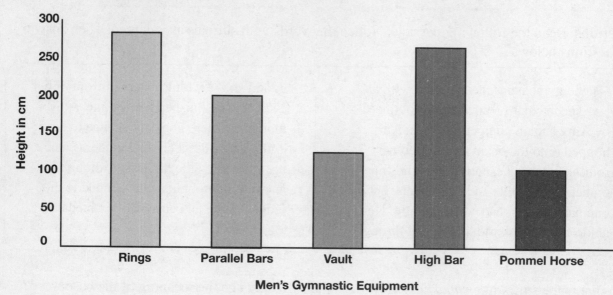

1. Explain what kind of graph this is and how you know.

_____

_____

2. What is the tallest piece of equipment? What is the shortest piece of equipment?

_____

_____

3. How many pieces of equipment are being compared?

_____

4. Approximately how tall are the parallel bars? The high bar?

_____

5. Would this graph be a good source for finding out information about equipment used by female gymnasts? Explain.

_____

_____

Name_____

Directions Use this graph to answer the questions below.

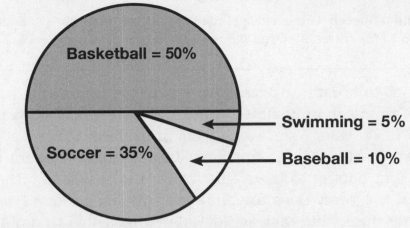

Favorite Sports of Sawyer School Fifth Graders

6. What kind of graph is this? How do you know?

_____

_____

7. What is the favorite sport of the fifth graders at Sawyer School? What percent of students prefer that sport?

_____

_____

8. What sport is second-most popular? What percent of students prefer that sport?

_____

_____

9. What sport is the least popular? What percent of students prefer that sport?

_____

_____

10. What is being compared in this graph? Explain why you think this type of graph displays this information effectively.

_____

_____

_____

© Pearson Education, Inc., 5

Home Activity Your child learned about using graphs as resources. With your child, look at a graph that appears in the newspaper or in a brochure. Ask your child what information is being compared. Ask your child specific questions about information the graph shows.

Research and Study Skills 299

Name _____

Negative Prefixes

Proofread a Speech Circle six spelling errors in the toymaker's speech. Write the words correctly. Write the run-on sentence as two sentences.

> "I want to create an irresistable toy for children. It will make the user innvisible. I need five independent teams to work on this. As always, I am impashent to get this project started! We do not have an indefinute amount of time. I'm hoping to have this toy on the market by the end of the year. Does anyone have any questions? Does anyone think this task is ilogical or inpossible to do? Do we all agree this can be done let's get to work!"

Spelling Words

invisible
illiterate
irregular
irresistible
impossible
informal
illegal
impatient
independent
incorrect

inactive
imperfect
impolite
immature
illogical
indefinite
inappropriate
immobile
irresponsible
inexpensive

1. _____   2. _____

3. _____   4. _____

5. _____   6. _____

7. _____

_____

Proofread Words Circle the word that is spelled correctly.

8. irresistible   unresistable   ilresistable

9. ilexpensive   imexpensive   inexpensive

10. inmature   immature   imature

11. imperfect   ilperfect   unperfect

12. imdependent   independent   ildependent

13. imactive   innactive   inactive

14. impolite   inpolite   unpolite

15. illiterate   iliterate   inliterate

16. imappropriate   inappropriate   inapropriate

Frequently Misspelled Words

through
always

© Pearson Education, Inc., 5

Home Activity Your child identified misspelled list words. Take turns spelling list words that begin with the four negative prefixes studied.

Using *Who* and *Whom*

Directions Read the passage. Then read each question. Circle the letter of the correct answer.

Making the Team

(1) When Coach Reed asked, "Whom would like to try out for the basketball team?" we all raised our hands. (2) "Who will make the team?" I wondered. (3) Some of the kids were already very good at basketball. (4) It wasn't hard to see who had not played much. (5) I could run and shoot, but I was never sure to whom I should pass the ball. (6) Whom could I ask for help? (7) Coach Reed saw me practice and asked me to be on the team.

1 What change, if any, should be made in sentence 1?

A Change *Coach* to **coach**

B Remove quotation marks

C Change *Whom* to **Who**

D Make no change

2 What change, if any, should be made in sentence 2?

A Change *I wondered* to **I wonder**

B Remove quotation marks

C Change *Who* to **Whom**

D Make no change

3 Which describes the underlined word in sentence 4?

A Subject

B Object of preposition

C Direct object

D None of the above

4 Which describes the underlined word in sentence 5?

A Subject

B Object of preposition

C Direct object

D None of the above

5 Which describes the underlined word in sentence 6?

A Subject

B Object of preposition

C Direct object

D None of the above

© Pearson Education, Inc., 5

Home Activity Your child prepared for taking tests on *who* and *whom*. Have your child read newspaper articles to highlight uses of *who* and *whom*. Then ask him or her to tell whether the words are used correctly, and why.

Words from Many Cultures

Spelling Words				
khaki	waltz	yogurt	cobra	buffet
hula	tomato	banquet	koala	stampede
banana	vanilla	macaroni	barbecue	karate
ballet	canyon	polka	safari	kiosk

Alphabetize Write the ten list words below in alphabetical order.

kiosk	stampede
safari	buffet
koala	polka
banquet	karate
ballet	khaki

1. _____   6. _____

2. _____   7. _____

3. _____   8. _____

4. _____   9. _____

5. _____   10. _____

Classifying Write the list word that belongs in each group.

11. lettuce, carrots, onion, _____

12. dance, ballroom, elegant, _____

13. rattlesnake, boa constrictor, _____

14. spaghetti, noodles, pasta, _____

15. gorge, valley, ravine, _____

16. Hawaii, dance, grass skirt, _____

17. milk, creamy, fruit, _____

18. fruit, yellow, plant, _____

19. chocolate, strawberry, _____

20. food, outdoors, grill, _____

Home Activity Your child has learned to spell words that come from a variety of cultures. With your child, look up several of the words in a dictionary and discuss what the dictionary says about the words' origins.

Subject and Object Pronouns

Directions Write *S* if the underlined word is a subject pronoun. Write *O* if the word is an object pronoun.

1. In *Weslandia*, Wesley is the main character. <u>He</u> has problems. _____

2. Wesley doesn't act like the other kids, and they pick on <u>him</u>. _____

3. His parents worry that <u>they</u> have raised an odd son. _____

4. Wesley creates a new civilization, and <u>it</u> fascinates everyone. _____

5. <u>I</u> really enjoyed reading this story. _____

6. Wesley's ingenious uses for his crop amused <u>me</u>. _____

7. My friend Winnie said the suntan oil was funniest to <u>her</u>. _____

8. <u>You</u> should read this story too! _____

9. Our teacher, Mr. Su, asked <u>us</u> about civilizations. _____

10. Native peoples create <u>them</u> based on climate and crops in their region. _____

Directions Underline the correct pronoun in ( ) to complete each sentence.

11. Corn has many uses. Many farmers plant (it, they).

12. (They, Them) can sell the grain as a food or as a raw material for fuel.

13. The stalks can be ground up. There are several uses for (it, them) as well.

14. John and (I, me) have learned about soybeans.

15. (We, Us) get nutritious foods from them.

16. Do you like tofu? (It, Them) is a curd made from soybeans.

17. Mom served tofu to Karl and (I, me).

18. She didn't tell (us, we) what we were eating.

19. When (he, him) found out it was bean curd, Karl laughed.

20. Mom had disguised it in pudding. That was clever of (her, she)!

Prefixes *over-*, *under-*, *sub-*, *super-*, *out-*

Spelling Words				
overlook	supermarket	undercurrent	submarine	output
underline	outlet	superstar	undercover	supernatural
subway	underground	overtime	overcast	subdivision
subset	overboard	supersonic	outfield	subhead

Analogies Write the list word that completes each comparison.

1. Light is to heavy as sunny is to _____.

2. Title is to subtitle as head is to _____.

3. Sky is to airplane as ocean is to _____.

4. Carpenter is to house as baseball player is to _____.

5. Shoes are to shoe store as food is to _____.

6. Living room is to outside as cabin is to _____.

7. Street is to bus as underground is to _____.

8. Strong is to athlete as famous is to _____.

9. Comedian is to funny as ghost is to _____.

10. Store is to mall as house is to _____.

Synonyms Write the list word that has the same, or nearly the same, meaning.

11. underscore _____

12. secret _____

13. category _____

14. extra _____

15. production _____

16. hint _____

17. buried _____

18. socket _____

19. fast _____

20. forget _____

 School + Home

Home Activity Your child has completed analogies containing words with prefixes. Ask your child to make up two analogies containing words from the list and explain how the analogies work.

Pronouns and Antecedents

Directions Match the pronoun with the noun or noun phrase that could be its antecedent. Write the letter of the correct antecedent next to the pronoun.

_____ 1. her   **A** Jinx and I

_____ 2. it   **B** Victoria

_____ 3. them   **C** Uncle Jeff

_____ 4. us   **D** other students

_____ 5. he   **E** fishing rod

Directions Circle the antecedent of the underlined pronoun in each sentence.

6. This story reminds me of my friend, and <u>she</u> is named Greta.

7. Greta and Jinx are similar because <u>they</u> fall a lot.

8. Greta has many casts, and <u>they</u> prove she has had many accidents.

9. Workers poured fresh cement, and Greta walked into <u>it</u>.

10. Will nearly lost the marathon when <u>he</u> tripped over Greta's crutch.

11. Cheerleaders made a pyramid, and Greta toppled <u>them</u>.

12. Greta is nicknamed Grace because <u>she</u> is not very graceful.

Directions Write a pronoun to replace each underlined noun or noun phrase.

13. Jinx doesn't trip over the lunch lady, but <u>Jinx</u> has other accidents. _____

14. Tony choked on some gum when Jinx bounced over <u>Tony</u>. _____

15. Jinx crawled into boxes and boots and got stuck in <u>boxes and boots</u>. _____

16. Jinx looked inside her locker and got stuck inside <u>her locker</u>. _____

17. She saw square dancers and wanted to be like <u>the square dancers</u>. _____

18. Victoria and Jinx tried square dancing, but <u>Victoria and Jinx</u> hurt themselves. _____

© Pearson Education, Inc., 5

Homophones

Spelling Words				
cent	through	there	tide	aloud
sent	weather	they're	tied	allowed
scent	whether	chili	pale	course
threw	their	chilly	pail	coarse

Crossword Puzzle Use the clues to find the list words. Write each letter in a box.

Across
2. gave permission
6. not here
7. fastened
8. pitched
9. place to play golf

Down
1. said so it could be heard
3. if
4. finished
5. smell
7. belonging to them

Classifying Write the list word that belongs in each group.

10. rain, snow, tornado, _____

11. cold, icy, frosty, _____

12. rough, thick, _____

13. taco, spaghetti, soup, _____

14. bucket, container, jug, _____

15. nickel, dime, quarter, _____

16. you're, we're, _____

17. white, colorless, sickly, _____

18. ocean, waves, high, low, _____

19. letter, mailed, transmitted, _____

School + Home
Home Activity Your child has learned to spell homophones. Ask your child to find some of the list words in a newspaper or magazine. Then ask your child to spell one or more homophones for each word and use them in sentences.

Possessive Pronouns

Directions Write the letter of the possessive pronoun that can replace the underlined word or words in each phrase.

_____ 1. <u>Lori's</u> idea   **A** her

_____ 2. <u>Nate's</u> paper   **B** their

_____ 3. <u>the twins'</u> pet   **C** our

_____ 4. <u>an owl's</u> eyes   **D** its

_____ 5. <u>Ti's and my</u> cat   **E** his

Directions Underline the pronoun that correctly completes each sentence.

6. Each ant colony has (its, their) own smell.

7. The ants can recognize an intruder in (theirs, their) nest.

8. They also know which eggs are not (theirs, we).

9. A female worker will help defend (her, she) home.

10. I know some ants can sting because an ant stung (mine, my) foot!

Directions Write the possessive pronoun that can replace the underlined word or words.

11. Dad and I love to have honey on <u>Dad's and my</u> toast. _____

12. Mom likes honey on <u>Mom's</u> oatmeal. _____

13. Sam puts honey on <u>Sam's</u> peanut butter sandwiches. _____

14. Bees make honey for <u>the bees'</u> food. _____

15. A bee can always fly back to <u>a bee's</u> hive. _____

16. I washed my plate, and now you can wash <u>the plate belonging to you.</u> _____

17. Paul put his glass in the dishwasher, and then I added <u>the glass belonging to me.</u> _____

18. He found his fork, but she couldn't find <u>the fork belonging to her.</u> _____

Suffixes *-ible, -able*

Spelling Words				
sensible	fashionable	favorable	laughable	hospitable
washable	valuable	breakable	sociable	reversible
available	flexible	convertible	allowable	responsible
agreeable	reasonable	forgettable	divisible	tolerable

Words in Context Complete each sentence with a list word.

1. Be careful with that vase because it is _____.

2. It is hot in the desert, but the dry air makes it _____.

3. Jim's mom was _____ and invited us to stay for dinner.

4. You can wear the jacket with that side in or out because it is _____.

5. A(n) _____ car is not practical in a cold climate.

6. Anita didn't go to the party because she was not feeling _____.

7. Gold and silver are _____ metals.

8. The critic liked the movie, so he gave it a(n) _____ review.

9. Is that number _____ by ten?

10. It's all right to get your uniform muddy because it is _____.

11. The magician's tricks were so obvious they were _____.

12. The soccer team took care to make plays that were _____.

13. Lizzy often wears new styles because she likes to be _____.

14. I can't recall the story's characters because they were _____.

15. The Henrys asked Carla to baby-sit, but she was not _____ that day.

16. Unlike the unpleasant dog next door, our pet is always _____.

17. Who is _____ for setting the table?

18. It is _____ to wear sturdy shoes on a long hike.

19. If you work on the problem, you will think of a(n) _____ answer.

20. Rubber is used for many items because it is _____.

© Pearson Education, Inc., 5

School + Home

Home Activity Your child has learned to spell words with the suffixes *-ible* and *-able*. Ask your child to make up several sentences containing list words and to spell each list word used.

Name _____

Indefinite and Reflexive Pronouns

Directions Underline the pronoun in each sentence. Write *indefinite* or *reflexive* to identify the kind of pronoun it is. Then write *singular* or *plural* to show its number.

1. Everybody eats lunch in the cafeteria. _____ _____

2. Many of the students bring a sack lunch. _____ _____

3. Others eat a hot lunch. _____ _____

4. Students help themselves to milk. _____ _____

5. Mom says, "Give yourself time to eat." _____ _____

Directions Underline the correct pronoun in ( ) to complete each sentence.

6. I chose a special place for (myself, myselves).

7. (Everybody, Many) needs a place to be alone and think.

8. (Few, No one) is immune to stress.

9. The teacher said, "Do your work by (theirself, yourself)."

10. (Several, Someone) of my friends have private places.

Directions Choose a pronoun from the box to complete each sentence correctly. Be sure indefinite pronouns used as subjects agree in number with their verbs.

> herself   many   myself   something   everybody

11. If I see someone new, I introduce _____.

12. I tell the new person _____ about the school.

13. The new girl said to _____, "I won't make any friends."

14. _____ appreciates a friendly welcome.

15. _____ try to make newcomers feel at home.

Negative Prefixes

Spelling Words				
invisible	impossible	independent	impolite	inappropriate
illiterate	informal	incorrect	immature	immobile
irregular	illegal	inactive	illogical	irresponsible
irresistible	impatient	imperfect	indefinite	inexpensive

Synonyms Write the list word that has the same, or nearly the same, meaning.

1. restless _____

2. cheap _____

3. rude _____

4. motionless _____

5. casual _____

6. vague _____

7. uneven _____

8. lazy _____

9. separate _____

10. fascinating _____

Antonyms Write the list word that has the opposite, or nearly the opposite, meaning.

11. lawful _____

12. experienced _____

13. excellent _____

14. reasonable _____

15. accurate _____

16. educated _____

17. suitable _____

18. likely _____

19. noticeable _____

20. dependable _____

Home Activity Your child has written synonyms and antonyms for words with negative prefixes. Name several list words. Ask your child to spell each word and to name a synonym and/or antonym for each.

Name _____

Using *Who* and *Whom*

Directions Write *subject, object of preposition,* or *direct object* to identify how the underlined word is used.

1. <u>Who</u> likes cheerleading? _____

2. Jim is the one for <u>whom</u> the crowd is applauding. _____

3. Everyone <u>who</u> is watching was impressed. _____

4. <u>Whom</u> will the judges select? _____

5. To <u>whom</u> were you speaking? _____

Directions Underline *who* or *whom* to complete each sentence correctly.

6. (Who, Whom) would like something to drink?

7. Stu is the person to (who, whom) you should give your money.

8. He is the fellow with (who, whom) I went to the concession stand.

9. Anyone (who, whom) watches a gymnastics meet gets thirsty.

10. The judges, (who, whom) are volunteers, do a fantastic job.

11. (Who, Whom) shall we invite next time?

12. It should be someone with (who, whom) you can spend hours.

13. Spectators (who, whom) are veterans bring seat cushions for the bleachers.

14. Everybody (who, whom) sits through the entire gymnastics meet gets sore.

15. For (who, whom) is the meet the most fun?

Directions Cross out mistakes in the use of *who* and *whom* in the paragraph. Write the correct pronoun above the line. One sentence is correct.

(16) The girl watched her older brother, whom was turning cartwheels. (17) He wondered whom else might be looking. (18) He fell, and the dog with who the girl had been playing ran to lick his face. (19) The girl shrieked with laughter, and the mother, whom had been doing laundry, rushed into the yard. (20) "Who is ready for a snack?" asked the mother.

Cause-and-Effect Chart

Directions Most events have more than one cause and effect. Fill in the chart with each cause and effect that helps explain the change that is the main idea or thesis of your essay.

Change (Main Idea or Thesis of My Essay)	
Cause	Effect

Use Cause-and-Effect Words

Directions Write three sentences or sets of sentences for your essay that tell about causes and/or effects. Add one of the following words or phrases to each sentence or set of sentences to make the cause and the effect clear. You may need to change some words.

Words and Phrases for Cause-and-Effect Essays	
Words and Phrases for Causes	**Words and Phrases for Effects**
because	so
since	therefore
due to	for this reason
for the reason that	as a result
	as a consequence

1. _____

_____

_____

2. _____

_____

_____

3. _____

_____

_____

Combining or Rearranging Sentences

If a subject, a verb, or both are repeated in two sentences, combine the sentences to make your writing less wordy.

Wordy	Thunderstorms often occur in hot weather. Thunderstorms occur when warm air rises.
Concise	Thunderstorms often occur in hot weather when warm air rises.

Rearrange your sentences to put the ideas in the most logical order.

Unclear	Spring comes. The seed grows into a sprout. The seed gets light.
Clear	Spring comes. The seed gets light. The seed grows into a sprout.

Directions Combine each pair of sentences. You may add, delete, or change words.

1. The chameleon was crawling on a brown wall. The chameleon turned from pale green to brown.

_____

_____

2. Jon began training for a marathon. He began by running one mile at a time.

_____

_____

3. Forest fires can destroy trees in forests. Hurricanes can destroy trees in forests.

_____

Directions Rearrange each group of sentences. You may add, delete, or change words.

4. Puddles turned to ice. The temperature fell below freezing. It rained all afternoon.

_____

_____

5. Mr. Parker planted after the last frost. The tomato plants grew bigger. Mr. Parker put fertilizer in the soil.

_____

_____

Name _____

Peer and Teacher Conferencing Compare-and-Effect Essay

Directions Read your partner's essay. Refer to the Revising Checklist as you write your comments or questions. Offer compliments as well as revision suggestions. Then take turns talking about each other's draft. Give your partner your notes. After you and your teacher talk about your essay, add your teacher's comments to the notes.

Revising Checklist

Focus/Ideas

☐ Is the cause-and-effect essay focused on why a person, animal, or object in nature changes?

☐ Does the essay contain details about all the causes and effects?

Organization

☐ Does the essay have an introduction, body, and conclusion?

☐ Do any sentences need to be combined or rearranged to better connect ideas?

Voice

☐ Is the voice knowledgeable yet conversational?

Word Choice

☐ Do cause-and-effect words and phrases make the cause-and-effect relationships clear?

Sentences

☐ Does the essay have a variety of sentence types and lengths?

Things I Thought Were Good _____

_____

Things I Thought Could Be Improved _____

_____

Teacher's Comments _____

_____

Character and Plot

- **Traits** are the qualities, such as bravery or shyness, of **characters,** or the people and animals in a story. We see characters' traits in their words and how other characters treat them.
- The **plot** is the pattern of events in a story. Usually, the events are told in sequence, from start to finish.

Directions Read the following passage. Then fill in the diagram.

Darcy Evans had been a rebel all her life. As a young woman, she marched for civil rights. She protested a plan to build the first mall in her small hometown. She was at the first Earth Day celebration in the 1970s, supporting efforts to protect the environment. Save the dolphins, save the whales, save the trees: Darcy could always find a good cause to support, no matter how old she was. So nobody was surprised when 83-year-old Darcy Evans was leading the fight to save the 200-year-old City Hall building in her hometown. "I'm nearly as old as City Hall," she joked. But everyone knew that if Darcy was fighting for it, the building must be worth saving.

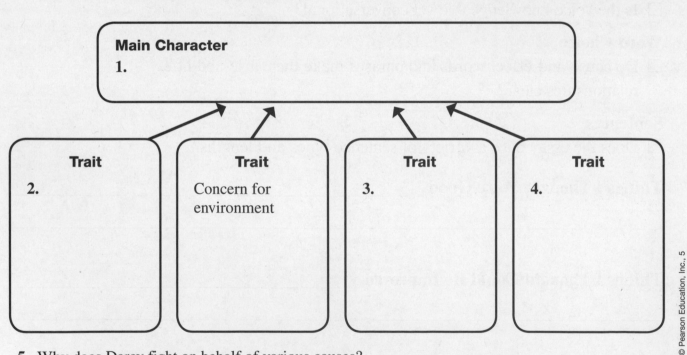

Main Character
1.

Trait
2.

Trait
Concern for environment

Trait
3.

Trait
4.

5. Why does Darcy fight on behalf of various causes?

_____

Home Activity Your child answered questions about characters and plot in a fictional passage. Have him or her describe to you a favorite character from a book.

© Pearson Education, Inc., 5

Writing • Rhyming Poem

Key Features of a Rhyming Poem

- contains rhyme and rhythm
- often uses figurative language, such as similes and metaphors, and sensory or vivid words
- often uses poetic techniques, such as alliteration and onomatopoeia
- uses graphic elements, such as capital letters

Street Beat

I walk down the street.
My icy hands tapping a beat.
When suddenly before me appears
A patch of ice like a frozen tear.

My foot touches it.
I slide and slip.
Try to catch my fall,
And think *What a close call!*

WHOOSH! BANG! BAM!
I'm thinking *Oh, man.*
The fall is pretty rough,
And I thought I was tough!

1. Which line from the poem contains a simile?

   _____

2. Name one line that contains alliteration. Explain why.

   _____

Vocabulary

Directions Draw a line to connect each word on the left with its definition on the right.

1. bellow   gave up on, dismissed

2. savage   try or make an effort

3. attempt   shout or roar like a bull

4. feat   wild, ferocious, angry

5. abandoned   a difficult or skillful act

Check the Words You Know

___abandoned
___attempt
___bellow
___cavern
___feat
___immensely
___savage

Directions Choose a word from the box that best matches each sentence. Write the word on the line.

_____ 6. The outlaw buried the gold in the _____ just before his arrest.

_____ 7. For her latest brave accomplishment, or _____ , the escape artist freed herself from chains just in time to pull the cord on the parachute.

_____ 8. Their effort, or _____, to hike the entire Appalachian Trail in two months had little chance of success.

_____ 9. The _____ popular rock music star was greeted at the coliseum by thousands of his adoring fans.

_____ 10. The _____ expression on her face would not have been out of place on a panther or some other wild animal.

Write a News Report

On a separate sheet of paper, write an imaginary news report that describes two local youth who surprise everyone by succeeding at a difficult task. Use as many vocabulary words as you can.

© Pearson Education, Inc., 5

Home Activity Your child identified and used vocabulary words from the story *The Skunk Ladder*. Together, come up with a list of accomplishments that you or your child performs regularly, but that might seem amazing to other people.

Contractions and Negatives

A **contraction** is a shortened form of two words. An **apostrophe** is used to show where one or more letters have been left out. Some contractions are made by combining pronouns and verbs: *I + have = I've; you + are = you're*. Other contractions are formed by joining a verb and *not: should + not = shouldn't; were + not = weren't*.

- *Won't* and *can't* are formed in special ways (*can + not = can't; will + not = won't*).

Negatives are words that mean "no" or "not": *no, not, never, none, nothing*. Contractions with *n't* are negatives too. To make a negative statement, use only one negative word.
   No: Don't never ask about his leg. There won't be none left.
   Yes: Don't ever ask about his leg. There won't be any left.

- Use positive words instead of the negative in a sentence with *not:*

Negative	Positive	Negative	Positive
nobody	anybody, somebody	nothing	anything, something
no one	anyone, someone	nowhere	anywhere, somewhere
none	any, all, some	never	ever, always

Directions Write the letter of the two words used to form each contraction.

_____ **1.** what's   **A** has not

_____ **2.** that'll   **B** that will

_____ **3.** didn't   **C** they are

_____ **4.** hasn't   **D** could not

_____ **5.** they're   **E** did not

_____ **6.** couldn't   **F** what has

Directions Write the contraction for each pair of words.

7. would + have = _____   **8.** it + is = _____

9. she + will = _____   **10.** will + not = _____

Directions Circle the word in ( ) that correctly completes each sentence.

11. You can't (never, ever) tell what those boys will do.

12. There wasn't (nobody, anything) in the hole.

© Pearson Education, Inc., 5

Home Activity Your child learned about contractions and negatives. With your child, scan articles in the newspaper to find contractions. Ask your child to write the words used to form each contraction.

Name _____

Multisyllabic Words

Spelling Words				
elementary	vehicle	miniature	probability	opportunity
substitute	variety	literature	elevator	Pennsylvania
ravioli	cafeteria	mosaic	tuxedo	meteorite
fascination	cylinder	intermediate	centennial	curiosity

Words in Context Write the list word that best completes each sentence.

1. I'm having lunch in the _____ today.

2. Did you know that cheese _____ is on the menu?

3. Eating a _____ of foods keeps you heathy.

4. Next year our town is 100 years old, so we'll have a _____ celebration.

5. The astronauts drove a lunar _____ on the moon.

6. The colorful _____ on the table top is made of tiny tiles.

7. A shooting star is really a falling _____.

8. The capital of _____ is Harrisburg.

9. The levels of swimming at my camp are beginner, _____, and advanced.

10. Books, poetry, and short stories are types of _____.

11. Let's take the _____ to the tenth floor.

12. We had a _____ teacher for one week.

13. He had a _____ with all types of model trains.

1. _____

2. _____

3. _____

4. _____

5. _____

6. _____

7. _____

8. _____

9. _____

10. _____

11. _____

12. _____

13. _____

Synonyms Write the list word that has the same or almost the same meaning as the word or phrase.

14. tube

15. tiny

16. basic

17. lucky chance

18. desire to know

19. formal suit

20. likelihood

14. _____

15. _____

16. _____

17. _____

18. _____

19. _____

20. _____

School + Home

Home Activity Your child wrote list words containing many syllables. Have your child draw a line between syllables. Use a dictionary to help you.

Three-Column Chart

Vocabulary • Greek and Latin Roots

- Many English words are based on **Greek** and **Latin** root words. Sometimes you can use Greek and Latin roots to figure out the meaning of an unfamiliar word.
- The Latin root *spec* means "look" or "see," as in the word *inspect.* The Latin root *sect* means "to cut," as in the word *dissect.* The Latin root *pond* means "to weigh," as in the word *ponderous.*

Directions Read the following passage. Then answer the questions below. Look for Greek and Latin roots to help you determine the meaning of the words in italics.

> The toughest section of Thursday was the morning, when I drove into town with my great-uncle Al. He couldn't see his hand in front of his face without his spectacles. So as we approached the stoplight with Uncle Al at the wheel, you can imagine my fright when I noticed he didn't have his glasses on. I pondered my options: Do I yell something? Do I scream and point? But then I saw his glasses sitting on top of his head. Not wanting to distract Uncle Al with any unnecessary interaction, I reached over and gently tapped his glasses. They slid right onto his nose, perfectly in place. We came to an easy stop at the red light.

1. What is the root of the word *section*? What does the word mean?

_____

_____

2. How does the Latin root of the word *spectacles* help you understand the meaning of the word?

_____

3. How does the Latin roots in the word *interaction* help you understand the meaning of the word?

_____

4. The Latin root word *distrahere* means "to pull away." Which word above comes from that root?

_____

5. How does the Latin root of the word *pondered* help you understand the meaning of the word?

_____

 Home Activity Your child identified and answered questions about Latin and Greek roots in words. Have your child look in the dictionary and find other words with Latin or Greek roots. Have him or her tell you the meanings of the roots he or she found. Together think of other words with the same roots.

© Pearson Education, Inc., 5

Print Sources

- Libraries contain many sources of information for students to use. You can use a library database or a card catalog to identify and locate these materials. In both cases, you can search for materials by author, title, or subject.
- **Print sources** include encyclopedias, newspapers, magazines, dictionaries, and other reference books.

Directions Read the following list of school library print sources for a report on U.S. Presidents.

Encyclopedias

Encyclopedia of U.S. Presidents, Vols. I & II

World History Encyclopedia, Vols. I–XX

Encyclopedia of American History, Vols. I–XII

Encyclopedia of Modern Science, Vols. I–VI

Encyclopedia of Entertainment, Vols. I–III

Newspapers

World News Daily (metropolitan paper)

Weekly Wrap-Up (community paper)

Kingsley Chronicle (school paper)

Magazines

News Weekly

The Historical Reader

History for Children

Skateboard Life

U.S. and the World

Dictionaries

Student Dictionary of American History

Cultural Dictionary of the United States

Anders' Dictionary of Places & Events

Dictionary of Who's Who & What's What

Directions Pretend you are writing a report on U.S. Presidents in the twentieth century. Use the list of print sources to answer the questions below.

1. Which type of print sources might be valuable to use for this report?

_____

2. Which would be the best source with which to start your report?

_____

3. Would all the magazines be valuable to your report? Why or why not?

_____

_____

4. Suggest a topic you might research in a library's card catalog for your report.

_____

5. If you knew an author had written a good book about U.S. Presidents, how could you use this knowledge to get information for your report?

_____

6. Explain how a newspaper would be helpful if you extended your report to include U.S. Presidents in the twenty-first century.

_____

7. How helpful would any of the newspapers be in gathering information for your report? Why?

_____

_____

8. If you didn't understand something that was referred to in the magazine *History for Children*, where would be a good place to find out what the reference meant?

_____

9. If you wanted to find out how many Presidents were from a certain state, where would you look?

_____

10. Would encyclopedias be more useful if you were writing a report on U.S. Presidents in the twentieth century or a report on children's movies currently showing in your neighborhood? Why?

_____

_____

Home Activity Your child answered questions about print and media sources. Discuss where media sources are located at your local library or bookstore. How are they organized? How are they organized similarly or differently from the print sources?

Name _____

Multisyllabic Words

Proofread an Article Circle six spelling errors. Write the words correctly. Find one capitalization error and write the sentence correctly.

© Pearson Education, Inc., 5

Fictional Detectives

Literture has its share of famous detectives. writers have created an enormous variaty of detectives. All have curiousity about and a fasination with crime. Usually, they are average people with an especially high probility of being right in the middle of a crime scene! As one famous detective said, "It's elamentry, my dear Watson!"

---

1. _____   2. _____

3. _____   4. _____

5. _____   6. _____

7. _____

    _____

Proofread Words Circle the word that is spelled correctly.

8. A ____ looks like a rock.

   metorit   meteoright   meteorite

9. I made a ____ out of glass tile.

   mosaic   mosesic   mosiac

10. My 99-year-old grandfather will have his ____ birthday next year.

    centenial   centennial   cintennial

11. William Penn was the founder of ____.

    Pennsylvania   Pennysylvania   Pennysalvenia

12. The tour ____ can go on land and water.

    veacle   vehicle   vehical

13. A soup can is a ____.

    cylindar   cylander   cylinder

14. My dog is a ____ poodle.

    miniature   miniture   miniatur

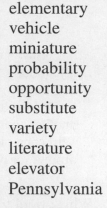

Spelling Words

elementary
vehicle
miniature
probability
opportunity
substitute
variety
literature
elevator
Pennsylvania

ravioli
cafeteria
mosaic
tuxedo
meteorite
fascination
cylinder
intermediate
centennial
curiosity

Frequently Misspelled Words

usually
especially

Home Activity Your child identified misspelled multisyllabic words. Ask your child to select four list words and tell you how many syllables are in each word.

Contractions and Negatives

Directions Read the passage. Then read each question. Circle the letter of the correct answer.

Will Potluck's Songs

(1) My uncle, Will Potluck, lived out in the country near a small river. (2) Nobody ever saw him. (3) Uncle Will was always bothered by the badgers that dug under his house and garden. (4) When he <u>could</u> <u>not</u> stand it anymore, <u>he would</u> walk down to the river to escape the troublesome creatures. (5) He had _____ seen another soul there in the shade of the tall trees. (6) Dozing under the cedars, Uncle Will sang old songs, and the badgers did not never bother him. (7) With _____ around for miles, _____ ever heard Uncle Will's songs.

1 Which word from sentence 2 is a negative?

   A didn't

   B ever

   C anybody

   D nobody

2 Which pair of contractions could you make from the underlined words in sentence 4?

   A couldn't/he'll

   B couldn't/he'd

   C wouldn't/he'll

   D can't/wouldn't

3 Which word best completes sentence 5?

   A never

   B ever

   C any

   D no one

4 What change, if any, could be made in sentence 6?

   A Change *cedars,* to **cedars**

   B Change *did not never* to **didn't ever**

   C Change *did not never* to **do not never**

   D Make no change

5 Which pair of words best completes sentence 7?

   A everybody/something

   B nobody/anyone

   C no one/no one

   D nothing/something

© Pearson Education, Inc., 5

Home Activity Your child prepared for taking tests on contractions and negatives. Ask your child to write contractions on one side of index cards and the words used to form them on the other side. Help your child practice identifying them.

Graphic Sources

- **Graphic sources** include charts, tables, graphs, maps, illustrations, and photographs.
- Before you read, look closely at graphic sources that accompany a selection. They will give you an idea of what you will read.

Directions Study the map of the *Titanic's* journey. Then answer the questions below.

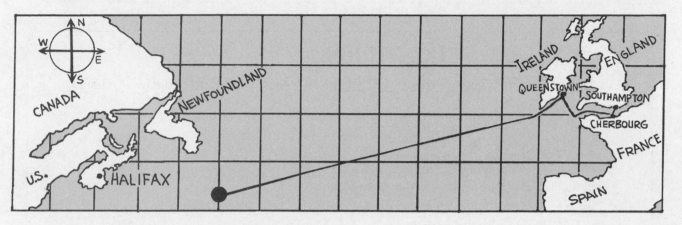

1. Where did the *Titanic* begin its journey?

_____

2. What other two ports in Europe did the *Titanic* visit?

_____

3. In which direction was the *Titanic* sailing?

_____

4. Which country was the *Titanic* closest to when it sank?

_____

5. The *Titanic* was headed to New York. About what portion of its journey had it completed when it sank?

_____

_____

_____

Home Activity Your child looked at a map and answered questions about it. With your child, draw a floor plan of your home. Label all the major rooms and areas.

Writing • Notes

Key Features of Notes

- Includes most important dates and facts
- Restates information in one's own words; avoids plagiarism
- Cites, or names, original source or sources

What Is Left of the Titanic

From <u>The Unsinkable Wreck of the R.M.S. Titanic</u> by Robert D. Ballard and Rick Archbold, pages 207–208.

Current status of ship
- First-class glass dome missing
- Titanic broken into two halves on ocean floor
- Two parts are 2,000 feet apart
- Edge of ship part is very mangled

Debris
- Very thin layer of sediment covering objects from inside the ship—Ballard thinks there should be more
- Items found include: a boiler, a tin cup, champagne bottles, the head of a porcelain doll, boots, and shoes.

---

1. Circle the two types of facts that appear in the notes.

2. How does the writer avoid plagiarism?

_____

3. Circle where the writer cites an original source.

Vocabulary

Directions Draw a line to connect each word on the left with its definition on the right.

1. cramped   soft mud or slime

2. sonar   scattered fragments, ruins

3. interior   device for finding water depth or
                          underwater objects

4. ooze   shut into a small space

5. debris   inner surface or part

Check the Words You Know

____cramped
____debris
____interior
____ooze
____robotic
____sediment
____sonar

Directions Choose words from the box to complete the crossword puzzle.

DOWN

6. litterbugs leave this behind

7. moving but not living

ACROSS

8. opposite of *exterior*

9. collected at the bottom of the ocean

10. locates objects underwater

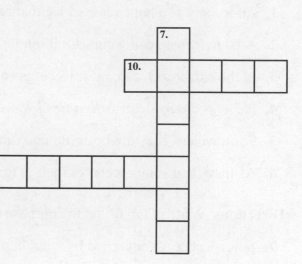

Write a Journal Entry

Pretend you are a passenger on a huge cruise ship crossing the ocean. On a separate sheet of paper, write your first journal entry as the ship sets sail. Use as many vocabulary words as you can.

Home Activity Your child identified and used vocabulary words from the story *The Unsinkable Wreck of the R.M.S. Titanic.* Have your child narrate a recent adventure he or she has experienced.

Name _____

Adjectives and Articles

An **adjective** describes a noun or pronoun. It tells what kind, how many, or which one.

What Kind	a <u>gigantic white</u> iceberg
How Many	<u>numerous</u> icebergs; <u>several</u> chances
Which One	<u>this</u> lifeboat

The **articles** *a, an,* and *the* appear before nouns or other adjectives.

- Use **a** before words that begin with a consonant sound: <u>a</u> disaster, <u>a</u> rapid speed.
- Use **an** before words that begin with a vowel sound or a silent *h:* <u>an</u> ending, <u>an</u> eerie noise.
- Use **the** before words beginning with any letter: <u>the</u> site, <u>the</u> passengers.

An adjective formed from a proper noun is a **proper adjective.** Proper adjectives are capitalized: <u>American</u> newspapers.

Directions Underline the articles and circle the adjectives in each sentence.

1. An iceberg is a huge mass of ice that has broken off from a glacier.

2. A large iceberg can weigh a million tons and stretch many miles.

3. In the Atlantic Ocean, most icebergs come from the island of Greenland.

4. Icebergs are made of frozen fresh water.

5. For travelers, they are beautiful and deadly.

6. As they float south, icebergs melt in the warm sun.

Directions Write *a, an,* or *the* to complete each sentence. Use the article that makes sense.

7. Some icebergs are carried by wind into _____ Atlantic Ocean.

8. Only _____ small part of an iceberg is visible above the water.

9. _____ iceberg is quite impressive to behold.

Directions Complete each sentence with an adjective or adjectives of your own.

10. The wreck of the _____ ship lies in _____ pieces on the ocean floor.

11. A litter of belongings tells the _____ tale of lost life.

12. The once _____ ship is now a _____ heap on the ocean floor.

Home Activity Your child learned about adjectives and articles. Ask your child to expand sentences such as the following by adding adjectives and articles: *The ship sank. It struck an iceberg. People died. Today it's a legend.*

Spelling Words

Spelling Words				
music	musician	select	selection	sign
signal	part	partial	haste	hasten
protect	protection	magic	magician	resign
resignation	electric	electrician	condemn	condemnation

Words in Context Complete each sentence with a list word.

1. John was forced to _____ as the class president.

1. _____

2. The string trio was missing one _____.

2. _____

3. She had a look of _____ on her face.

3. _____

4. A(n) _____ works with electricity.

4. _____

5. The _____ pulled a rabbit out of a hat.

5. _____

6. We need a piano for _____ class.

6. _____

7. The crowd's noises are a _____ of discontent.

7. _____

8. She left in _____ and lost her shoe.

8. _____

9. Mom said the _____ bill was due today.

9. _____

10. The clown performed a few _____ tricks.

10. _____

Antonyms Write the list word that has the opposite or nearly opposite meaning.

11. whole

11. _____

12. do not choose

12. _____

13. harm

13. _____

14. recommendation

14. _____

15. delay

15. _____

Synonyms Write the list word that has the same or nearly the same meaning.

16. incomplete

16. _____

17. indicator

17. _____

18. security

18. _____

19. choice

19. _____

20. denounce

20. _____

School + Home **Home Activity** Your child wrote related words. Have your child tell you a synonym or an antonym for a list word.

Outline Form A

Title _____

A. _____

   1. _____

   2. _____

   3. _____

B. _____

   1. _____

   2. _____

   3. _____

C. _____

   1. _____

   2. _____

   3. _____

Vocabulary • Unknown Words

- A dictionary lists words in alphabetical order and gives their meanings, part of speech, and pronunciations. A glossary is an alphabetical list of important words and their meanings that are used in a book. Glossaries are located at the back of a book.
- Sometimes an **unknown word** doesn't have context clues to help you find its meaning. Then you should look up the word in a dictionary or glossary.

Directions Read the following passage. Then use the glossary in the back of your book or a dictionary to answer the questions below.

> One of the pioneers of underwater research was Jacques Cousteau. He invented the "Aqua-Lung" in 1943. The Aqua-Lung was the first compressed air diving tank that allowed divers to stay underwater for long periods of time. This tank allowed Cousteau to move freely among the fish he studied. Cousteau also helped create, or invent, a camera for filming underwater. His television series, *The Undersea World of Jacques Cousteau,* was extremely popular. People were compelled by images of the deep sea that they were able to view without leaving their homes.

1. What is the meaning of *compressed*?

_____

2. What is the meaning of *pioneer*? Is *pioneer* used as a verb or a noun in this passage?

_____

_____

3. What is the meaning of *invent*?

_____

4. Look up *Jacques Cousteau* in your dictionary. Did you find him listed under *C* or *J*? When was he born?

_____

5. Find an unfamiliar word in the passage. Write a sentence using this word.

_____

_____

© Pearson Education, Inc., 5

Home Activity Your child read a short passage and used a dictionary and glossary to find the meanings of unknown words. Read an article together and pick a few unknown words. If your child cannot find context clues to help with the meanings, ask him or her to find the meanings in a dictionary.

Note Taking

Taking notes about what you read can help you understand and remember the text better. It can also help you organize information to study for a test or to include in a research report. There is no one right way to take notes. You might make a list, an outline, or a story map or paraphrase what you've read. When you **paraphrase,** you rewrite what you've read using your own words. Avoid plagiarism, or copying another person's words. When you record findings, you synthesize, or combine information. Use key words, phrases, or short sentences when taking notes.

Directions Read the following article. On a separate sheet of paper, take notes properly as you read.

Remotely-operated vehicles, or ROVs, are the primary means for underwater exploration to take place in deep waters. The first ROV was created by a Russian photographer, Demitri Rebikoff, in 1953. Since the first ROV, which was connected by rope or cable above water, many improvements have been made to the technology. The earliest innovations in ROV technology were made by the U.S. Navy in the 1960s. The Navy used CURV, Cable-Controlled Underwater Recovery Vehicle, to recover a hydrogen bomb lost off the coast of Spain. CURV was also used to save the lives of the pilots of a submersible that sunk off the coast of Cork, Ireland, in 1973. In the past two decades, private oil companies have searched ever deeper for new oil resources. As a result, they are responsible for the greatest developments in ROV technology.

The most famous development in ROV technology, however, came in 1986 when *Alvin* was "flown" down to the wreck of the *Titanic* in the Atlantic Ocean. Created by the scientists at Woods Hole Oceanographic Institution, *Alvin* was a human-driven submersible tethered by a line that reached the water's surface. A person was able to steer it and operate the camera equipment attached to the exterior. Scientist Martin Bowen was the first person to take *Alvin* to the wreck of the *Titanic,* some 13,000 feet below sea level. Because the pressure at such a depth is far too great for the human body to withstand, only a protective submersible like *Alvin* could provide the necessary protection for such a journey.

Currently, more advanced ROVs, like Triton XL (which is about the size of a small car), can perform a variety of tasks deep underwater. Construction, underwater surveying, and pipeline maintenance are a few of the things these advanced ROVs can accomplish.

Directions Answer the questions below based on the article you read and the notes you took.

1. When was the first ROV developed?

_____

2. Why did the U.S. Navy develop ROV technology?

_____

3. Why was *Alvin* developed?

_____

4. How far below sea level is the wreck of the *Titanic* located?

_____

5. Paraphrase the last two sentences of the first paragraph.

_____

_____

6. Synthesize the information in the second paragraph.

_____

_____

_____

7. How would you organize your notes about this article? Why?

_____

_____

8. Why is it important for you to take notes about what you read?

_____

_____

9. How does paraphrasing help you to understand and recall material that you read?

_____

_____

10. On a separate piece of paper, make a simple time line of the major developments in ROV technology.

Home Activity Your child read a short article, took notes, and recorded findings from it. With your child, read an article from a newspaper or magazine and practice taking notes and recording findings from the article.

Related Words

Proofread an E-Mail Shawnelle wrote an e-mail to her friend. Circle six spelling errors and one capitalization error. Write the corrections on the lines.

Dear nancy,

I had a great time at the outdoor musick festival. The hole group played so well. I especially liked the selecshun played by the alectric guitars. Playing without a conductor must be hard. It was difficult to see who gave the signle to start. When it began raining I wondered what they would do to protek the instruments. Luckily I had a raincoat which kept me dry! Thanks again for giving me your extra ticket.

Your friend,

Kim

1. _____   2. _____

3. _____   4. _____

5. _____   6. _____

7. _____

Spelling Words

music
musician
select
selection
sign
signal
part
partial
haste
hasten

protect
protection
magic
magician
resign
resignation
electric
electrician
condemn
condemnation

Proofread Words Circle the correct spelling of the word.

8. musishun   musician   musicshun

9. magisshun   magicshun   magician

10. partial   partshel   parshel

11. select   selekt   selek

12. haston   hastin   hasten

13. resignashun   resinashun   resignation

14. finaly   finally   finely

15. electrician   electreshun   aletrician

16. condemnation   condemmation   condennation

Frequently Misspelled Words

finally
whole
want

© Pearson Education, Inc., 5

Home Activity Your child identified misspelled words in a paragraph. Ask your child to name a pair of list words and describe how one of the consonants is pronounced differently in each.

Adjectives and Articles

Directions Read the passage. Then read each question. Circle the letter of the correct answer.

Trouble at Sea

(1) From the deck of the <u>small</u> boat, the waves were giant mountains crashing down on us every few seconds. (2) It was a great feat to catch our breath. (3) There was nothing we could do to keep out of the way of the _____ waves. (4) We could only hope that our tiny boat was strong enough to hold up against _____ force of _____ storm and _____ battering of _____ huge waves. (5) The storm seemed endless, and all hope appeared lost. (6) Suddenly, _____ small flash of sunlight streaked across the _____ deck. (7) The waves began to recede, and we looked at each other with joy.

1 In sentence 1, the underlined word answers which question about the boat?

   A What kind?

   B How many?

   C Which one?

   D How much?

2 What is the article in sentence 2?

   A It

   B was

   C a

   D to

3 Which adjective best completes sentence 3?

   A wonderful

   B colossal

   C soft

   D boring

4 Which article could be used in all four places in sentence 4?

   A a

   B an

   C the

   D None of the above

5 Which pair of words best completes sentence 6?

   A an/distraught

   B the/relieved

   C a/happy

   D a/battered

Home Activity Your child prepared for taking tests on adjectives and articles. Copy a page from a storybook. Have your child highlight the adjectives in red and the articles in blue.

Author's Purpose

- The **author's purpose** is the main reason an author writes a selection. An author may write to persuade, to inform, to entertain, or to express ideas or feelings.
- Sometimes an author may write with more than one purpose in mind.
- What the author says and the details given help you figure out the author's purpose.

Directions Read the following passage and fill in the diagram below.

> Jenna dreamed of being an astronaut. She read books about astronauts, she watched documentaries on TV about space exploration, and she even insisted her parents take her on vacation to the NASA launch site in Florida. At school, Jenna's science projects always had something to do with the planets or space or famous astronauts. It seemed she knew more about the space shuttle than some of her teachers did. Although she had only been in an airplane once, she spent the whole three-hour flight staring out the window at the clouds and the vast sky. Jenna wasn't sure how long it would take, but she knew one day she would see the Earth from as far away as the moon.

AUTHOR'S PURPOSE	1.
DETAIL What is one example of Jenna's interest in astronauts?	2.
DETAIL What is another example of Jenna's interest in astronauts?	3.

4. Does the author meet his or her purpose successfully? Why do you feel this way?

_____

_____

5. If you did not understand the passage, what could you do to help yourself understand?

_____

Home Activity Your child answered questions about an author's purpose in a fictional passage. Read a favorite book and have your child describe the author's purpose for writing.

Writing • Biographical Sketch

Key Features of a Biographical Sketch

- tells about a real person's life
- uses precise language and sensory details
- can show the subject's personality
- may use quotations to reveal the subject's personality

Tonya's Sweet Tea Stand

My friend Tonya is a natural business person. She can sell anything to anyone, from cookies to T-shirts with a special pattern that she has made. Last summer, Tonya decided to try a new kind of business: selling sweet tea from a stand in front of her house.

I helped Tonya prepare a tall pitcher of tea on the first day of her new enterprise. As we worked in her mother's kitchen, she told me, "This'll be a great idea. The key to any good business is giving people what they want. It's so hot in the summertime that everyone will want a cool, refreshing drink."

But that first day didn't go quite as well as she had hoped. She sat in front of her house next to a big, bright sign advertising "Tea 25 cents." The afternoon was dry and hot. It was the perfect weather for a cool drink. But only a few cars passed by her narrow yard, and only one car stopped.

That night, Tonya asked her mother for advice. Tonya gets a lot of her business knowledge from her mother, who's a buyer for the department store downtown. Her mother told her, "Tonya, you can't wait for your customers to come to you. You have to go where your customers are."

Early the next morning, I helped Tonya set up her stand in a different spot. We went to the park by the train station, where crowds of people were on their way to work. The morning was hot, the people were thirsty, and by ten-thirty we'd sold out of all the tea we'd brought. Tonya was right: her tea stand was a great idea!

1. What sensory details does the author use to describe the weather?

_____

2. Underline the quotation from Tonya. What does this quotation show about her?

_____

_____

Name_____

Vocabulary

Directions Draw a line to connect each word on the left with its definition on the right.

1. monitors   part played in real life

2. role   the force that causes objects to move or tend to move toward the center of the Earth

3. gravity   computer screens

4. accomplishments   definite

5. specific   achievements

Check the Words You Know

___accomplishments
___focus
___gravity
___monitors
___role
___specific

Directions Choose a word from the box that best matches each clue. Write the word on the line.

_____ **6.** what gets the most attention

_____ **7.** this keeps our feet on the ground

_____ **8.** they show information

_____ **9.** things you can successfully complete

_____ **10.** not just anything

Write a Scene from a Play

On a separate sheet of paper, write a short scene from a play about an astronaut telling his granddaughter what it was like to fly to the moon. Use as many vocabulary words as you can.

Home Activity Your child identified and used vocabulary words from the interview *Talk with an Astronaut.* Have your child interview you about the work you do.

This, That, These, and *Those*

The adjectives *this, that, these,* and *those* tell which one or which ones. *This* and *that* modify singular nouns. *These* and *those* modify plural nouns. *This* and *these* refer to objects that are close by. *That* and *those* refer to objects farther away.

This shirt I have on is like that one in the store window.
These pencils just fit in the pocket, but those pens on the desk did not fit.

- Do not use *here* or *there* after *this, that, these,* or *those.*
   No: This here article is about NASA. That there one is about new computers.
   Yes: This article is about NASA. That one is about new computers.

- Do not use *them* in place of *these* or *those.*
   No: She wrote them articles for *Newsweek.*
   Yes: She wrote those articles for *Newsweek.*

Directions Write the letter of the sentence in which the underlined part is correct.

_____ 1. **A** That there space capsule is smaller than I realized.
   B That space capsule is smaller than I realized.

_____ 2. **A** I think them astronauts were brave to travel in it.
   B I think those astronauts were brave to travel in it.

_____ 3. **A** Is that spacesuit the one worn by John Glenn?
   B Is those spacesuit the one worn by John Glenn?

_____ 4. **A** This here time line shows the history of space flight.
   B This time line shows the history of space flight.

_____ 5. **A** Robert Goddard helped design these early rockets.
   B Robert Goddard helped design them early rockets.

Directions Write each sentence. Use the correct adjective in ( ).

6. Will (that, those) storm reach Florida today?

_____

7. If it does, NASA will postpone (this, these) shuttle launch.

_____

8. Use (them, those) binoculars to view the launch.

_____

Home Activity Your child learned about *this, that, these,* and *those.* Write the words on four index cards. Ask your child to match each word with the appropriate category: singular near, singular far, plural near, plural far.

Greek Word Parts

Spelling Words				
artist	tourism	biology	phobia	heroism
geology	cartoonist	technology	journalism	hydrophobia
violinist	ecology	patriotism	vocalist	meteorology
zoology	claustrophobia	capitalism	novelist	technophobia

Classifying Write the list word that best fits each group.

1. animal, study, science, ____

2. travel, pleasure, recreation, ____

3. soprano, bass, tenor, ____

4. paint, canvas, sculpture, ____

5. rocks, minerals, earth, ____

6. plants, animals, study, ____

7. courage, bravery, fortitude, ____

8. weather, forecast, barometer, ____

9. writing, reporting, news, ____

10. fear, water, abnormal, ____

1. _____

2. _____

3. _____

4. _____

5. _____

6. _____

7. _____

8. _____

9. _____

10. _____

Definitions

11. a persistent, abnormal fear or dislike

12. one who draws a comic strip

13. a person who writes novels

14. the development of new ways to solve problems

15. an abnormal fear of technology

16. a person who plays the violin

17. love and devotion to one's country

18. economic system based on the private ownership of industry

19. fear of being in small or enclosed spaces

20. study of the relation of living things to their environment and one another

11. _____

12. _____

13. _____

14. _____

15. _____

16. _____

17. _____

18. _____

19. _____

20. _____

© Pearson Education, Inc., 5

Home Activity Your child wrote words that have Greek word parts. Have your child underline the Greek word part in each word.

Story Sequence B

```
┌─────────────────────────────────────────┐
│                  Title                    │
│                                           │
│                                           │
└─────────────────────────────────────────┘
```

```
┌─────────────────────────────────────────┐
│               Characters                  │
│                                           │
│                                           │
└─────────────────────────────────────────┘
```

```
┌─────────────────────────────────────────┐
│                 Setting                   │
│                                           │
│                                           │
└─────────────────────────────────────────┘
```

```
┌─────────────────────────────────────────┐
│                 Events                    │
│  _____ │
│  _____ │
│  _____ │
│  _____ │
│  _____ │
│  _____ │
│  _____ │
│  _____ │
│  _____ │
└─────────────────────────────────────────┘
```

Vocabulary · Multiple-Meaning Words

- Some words have more than one meaning. They are called **multiple-meaning words.**
- If you read a word that you recognize, but it is used in an unfamiliar way, look for clues about its meaning in the words nearby. Then use a dictionary to help you understand its meaning.

Directions Read the following passage. Then answer the questions below. Look for context clues to help you understand words with multiple meanings.

> You could say astronomers are monitors of the skies. They focus in on the details of our vast universe so we can understand the bigger picture. Even though the serious work astronomers do has a lot of gravity, or seriousness, most of them will admit they feel as excited as kids when a major discovery is made.
>
> To become an astronomer, you have to study many elements of science, such as gravity, with a dedication and focus most people find hard to have. But once you complete your education and are a working astronomer studying space, the sky truly is the limit.

1. How would you define the word *monitors* as it is used in the passage?

_____

_____

2. What is another definition for the word *monitors*?

_____

_____

3. What context clues helped you understand the way the word *gravity* was used in the passage the first time?

_____

4. What does *focus* mean the first time it is used in the passage?

_____

_____

5. What does *focus* mean the second time it is used in the passage?

_____

_____

Home Activity Your child used context clues to help define words with multiple meanings. Work together to try to use other words with multiple meanings to make up a silly poem.

© Pearson Education, Inc., 5

Readers' Guide to Periodical Literature

- The **Readers' Guide to Periodical Literature** is a set of books that lists, alphabetically by author and subject, the articles that are published in more than 200 periodicals. Each entry provides an article's title, author, volume, pages, and date.
- You can find a *Readers' Guide* in most libraries.

Directions Read the following page, which is similar to one you would find in the *Readers' Guide to Periodical Literature*. Then answer the questions below.

ASTRONAUTS—
    See also
    Moonwalk
    NASA
    Shuttle
Astronaut interviews. *School Zone* v496 p18 Ja '02
Astrophysics. L. Jones. *Science Explorers* v117 p87 My '02
Calling Earth [astronaut talks about mission] G. Calwell. *The Northwest Herald* Sec D p1
    Au 17 '02
Miraculous Adventure [astronaut orbits Earth] R. Gold. *Discover the World* v198 p29 Jy '03
Where is NASA's Latest Mission? S. Bobrick. *Mysteries of Space* v48 p31 Mr '03
The Years Before Space Exploration [training astronauts in 1950s] A. Hether. *Our Times* p44
    F '03

---

1. Which article would probably be the best to read if you were writing a research paper on the training of the first astronauts?

_____

2. In each listing, where does the title of the article appear?

_____

3. What do the words in brackets tell you?

_____

4. Are there any books listed in this section? How do you know?

_____

5. Why is the *Readers' Guide to Periodical Literature* a valuable tool?

_____

_____

Directions Read the following page. Then answer the questions below.

MARS

     See also
     Martians
     Red Planet
     Solar System–Planets
     Space Exploration
Are the Martians Coming? A. Wilson. *Mysteries of Space* v22 p24 D '03
Astral Recordings. *Science Sounds* v6 p33 F '04
Earth's Neighbors [Venus and Mars] T. Charleston. *The Jersey Times* Sec 1 p3 O 7 '03
Ice on Mars [NASA's report on ice deposits] W. M. Walters. *This Great Planet* v8 p29 Ja '04
Life on Mars? [research by University of Minnesota] L. Fulkner. *Science Research Weekly* p8
   S 18 '03
The Trouble with Hubble [information on Hubble] J. Randolph. *Astrophysical Magazine* v68
   p356 Mr '04

---

6. Why do you think the *"See also"* references are placed at the top of the listing?

_____

7. According to the listing above, what is the focus of the article in *The Jersey Times?*

_____

_____

8. If you were writing a report on the possibility of water existing on Mars, which article or articles would be most helpful?

_____

_____

9. How would you describe one of the major differences between a library card catalog and the *Readers' Guide*?

_____

_____

10. If you were writing a research paper, why might you use the *Readers' Guide?*

_____

_____

Home Activity Your child answered questions about the *Readers' Guide to Periodical Literature*. Together, gather several magazines and create your own *Readers' Guide* listings for them. Encourage your child to catalog as many articles from the magazines as possible.

Greek Word Parts

Proofread an Article Circle six spelling errors in the article. Write the corrections on the lines. Find the sentence with two punctuation errors and write the sentence correctly.

Vacation in Millville

This year many of Millville's families will spend their summer vacations at home. The city's bureau of torism has great ideas on where to go and what to see. The Museum of Natural History has exhibits on geology and metorology. Meanwhile Millville's war memorial holds stories of local herosm and patritism Kids of all ages are invited to the park's month-long festival of ecology and zology. With all that Millville has to offer, its bound to be a fun summer!

1. _____   2. _____

3. _____   4. _____

5. _____   6. _____

7. _____

_____

Proofread Words Circle the correct spelling of the word.

8. journlism   journalism   jurnalism

9. violinist   vilinist   vylinist

10. captalism   capitalism   capetlism

11. tecknology   teknology   technology

12. cartoonist   cartunist   cartoonis

13. eclogy   ekology   ecology

14. biology   bilogy   biologie

15. clastrofobia   claustraphobia   claustrophobia

16. hidrofobia   hydrophobia   hydrofobia

Home Activity Your child identified misspelled list words. Ask your child to spell four words, each with a different Greek word part, and tell you what the words mean.

Name _____

This, That, These, and Those

Directions Read the passage. Then read each question. Circle the letter of the correct answer.

Man on the Moon

(1) Today, we continued to analyze the surface of <u>this</u> dark moon.
(2) Temperatures here are very low, and we would freeze without these here suits.
(3) Them early astronauts were extremely brave to come here. (4) Regarding those rumors of life on this moon, we believe they are false. (5) _____ old report submitted by Colonel Brown appears to be correct. (6) We have collected rocks and soil samples. (7) We have found no evidence in those there rocks that water ever ran here.

1 In sentence 1, the underlined word suggests what?

  A The author is cold.

  B The author is on the moon.

  C The author is lonely.

  D The author had once gone to the moon.

2 What change, if any, should be made in sentence 2?

  A Change *here* to **there**

  B Change *we would* to **we did**

  C Change *these here suits* to **these suits**

  D Make no change

3 What change, if any, should be made in sentence 3?

  A Change *Them* to **Those**

  B Change *Them* to **This**

  C Change *were* to **was**

  D Make no change

4 Which article could be used to complete sentence 5?

  A These

  B That

  C Those

  D All could be used

5 What change, if any, should be made in sentence 7?

  A Change *those* to **this**

  B Change *those* to **these**

  C Change *those there* to **those**

  D Make no change

Home Activity Your child prepared for taking tests on *this, that, these,* and *those.* Ask your child to use these adjectives with the names of objects you point out in a room to describe their number and location.

Cause and Effect

- A **cause** (what makes something happen) may have several effects. An **effect** (what happens as a result of a cause) may have several causes.
- Sometimes clue words such as *since, as a result, caused, thus, therefore,* and *consequently* are used to show cause-and-effect relationships.

Directions Read the following passage. Then complete the diagram below.

Kai was determined to dig straight through to the other side of the Earth. He had the tools: his mom's garden shovel and his dad's metal rake. When he started digging, things went smoothly. As he dug deeper, the digging got harder. As Kai pounded away at the clay below the topsoil, the tip of his shovel began to flatten. He knew he'd need a sharp tip on his shovel to dig deep into the mantle of the Earth, so he went back to the garage and got another shovel. The harder he dug, the sweatier he became. Pretty soon, Kai was exhausted. He sat down in the shade of a nearby tree and quickly fell asleep.

He dreamed he had dug through Earth's mantle, through the boiling hot core, and was making his way out on the other side of the globe. Dream-digging was so much easier.

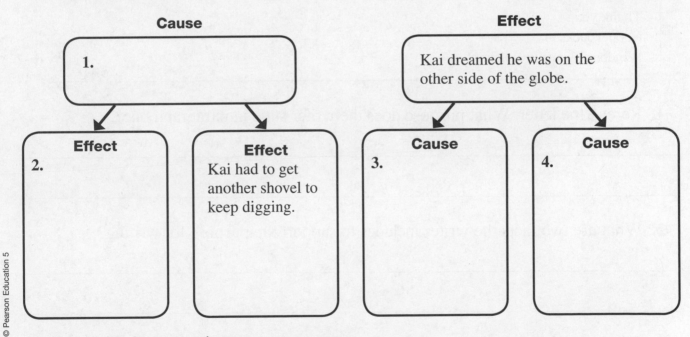

Cause

1.

Effect

Kai dreamed he was on the other side of the globe.

Effect

2.

Effect

Kai had to get another shovel to keep digging.

Cause

3.

Cause

4.

5. Summarize the passage in one or two sentences.

_____

Home Activity Your child read a short passage and identified causes and effects. Read a favorite story together and discuss the causes and effects you find.

Comprehension 349

© Pearson Education 5

Writing · Writing for Tests

To the Editor:

The Oregon Street Park is in desperate need of repair and renovation. Between the crumbling pavement on the basketball and tennis courts and the rusty, broken slides and swing sets, the park is unsafe for the many children who visit it daily. The park must be fixed before someone gets hurt.

First, the park must be cleaned up. Broken bottles and pieces of litter are scattered all over the ground. My fifth-grade class at Windber Elementary has arranged a field trip to clean up the park. We will gather at Oregon Park at 9 AM on October 11th. We ask our neighbors in the community to join us and help clean up our park.

Next, we ask the members of the city government to visit the park and see the problems for themselves. It is up to the city government to remove the old, broken parts of the park and replace them with safe, new materials. Specifically, we believe that the basketball and tennis courts, along with the slides and swing sets, should be replaced.

If we work together as a community, we could have the safest, cleanest, and most enjoyable park around. A new park will provide the community with a place to meet, to exercise, and to play. We students are ready to help make this change. We hope we can count on the support of the adults in our community.

Thank you,
Cooper Jackson
Windber Elementary School

1. Reread the letter. What purpose does the writer state in paragraph one?

_____

_____

2. What are two facts the writer includes to support the purpose for writing?

_____

_____

_____

3. From whom does the writer ask support for this purpose?

_____

Name_____

Vocabulary

Directions Choose the word from the box that best completes each sentence. Write the word on the line shown to the left.

_____ 1. No one is really sure how the dinosaurs vanished, or became _____.

_____ 2. Some think a giant asteroid collided with the Earth and _____ it into darkness.

_____ 3. Some dinosaurs looked as though they were covered in heavy, protective _____.

_____ 4. Although they looked strong, they were not protected from starvation, a painful and _____ way to die.

_____ 5. Today, a scientist who finds any remains from the age of the dinosaurs covers, or _____, them in special boxes that will preserve them into the future.

Check the Words You Know

___armor
___encases
___extinct
___hideous
___plunged
___serpent

Directions Fill in the crossword puzzle using the clues below.

DOWN
6. very ugly, horrible
7. protective covering
8. covers completely

ACROSS
9. snake
10. no longer existing

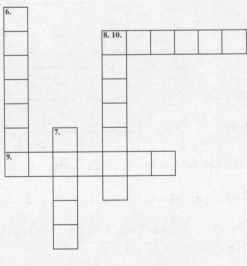

Write a Newspaper Article

On a separate sheet of paper, pretend you are a news reporter and dinosaur fossils have been discovered somewhere in your town. Use as many vocabulary words as you can to write an article about the fossils.

Home Activity Your child identified and used vocabulary words from the story *Journey to the Center of the Earth*. With your child, make up a story about what is at the center of the Earth using the vocabulary words.

Comparative and Superlative Adjectives

Comparative adjectives are used to compare two people, places, things, or groups. Add *-er* to most short adjectives to make their comparative forms. Use *more* with longer adjectives.
Superlative adjectives are used to compare three or more people, places, things, or groups. Add *-est* to most short adjectives to make their superlative forms. Use *most* with longer adjectives.

Adjective	Comparative	Superlative
great	great<u>er</u>	great<u>est</u>
enormous	<u>more</u> enormous	<u>most</u> enormous

- Adjectives such as *good* and *bad* have irregular comparative and superlative forms: *good, better, best; bad, worse, worst.*

- Never use *more* or *most* with *-er* and *-est.*
  No: more sillier, most ancientest
  Yes: sillier, most ancient

Directions Complete the table. Add *-er*, *-est*, *more*, or *most* as needed.

Adjective	Comparative	Superlative
primitive	1. _____	2. _____
great	3. _____	4. _____
calm	5. _____	6. _____
wet	7. _____	8. _____
frightening	9. _____	10. _____
exciting	11. _____	12. _____

Directions Write the correct forms of the adjectives in ( ) to complete the sentences.

13. Is Ray Bradbury _____ (famous) than Jules Verne was?

14. Readers might think Jules Verne was the _____ (lucky) science fiction writer of all.

15. Did Verne write _____ (good) fiction than Lewis Carroll?

16. His _____ (important) legacy of all was his influence on twentieth-century scientists, inventors, and explorers.

Home Activity Your child learned about comparative and superlative adjectives. Ask your child to use these forms to expand these sentences: *Science fiction is* <u>fascinating</u>. *Reading is* <u>fun</u>. ____ *is a* <u>good</u> book.

Name _____

Latin Roots

Spelling Words				
describe	interruption	inspection	scribble	respectful
bankrupt	project	injection	manuscript	suspect
subscription	spectacular	eruption	eject	abruptly
prescribe	reject	aspect	rupture	inscribe

Words in Context Write the list words that complete each sentence.

She paged through the mystery **(1)**____ and became convinced that the **(2)**____ was guilty.

1. _____   2. _____

She needed to give it a close **(3)**____ before she announced that she would **(4)**____ it.

3. _____   4. _____

It was a long-term **(5)**____ and would look bad if it ended **(6)**____.

5. _____   6. _____

She had to **(7)**____ in detail any pause or **(8)**____ that occurred.

7. _____   8. _____

Even when the company lost money and went **(9)**____, she remained **(10)**____.

9. _____   10. _____

Word Definitions Write the list word that has the same meaning.

11. purchase of a series of things   11. _____

12. a burst, split, or break   12. _____

13. write carelessly   13. _____

14. an element to be considered   14. _____

15. a way of administering a substance, such as a drug   15. _____

16. an order, set down as a rule or guide   16. _____

17. carve into a material   17. _____

18. put out from a place   18. _____

Home Activity Your child wrote words that have Latin roots. Have your child tell you five list words and identify the Latin root in each word. Have your child spell each word.

© Pearson Education, Inc., 5

Scoring Rubric: Letter to the Editor

	4	3	2	1
Focus/Ideas	Focused argument with clearly stated opinion or claim; inclusion of supporting reasons and evidence	Somewhat focused argument with clearly stated opinion or claim; some supporting reasons and evidence included	Unfocused argument; opinion or claim apparent but not stated; few supporting reasons or evidence included	Argument with no clear opinion or claim; no supporting reasons or evidence included
Organization	Logical organization supported by facts and details; proper letter conventions	Mostly logical organization with some facts; some letter conventions missing or incorrect	Weak organization; letter conventions missing or incorrect	No identifiable organizational scheme; letter conventions missing or incorrect
Voice	Engaging, effective, and confident; shows writer's opinion about stated purpose	Fairly engaging voice; shows writer's opinion about stated purpose	Weak voice showing few feelings about stated purpose	Flat writing with no identifiable voice
Word Choice	Vivid, precise word choice including words that appeal to the reader's thoughts and emotions	Accurate word choice including some words that appeal to the reader's thoughts and emotions	Limited or repetitive word choice with few or no words that appeal to the reader's thoughts and emotions	Incorrect or very limited word choice with no words that appeal to the reader's thoughts and emotions
Sentences	Varied sentences in logical progression	Not as much variety; order mostly logical	Too many similar sentences; order lacking	Many fragments and run-ons
Conventions	Excellent control and accuracy; comparative and superlative adjectives used correctly	Good control, few errors; comparative and superlative adjectives generally used correctly	Weak control, many errors; comparative and superlative adjectives used incorrectly	Serious errors that obscure meaning

Vocabulary • Unfamiliar Words

- As you read, you may come to a word you do not know. Look for **context clues,** or words and sentences around the words, to help you figure out the meaning of the unknown word.

Directions Read the following passage. Then answer the questions below.

> The *ichthyosaurus* isn't one specific dinosaur; it refers to a category of dinosaurs. Throughout history, *Ichthyosaurs* have been described as hideous, or disgusting to look at, creatures. That description has more to do with the imagination of artists than with actual fact.
>
> *Icthyosaurs* were the ancestors that came before modern dolphins and serpents (or snakes). Though extinct for millions of years, we can see similarities between *ichthyosaurs* and snakes and dolphins today: they can live in water, they can be up to 10 feet long, and they have flexible spines. They all have sharp teeth.

1. What do you think *hideous* means?

_____

_____

2. What context clue helped you understand its meaning?

_____

_____

3. How do context clues help you understand the meaning of *serpent*?

_____

_____

4. How do context clues help you understand the meaning *ancestor*?

_____

_____

5. What context clues help you to figure out what *extinct* means?

_____

_____

Home Activity Your child read a short passage and used context clues to understand unfamiliar words. With your child, read a piece of mail you received and help him or her use context clues to understand unfamiliar words.

© Pearson Education, Inc., 5

Diagram/Scale Drawing

- A **diagram** is a drawing that shows how something is put together, how its parts relate to one another, or how it works. The parts are usually labeled in a diagram, and they often have text that explains how the different parts work.

- A **scale drawing** is a diagram that uses a mathematical scale, such as 1 inch on the drawing equals 1 foot in "real life."

Directions Use this Web page to answer the questions below.

GEOLOGY SITE

Search

Note: The more specific your search terms, the more successful your search will be.

Student Question of the Day

How hot is magma?
Click here to find out.

Today in History

1891: British spelunker Ed Jensen discovers new mineral in Southeast Asia.

1. Where would you begin your search on this site for a diagram of the Earth's layers?

_____

2. What keywords would you use to search for a diagram of the Earth's layers?

_____

3. If you want to get an idea of the size of the diagram area, what specific keyword would you need to use?

_____

4. If you wanted help understanding the diagram, what might be a helpful keyword to include in a search?

_____

5. Why would a geology site be a good place to start looking for your diagram?

_____

_____

Directions Use the diagram below to answer the questions.

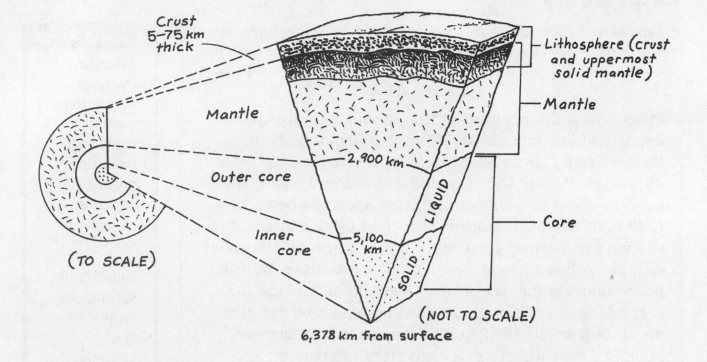

Crust 5–75 km thick

Mantle

2,900 km

Outer core

Inner core

5,100 km

(TO SCALE)

LIQUID

SOLID

Lithosphere (crust and uppermost solid mantle)

Mantle

Core

(NOT TO SCALE)

6,378 km from surface

6. Which of the two images of the Earth's layers is to scale?

_____

7. What is the Earth's core made of?

_____

8. Looking at the "To Scale" image, what makes up the largest part of the Earth: the core, the mantle, or the crust?

_____

9. The Earth is 8,000 miles in diameter. If you made a scale drawing with a scale of 1 inch to 2,000 miles, how big would the drawing be?

_____

10. How might you interpret what the drawing shows about the Earth's core?

_____

_____

Home Activity Your child learned how to locate and interpret a scale drawing. With your child, create a scale drawing of your home using a size ratio of 1 inch equaling 2 feet (this should fit on a standard piece of paper).

Name _____

Latin Roots

Proofread an Article Circle six spelling errors in the article. Write the words correctly. Find a punctuation error and write the sentence correctly.

describe
interruption
inspection
scribble
respectful
bankrupt
project
injection
manuscript
suspect

subscription
spectacular
eruption
eject
abruptly
prescribe
reject
aspect
rupture
inscribe

Library News

Police spent all morning in the ancient manuscript department of our library. They left about an hour later, shaking their heads, barely able to discribe what happened. During the morning inspection, I found the suspect about to scribbel his name apon the cover of a rare manuscript. I gasped. Surprised by the interuption the suspect turned abruptly. I grabbed him by the collar and proceeded to eject him from the premises. During police questioning, the suspect revealed his plans for a spectacilar project. He intended to enscribe his name on all 600 volumes of ancient and rare manuscripts. Luckily, I was able to stop that from happening.

1. _____   2. _____

3. _____   4. _____

5. _____   6. _____

7. _____

_____

Proofread Words Circle the correct spelling of each word.

8. bankupt   bankrupt   bankrup

9. injection   enjection   injekshun

10. aruption   erubtion   eruption

11. respectfull   respectful   rispectful

12. prescribe   preescribe   preskribe

13. subsription   subscription   subscreption

14. rejekt   rejict   reject

15. rupshure   repture   rupture

16. aspect   espekt   aspict

Home Activity Your child identified misspelled list words. Ask your child to say five list words, tell the Latin root for each, and then spell and define each word.

© Pearson Education, Inc., 5

Name _____

Comparative and Superlative Adjectives

Directions Read the passage. Then read each question. Circle the letter of the correct answer.

Uncovering Dinosaurs

(1) Most dinosaurs were (big) than today's reptiles. (2) Although he was not the (large), the *Tyrannosaurus rex* was the (scary) dinosaur of them all. (3) Scientists today have a _____ idea of what dinosaurs looked like than they used to. (4) Sue is the largest *T. rex* ever found. (5) She stands in the Field Museum, one of the country's _____ museums. (6) Their collection of dinosaurs is exquisite. (7) Most dinosaurs at the Field Museum are much (small) than *T. rex* and much (frightening)!

1 Which form of the word in parentheses best completes sentence 1?

  A big

  B bigger

  C biggest

  D more big

2 Which forms of the words in parentheses best completes sentence 2?

  A larger/scarier

  B larger/scariest

  C largest/scary

  D largest/scariest

3 Which word best completes sentence 3?

  A good

  B better

  C best

  D great

4 Which superlative adjective would not be used to complete sentence 5?

  A finest

  B dirtiest

  C best known

  D most respected

5 Sentence 7 could best be replaced with which sentence?

  A Most dinosaurs at the Field Museum are much smaller than *T. rex* and much less frightening!

  B Most dinosaurs at the Field Museum are much more smaller than *T. rex* and much less frightening!

  C Most dinosaurs at the Field Museum are much small than *T. rex* and much less frightening!

  D Most dinosaurs at the Field Museum are much more small than *T. rex* and much less frightening!

© Pearson Education, Inc., 5

Home Activity Your child prepared for taking tests on comparative and superlative adjectives. Ask your child to use the correct adjective forms on this page in sentences to compare sets of two objects, then sets of three objects.

Name_____

Generalize

- To **generalize** means to make a broad statement or rule that applies to several examples. Clue words such as *all, many,* and *most* can signal generalizations.
- If generalizations are supported by the text, they are *valid generalizations.* If they are not supported by the text or by logic, they are *faulty generalizations.*

Directions Read the following passage. Then complete the diagram below by writing a valid generalization and two ideas that support your generalization.

> President Thomas Jefferson led an effort to make the Louisiana Purchase in 1803. The United States bought an 828,000-square-mile stretch of land west of the Mississippi River from France for a mere three cents per acre. The Louisiana Purchase is widely considered to be the greatest land bargain in American history.
>
> Jefferson asked Lewis and Clark to explore the territory. For more than two years they investigated the land along the Missouri River seeking a route to the Pacific Ocean. They were greeted as heroes when they returned to St. Louis in 1806. President Jefferson was pleased, as he had doubled the size of the United States. You might say that he got the deal of the century!

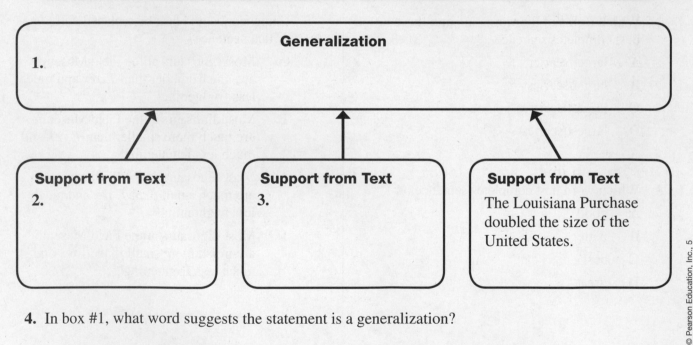

Generalization

1.

Support from Text

2.

Support from Text

3.

Support from Text

The Louisiana Purchase doubled the size of the United States.

4. In box #1, what word suggests the statement is a generalization?

_____

5. Would you say this generalization is valid or faulty? Why?

_____

Home Activity Your child made and supported a generalization about a nonfiction text. Choose a familiar generalization from everyday life, and discuss with your child whether or not it is valid.

Writing • Summary

Key Features of a Summary

- uses the writer's own words
- restates the most important facts and details
- leaves out unimportant details

Summary of "Going West"

During the 1800s, the Homestead Act caused many people to pack up their belongings and move to a place they had never seen before. Under the Homestead Act, the government freely gave away 160 acres of land to anyone who would build a house on it, dig a well, farm it, and live on it for five years.

The journey west could be extremely difficult for these pioneers. Their lives were certainly not easy. But if they made it through all the hardships, they had something to show for it in the end—the American Dream!

---

1. Which sentence expresses the main idea?

_____

_____

_____

2. Circle an important detail the writer included in the summary.

Vocabulary

Directions Draw a line to connect each word on the left with its definition on the right.

1. **scrawled**   not occupied

2. **independence**   to spread over

3. **vacant**   written or drawn poorly or carelessly

4. **overrun**   of or about the management of the
                                             income, supplies, and expenses of a
                                             household, government, etc.

5. **economic**   freedom from the control, influence,
                                             support, or help of others

Directions Choose the word from the box that best completes the sentences below. Write the word on the line.

6. You can find evidence of the Old West in the run-down, _____

old buildings that stand like ghosts in Colorado. **7.** At one time these booming towns were

_____ with prospectors. **8.** The prospectors had come in search of gold

and _____ freedom. **9.** _____ on old walls and

doors are the names and dates of particularly wealthy gold rushers. **10.** Unfortunately, their

financial success and _____, or freedom, was short-lived, as the gold

boom busted within a few years.

Write an Advertisement

On a separate sheet of paper, write an advertisement for a new theme park celebrating the Old West. Your advertisement should describe some appealing exhibits and activities, as well as noting details that reflect ways of life in the Old West. Try to use as many vocabulary words as possible.

© Pearson Education, Inc., 5

Home Activity Your child identified and used vocabulary words from the story *Ghost Towns Of the American West*. Together, make up a story about a relative who lived in the Old West.

Adverbs

Adverbs tell more about verbs. They explain *how, when,* or *where* actions happen. Many adverbs that tell *how* end in *-ly.* Adverbs can appear before or after the verbs they describe.

How	Cowboys rode expertly. They worked hard.
When	They seldom slept past daybreak. They always took care of their horses.
Where	A cowtown existed here. Cowboys visited there for entertainment.

Some adverbs tell more about an adjective or another adverb:

A ghost town seems rather spooky to me. I very rarely go to such places.

Comparative adverbs compare two actions. Add *-er* to form a comparative adverb. **Superlative adverbs** compare three or more actions. Add *-est* to form a superlative adverb. If an adverb ends in *-ly,* use *more* or *most* instead of *-er* or *-est.*

Comparative Adverb   The stagecoach rolled more slowly going up the mountain than going down.

Superlative Adverb   When they were fresh, the horses pulled most quickly of all.

- The adverbs *well* and *badly* use special forms to show comparison.

Adverb	Comparative	Superlative
well	better	best
badly	worse	worst

Directions Underline the adverb or adverbs in each sentence. Circle the word that each adverb tells more about.

1. Pioneer women bravely risked their lives.

2. They worked tirelessly to feed and clothe their families.

3. They seldom shopped at a store.

4. They were often lonely in their isolated homes.

5. They toiled outdoors in gardens and indoors at wood stoves.

Directions Underline the correct adverb in ( ) to complete each sentence.

6. We can point (proudly, more proudly) at the staying power of pioneers.

7. They lived with hardship (better, more better) than I would have.

8. If crops failed, they faced a (terrible, terribly) hard winter.

9. Towns needed railroads (more desperately, most desperately) than they needed settlers.

10. Railroads connected settlers (direct, directly) to supplies and goods.

School + Home   **Home Activity** Your child learned about adverbs. Ask your child to expand these sentences using adverbs to tell how, when, and where: *Settlers traveled. They built homes and towns. They raised food.*

Greek Word Parts

Spelling Words				
telephone	graphic	thermometer	photographer	centimeter
paragraph	telescope	diameter	photocopy	speedometer
telegraph	millimeter	autograph	television	barometer
telecommute	pedometer	phonograph	kilometer	telephoto

Classifying Write the list word that best fits each group.

1. circle, radius, circumference, _____

2. microscope, binoculars, _____

3. letters, words, sentences, _____

4. tape cassette, compact disc, mp3 player, _____

5. air pressure, weather, instrument, _____

6. instrument, measure, speed, _____

7. communicate, wire, electric, _____

8. call, dial, talk, _____

9. camera, pictures, person, _____

10. mile, furlong, fathom, _____

Definitions Write the list word that has the same meaning.

11. one hundredth of a meter

12. a person's own signature

13. a photographic copy of written or printed work

14. instrument for measuring temperature

15. electronic device that shows images on a screen

16. instrument for measuring distance walked

17. one thousandth of a meter

18. to work at a location remote from one's place of employment, making use of a computer

19. a lens that makes distant objects appear magnified

20. a picture, design, or visual display

11. _____

12. _____

13. _____

14. _____

15. _____

16. _____

17. _____

18. _____

19. _____

20. _____

Home Activity Your child wrote related words that are spelled similarly but pronounced differently. Say list words and have your child say and spell the list word that is related.

Name _____

Outline Form A

Title _____

A. _____

   1. _____

   2. _____

   3. _____

B. _____

   1. _____

   2. _____

   3. _____

C. _____

   1. _____

   2. _____

   3. _____

Vocabulary • Prefixes

- A **prefix** is a word part added at the beginning of a base word that has a meaning of its own.
- Prefixes do not stand alone in sentences. They usually have their own definitions listed in dictionaries, as well as their own origins, such as the Greek or Latin languages.
- Sometimes you can use prefixes to figure out the meaning of an unfamiliar word. For example, one meaning of the prefix *over-* is "too much." An *overheated* engine is too hot. The prefix *in-* can mean "not." An *informal* party is not formal.

Directions Read the following passage. Then answer the questions below. Look for prefixes in words to help determine their meanings.

> Independence is something that many people strive to attain. In fact, the United States of America was established in response to such an idea. You might say the founders of our nation were overrun with ideas of freedom and independence.
>
> They believed that any form of government that limited freedom was invalid. The patriots' ability to overpower the stronger and more experienced British army illustrates how strong this urge to be free really was.

1. If *independence* means "freedom from the control, influence, support, or help of others," what does its base word mean and why? Use a dictionary to help you.

_____

2. What word uses the prefix *over-*? How does this prefix change the meaning of its base word?

_____

3. If *invalid* means "not acceptable under the law," what does its base word mean and why?

_____

_____

4. What do you think might be the definition of *overpower*? Why? Use a dictionary to help you.

_____

_____

5. What prefix could you add to the word *experienced* to describe the colonial army? How would the prefix change the meaning of the base word?

_____

_____

 Home Activity Your child identified prefixes as a way of understanding the meanings of words. Together, try to make a rhyming song featuring base words with different prefixes. For example, the base word *view* could be used to make the rhyming words *review* and *preview,* and the base word *done* could be used to create the rhyming pair *overdone* and *underdone.*

© Pearson Education, Inc., 5

Outline

- An **outline** is a good way to organize information that you find in an article, report, or other nonfiction text. Creating an outline can help you better understand a text. It can also help you focus your own thoughts before you write something of your own.
- An outline includes a title, main topics, subtopics, and details.

Directions Read the following outline. Then answer the questions below.

The Gold Rush

I. Traveling West
  A. Searching for new lands
  B. Meeting the natives
    1. Establishing friendships
    2. Conflicts arise
  C. The California coast
    1. New settlements
    2. Towns are established

II. The Rush for Gold
  A. They came in droves
    1. Prospectors
    2. Easterners flock to new towns
  B. The newly rich
  C. An overnight economy
    1. Merchants and merrymakers
    2. Banking and loan sharks
    3. Golden staircases

1. What are the two main topics of this outline?

_____

2. Under the first subtopic of "The Rush for Gold," what details are listed?

_____

_____

3. Which subtopic describes dealings with Native Americans?

_____

4. Which is the first subtopic to contain information about people striking it rich during the Gold Rush?

_____

5. How can an outline help you plan a report?

_____

_____

Name_____

Research and Study Skills

Directions Read the following passage. Then complete the outline below.

Purchase of the Louisiana Territory

The Louisiana Territory covered 828,000 square miles of North America west of the Mississippi River.

A Spanish Territory With Spain's permission, Americans used the Mississippi and Missouri Rivers, and the port of New Orleans for trade. However, President Jefferson believed that the United States should control both waterways.

French Acquisition France's leader, Napoleon, also wanted more control in North America. In April 1802, Jefferson wrote a letter to the U.S. Minister to France. He discussed his interest in obtaining the territory around New Orleans. In October 1802, France acquired the territory from Spain. Americans were angered, and a conflict between the U.S. and France seemed unavoidable.

The U.S. Purchase In spring 1803, President Jefferson sent James Monroe to France to purchase the area around the mouth of the Mississippi, including New Orleans. When Monroe arrived, he found France in an uneasy position. Disease had weakened the French army. Moreover, French officials were worried that Britain would soon declare war on them. Napoleon was convinced that he should forget about establishing French power in North America. For these reasons, James Monroe made a deal with Napoleon to purchase the Louisiana Territory by the end of 1803. The size of the United States was doubled in a day.

Purchase of the Louisiana Territory

I. _____

   A. Spain allows U.S. to use Mississippi River, port of New Orleans for trade

   B. President Jefferson wants control of Mississippi and New Orleans

   C. _____

II. France Acquires Louisiana Territory from Spain

III. United States and France at Bargaining Table

   A. _____

   B. _____

      1. French army weakened by disease

      2. Napoleon fearing war with Britain

   C. _____

Home Activity Your child answered questions about outlines and completed an outline, using information from a nonfiction article. Together, make an outline that organizes your family's daily activities. Try to break down the day into main sections, subtopics, and important details.

Greek Word Parts

Proofread an Article Circle six spelling errors in the article. Write the words correctly. Find a punctuation error and write the sentence correctly.

From Feet to Kilometers

Each time your feet hit the pavement, your body vibrates. A pedimeter senses these vibrations and moves a counter forward, counting the total number of steps. Then it's computer changes the number of steps into miles or meters. A bicycle odometer does something similar. It counts the number of times a wheel goes around. A computer uses the dimeter of the wheel to compute the distance traveled, changing centameters to meters. Rather than counting wheel revolutions, automobile odometers count the number of turns made by the car's transmission gears. A computer changes the milimeters the gears move to the kilometers the automobile moves. Can you guess how a speedameter works.

Spelling Words

telephone
graphic
thermometer
photographer
centimeter
paragraph
telescope
diameter
photocopy
speedometer

telegraph
millimeter
autograph
television
barometer
telecommute
pedometer
phonograph
kilometer
telephoto

1. _____   2. _____

3. _____   4. _____

5. _____   6. _____

7. _____

Proofread Words Circle the correct spelling of each word.

8. telecomute   telacommute   telecommute

9. photacopy   photocopy   photocoppy

10. telescope   telascope   teliscope

11. grafic   graphik   graphic

12. thermameter   thermometer   thermemeter

13. photographer   photagrapher   photographor

14. barameter   barimeter   barometer

Frequently Misspelled Words

I'm
it's
let's

Home Activity Your child identified misspelled words. Ask your child to spell four words, each with a different Greek word part, and tell you what the words mean.

© Pearson Education, Inc., 5

Adverbs

Directions Read the passage. Then read each question. Circle the letter of the correct answer.

Gold Rush

(1) In 1848, James Marshall discovered gold in northern California. (2) Although Marshall quietly tried to keep his discovery secret, word <u>eventually</u> spread to San Francisco and other western towns. (3) Gold was free to anyone who could find it, so people went <u>hurriedly</u> to California seeking riches. (4) Mining towns were hastily built to house the miners and families who emigrated west. (5) While some miners found wealth, others fought _____ over the gold. (6) Some mining towns died <u>more suddenly</u> than others as the mines were gradually spent. (7) San Francisco watched its population grow rapidly, and it became the <u>most important</u> city in the west.

1 Which question is answered by the underlined adverb in sentence 2?

   A How?

   B When?

   C Where?

   D None of the above

2 The underlined word in sentence 3 tells about which word?

   A Gold

   B free

   C people

   D went

3 Which adverb best completes sentence 5?

   A most greedy

   B more greedy

   C greedily

   D greediest

4 Which best describes the underlined adverb in sentence 6?

   A Comparative adverb

   B Superlative adverb

   C Incorrect adverb

   D Not an adverb

5 Which best describes the underlined adverb in sentence 7?

   A Comparative adverb

   B Superlative adverb

   C Incorrect adverb

   D Not an adverb

Home Activity Your child prepared for taking tests on adverbs. Have your child read a favorite story aloud, point out the adverbs, and tell what words they describe. Encourage your child to add adverbs to the story.

Multisyllabic Words

Spelling Words				
elementary	opportunity	elevator	mosaic	cylinder
vehicle	substitute	Pennsylvania	tuxedo	intermediate
miniature	variety	ravioli	meteorite	centennial
probability	literature	cafeteria	fascination	curiosity

Analogies Write the list word that completes each comparison.

1. Store is to shop as lunchroom is to _____.

2. Poodle is to dog as poem is to _____.

3. Building block is to cube as tin can is to _____.

4. Huge is to giant as tiny is to _____.

5. Chicago is to Illinois as Philadelphia is to _____.

6. Silk is to fabric as car is to _____.

7. Apple is to fruit as _____ is to pasta.

8. Pleasant is to nice as basic is to _____.

9. Casual is to jeans as formal is to _____.

10. Beginning is to elementary as middle is to _____.

Alphabetize Write the ten list words below in alphabetical order.

meteorite	elevator
curiosity	opportunity
probability	substitute
fascination	centennial
mosaic	variety

11. _____

12. _____

13. _____

14. _____

15. _____

16. _____

17. _____

18. _____

19. _____

20. _____

Home Activity Your child has completed analogies for multisyllabic words. Take turns making up analogies for list words and completing them.

Contractions and Negatives

Directions Write the words used to form the contractions.

1. wouldn't _____

2. she'll _____

3. he's _____

4. we're _____

5. isn't _____

6. can't _____

Directions Write the contraction for each pair of words.

7. will + not _____

8. I + am _____

9. he + had _____

10. you + are _____

Directions Write the contraction for the underlined words.

11. What is the craziest project <u>you have</u> ever done? _____

12. Ashley says <u>she has</u> started a zoo. _____

13. <u>She had</u> collected a turtle, a mouse, and a snake. _____

14. Ashley says <u>she will</u> make another zoo in the future. _____

Directions Circle the word in ( ) that correctly completes each sentence.

15. My friend and I aren't (ever, never) without a new plan.

16. We don't ever do (anything, nothing) without our parents' permission.

17. They wouldn't (ever, never) let us do anything dangerous.

18. We don't want (anybody, nobody) to get hurt.

© Pearson Education, Inc., 5

Related Words

Spelling Words				
music	musician	select	selection	sign
signal	part	partial	haste	hasten
protect	protection	magic	magician	resign
resignation	electric	electrician	condemn	condemnation

Analogies Write the word that completes each sentence.

1. Pieces are to puzzle as notes are to _____.

2. Postpone is to delay as speed up is to _____.

3. Pipes are to plumber as lights are to _____.

4. Complete is to undone as whole is to _____.

5. Food is to nourishment as defense is to _____.

6. Sign up is to enroll as drop out is to _____.

7. Approve is to disapprove as praise is to _____.

8. Route is to path as choice is to _____.

9. Smart is to intelligent as symbol is to _____.

10. Drill is to carpenter as wand is to _____.

Word Clues Write the list word that fits each clue.

11. a strong statement of disapproval _____

12. a person who plays music _____

13. to choose _____

14. a portion _____

15. tricks and illusions _____

16. an action or gesture to communicate _____

17. great speed _____

18. watch over _____

19. full of electricity _____

20. a formal letter that you're leaving _____

Home Activity Your child has learned to spell related words. To practice at home, make up clues about related words and ask your child to spell the words.

Adjectives and Articles

Directions Underline the articles and circle the adjectives in each sentence.

1. A few brave adventurers are searching for shipwrecks.

2. They dive deep beneath the surface in search of an exciting find.

3. One group of divers found the treasure of a Spanish galleon.

4. The jewels, coins, and other artifacts are priceless.

5. Five hundred years ago, these ships sailed from Mexico loaded with silver and gold.

Directions Write *what kind, how many,* or *which one* to tell what question each underlined adjective answers about a noun.

6. That sunken ship is scary.   _____

7. All tour boats pass by it.   _____

8. The captain explains its tragic wreck.   _____

9. A million tourists have seen it.   _____

10. Some sad songs have been written about it. _____

11. This song tells about a sailor's wife.   _____

12. She looked for her husband for ten years. _____

Directions Write *a, an,* or *the* to complete each sentence. Choose the article that makes sense and follows the rules for articles.

13. Have you ever found _____ real treasure?

14. Once I found _____ old box.

15. It was buried in _____ bushes behind my house.

16. Inside _____ box were some rocks.

17. It was _____ disappointing moment.

18. Later, I found out _____ rocks were valuable.

19. One rock was _____ rare geode.

20. It was _____ amazing experience.

© Pearson Education, Inc., 5

Greek Word Parts

Spelling Words				
artist	tourism	biology	phobia	heroism
geology	cartoonist	technology	journalism	hydrophobia
violinist	ecology	patriotism	vocalist	meteorology
zoology	claustrophobia	capitalism	novelist	technophobia

Words in Context Write the list words that complete each sentence.

The School of the Arts is the best if you want to be an **(1)** _____ and paint or a **(2)** _____ and write.

1. _____   2. _____

The soldiers in the platoon showed great courage, **(3)** _____, and **(4)** _____.

3. _____   4. _____

Rafael studies environmental science, or **(5)** _____; he wants to use engineering science, or **(6)** _____, to improve the environment.

5. _____   6. _____

The **(7)** _____ titled his humorous drawing about the market economy, "**(8)** _____ at Work."

7. _____   8. _____

The **(9)** _____ students presented a news program about **(10)** _____, the fear of small, enclosed spaces.

9. _____   10. _____

Azir studied all living things, or **(11)** _____, before he decided to major in **(12)** _____, the study of animals.

11. _____   12. _____

Earth science courses include **(13)** _____, the study of rocks, and **(14)** _____ the study of weather and climate.

13. _____   14. _____

Synonyms Write the list word that has the same, or nearly the same, meaning.

15. violin player _____   16. recreational travel _____

17. singer _____   18. fear of technology _____

19. strong fear _____   20. fear of water _____

School + Home

Home Activity Your child has learned to spell words with Greek word parts. Ask your child to organize the list words into groups according to word parts and tell what each word part means.

Name _____

This, That, These, and Those

Directions Write *this, that, these,* or *those* to describe each object.

1. a book in your hands   _____ book

2. a store a mile away   _____ store

3. dogs in a neighbor's yard   _____ dogs

4. shoes on your feet   _____ shoes

Directions Underline the word in ( ) that completes each sentence correctly.

5. (That there, That) constellation is called Orion.

6. (This, This here) observatory will give us a good view.

7. (Them, Those) astronauts who have gone into space have not reached the stars.

8. (These, Them) articles tell about their trips to the moon.

9. I have reached (this, those) conclusion: Astronauts must be brave.

10. Can someone tell me if (this, these) facts are accurate?

Directions Write each sentence correctly.

11. That there telescope is called the Hubble Telescope.

_____

_____

12. These here photographs I'm showing you were made by that telescope.

_____

_____

13. Can you believe that this here photograph shows the birth of a galaxy?

_____

_____

14. A telescope on Earth could not take them photographs.

_____

_____

Latin Roots

Spelling Words

describe	interruption	inspection	scribble	respectful
bankrupt	project	injection	manuscript	suspect
subscription	spectacular	eruption	eject	abruptly
prescribe	reject	aspect	rupture	inscribe

Classifying Write the list word that belongs in each group.

1. book, pamphlet, brochure, _____

2. shot, vaccine, inoculation, _____

3. draw, write, doodle, _____

4. write, etch, chisel, _____

5. tear, void, break, _____

6. break, gap, discontinuity, _____

7. ejection, geyser, outburst, _____

8. appearance, part, perspective, _____

9. review, survey, examination, _____

10. magazines, monthly, newspapers, _____

Synonyms Write the list word that has the same, or nearly the same, meaning.

11. turn down _____

12. distrust _____

13. suddenly _____

14. broke _____

15. dictate _____

16. task _____

17. throw out _____

18. tell details _____

19. courteous _____

20. wonderful _____

Home Activity Your child has learned to spell words with Latin roots. Take turns brainstorming a word that has one of the list word roots. Look up each word in the dictionary to confirm it comes from a Latin word.

Comparative and Superlative Adjectives

Directions Complete the table. Add *-er, -est, more,* or *most* as needed.

Adjective	Comparative	Superlative
fierce	1. _____	2. _____
small	3. _____	4. _____
ridiculous	5. _____	6. _____
icy	7. _____	8. _____
hot	9. _____	10. _____

Directions Underline the adjective form in ( ) to complete each sentence correctly.

11. Which dinosaur was the (stronger, strongest) of all?

12. *Triceratops* had a (more dangerous, most dangerous) horn and tail than *Tyrannosaurus*.

13. However, *Tyrannosaurus* probably had the (greater, greatest) speed and strength of all the dinosaurs.

14. Bill has a (larger, largest) collection of dinosaur figures than I do.

15. He has the (more complete, most complete) collection of anyone I know.

Directions Write the correct forms of the adjectives in ( ) to complete the sentences.

16. Do you think description is _____ than plot in a story? (important)

17. I think stories with good characters are _____ than stories with good plots. (memorable)

18. The _____ characters of all are the villains. (interesting)

19. A _____ book may not be better than a shorter one. (long)

20. The _____ books of all are the ones that make you think. (good)

Greek Word Parts

Spelling Words				
telephone	graphic	thermometer	photographer	centimeter
paragraph	telescope	diameter	photocopy	speedometer
telegraph	millimeter	autograph	television	barometer
telecommute	pedometer	phonograph	kilometer	telephoto

Words in Context Write the list words that complete each sentence.

A **(1)** _____ lens magnifies distant objects; a **(2)** _____ also magnifies distant objects.

1. _____   2. _____

A **(3)** _____ keeps track of the distance walked; a **(4)** _____ keeps track of a vehicle's speed.

3. _____   4. _____

A **(5)** _____ and a land line **(6)** _____ both carry communication over wires.

5. _____   6. _____

A **(7)** _____ and a **(8)** _____ are each smaller than an inch.

7. _____   8. _____

You can use a **(9)** _____ and a **(10)** _____ to learn about the weather.

9. _____   10. _____

Word Definitions Write the list word that matches the definition.

11. a group of sentences developing a single idea   11. _____

12. record player   12. _____

13. picture or other visual representation   13. _____

14. a copy made with a photocopier   14. _____

15. twice the length of a circle's radius   15. _____

16. a person's own signature   16. _____

17. one thousand meters   17. _____

18. person who takes photographs   18. _____

19. work from home using computers, and other electronic devices   19. _____

20. a device that shows images on a screen   20. _____

 Home Activity Your child has learned to spell words with Greek word parts. Ask your child to organize the list words into groups according to word parts and tell what each word part means.

Adverbs

Directions Write the comparative and superlative forms of each adverb.

Adverb	Comparative	Superlative
sadly	1. _____	2. _____
wildly	3. _____	4. _____
late	5. _____	6. _____
well	7. _____	8. _____

Directions Underline the adverb in each sentence. Circle the word or words that each adverb tells more about.

9. Settlers waited impatiently for the mail.

10. Mail traveled slowly by stagecoach.

11. The Pony Express was a very welcome change.

12. Riders on horseback raced westward day and night.

13. The mail had never moved faster.

14. Soon railroads replaced the Pony Express.

Directions Underline the correct word in ( ) to complete each sentence.

15. The Pony Express moved the mail (most quickly, more quickly) than stagecoaches did.

16. The daring riders (certain, certainly) appealed to the public.

17. Of all western heroes, these young men lived (more dangerously, most dangerously).

18. The Pony Express worked (better, best) for some than for others.

19. It cost more to send a letter than most people could (possible, possibly) afford.

20. Today, airplanes serve the public (better, best) of all.

Persuasive Essay Chart

Directions Fill in the graphic organizer with ideas for the introduction, supporting reasons, and conclusion in your persuasive essay.

```
┌─────────────────────────────────────────────────────────────┐
│                                                               │
│   Introduction: State your position or thesis                 │
│                                                               │
│                                                               │
│                                                               │
└─────────────────────────────────────────────────────────────┘
                               ↓
┌─────────────────────────────────────────────────────────────┐
│                                                               │
│   First reason                                                │
│                                                               │
│                                                               │
│                                                               │
└─────────────────────────────────────────────────────────────┘
                               ↓
┌─────────────────────────────────────────────────────────────┐
│                                                               │
│   Second reason                                               │
│                                                               │
│                                                               │
│                                                               │
└─────────────────────────────────────────────────────────────┘
                               ↓
┌─────────────────────────────────────────────────────────────┐
│                                                               │
│   Third reason (most important)                               │
│                                                               │
│                                                               │
│                                                               │
└─────────────────────────────────────────────────────────────┘
                               ↓
┌─────────────────────────────────────────────────────────────┐
│                                                               │
│   Conclusion                                                  │
│                                                               │
│                                                               │
│                                                               │
└─────────────────────────────────────────────────────────────┘
```

Persuasive Words

Directions Add a persuasive word from the box or a word of your own to each sentence. Rewrite the sentence.

Persuasive Words

better	worse	should	never	most important
best	worst	must	necessary	effective

1. A camping trip in the Alaskan wilderness is the _____ excursion for our class.

_____

_____

2. It is _____ to set up camp away from any bear habitats.

_____

_____

3. Plenty of protective gear is _____ for survival.

_____

_____

4. While camping in Alaska, we'll learn that teamwork is _____ than working alone.

_____

_____

5. You _____ experience the wide-open spaces on our adventure in Alaska.

_____

_____

Adding, Deleting, or Rearranging Sentences

Directions Revise this paragraph by adding, deleting, or rearranging sentences as instructed below.

(1) Scores of people attempt to climb Mount Everest each year. (2) Many dangers are involved in climbing this mountain. (3) The air is very thin above 26,000 feet. (4) The weather is extremely harsh on the top of the mountain. (5) Many climbers take bottled oxygen because of the thin air. (6) The weather can also be unpredictable. (7) A huge blizzard can occur in a matter of minutes. (8) Finally, the mountain itself presents many dangers. (9) There are wide crevasses, or canyons, as well as moving ice blocks. (10) Many climbers have died on the mountain. (11) Another dangerous mountain is Mount Rainier in Washington. (12) Despite the dangers, Mount Everest is a popular destination for both professional and amateur climbers.

1. Write the number of the sentence that should be deleted. Tell why you think it should be deleted.

_____

_____

2. Underline the two sentences that need to be rearranged. Write the sentences in the correct order.

_____

_____

_____

_____

3. Tell where you would add each fact below to the paragraph.

   A. Some professional mountain climbers object to the use of oxygen, though.

   _____

   B. In 1996 alone, fifteen people died while climbing Mount Everest.

   _____

   C. At 29,029 feet, Everest is the highest mountain in the world.

   _____

Editing 3

Directions This is part of a persuasive essay. Edit the paragraph. Look for errors in spelling, grammar, and mechanics. Use proofreading marks to show the corrections.

Proofreading Marks	
Delete (Take out)	℔
Add	∧
Spelling	⬭
Uppercase letter	≡
Lowercase letter	/

Astronauts have preformed many exciting feats. Some astronauts have walked on the moon. Others have lived in a space station for more than a year. These amazeing adventures began in 1962 with a trip that seems simple today. In that year an astronaut named John Glenn became the first american to orbit Earth. He was launched into space by a rocket and was soon orbiting Earth in his spacecraft, *Friendship 7*. One of the first people in the world to see Earth from space. He said, It's a beautiful sight, looking eastward across the Atlantic." Soon he flown over Perth Australia, where it was allready night. People in Perth had turned on their lights so Glenn could spot them from space. Glenn's spacecraft orbited Earth three times the flight took about five hours. Then the spacecraft splashed down in the Atlantic ocean. The first orbit of Earth went smooth, paving the way for many future space journies.

Draw Conclusions

- Active readers **draw conclusions,** or make decisions, based on information in the text and their own knowledge.

- Examine your own conclusions as you read. Ask yourself, "Can I support them with information from the text or with facts I already know?"

Directions Read the following story. Then complete the diagram by writing a conclusion and listing details from the story that support your conclusion.

On most summer weekends, Tina went to the beach with her aunt and younger cousins. She built sand castles with her cousins and watched the kids carefully as they toddled near the shore. If they waded into the water, Tina held their hands. She taught them to watch out for big waves, and she showed the older cousins how to swim. She also brought snacks for all the children to share. When it was time to go home, Tina carried the youngest cousins to keep their feet from burning on the sand. On the way home, she was already looking forward to the next day at the beach.

What Can I Conclude?

1.

↑

What Does the Text Say?

2.

3.

4.

What Do I Already Know?

5.

Home Activity Your child drew a conclusion based on the details of a passage. Together, read a story about children. Work with your child to draw one or more conclusions about a character or event, using the text and prior knowledge.

Writing · Journal

Sunday, June 5

Dear Journal,

What a crazy week it has been! It all started last Saturday. You see, Dad has been planning a surprise party for Mom's birthday this year. Each member of the family had a task to do to help make the party happen. It was my job to ride my bike around the neighborhood and drop off the party invitations to people.

So last Saturday, I told Mom I was going to ride my bike to my friend Derek's house. I put all of the invitations in my backpack, so Mom had no clue what I was doing. Well, while I was out delivering invitations, Derek called my house and asked for me! I can't believe I forgot to let him in on the secret! Needless to say, Mom was furious at me when I got home. She wanted to know where I was and why I lied to her. Well, I couldn't tell her! I'd ruin the whole surprise party just to save myself from trouble. Mom grounded me for a week because I refused to answer her.

Her party was the next Saturday, and the surprise went off just perfectly. She cried when she saw everyone. When I walked up to her to say happy birthday, she hugged me and asked, "Did your lie last Saturday have to do with this party?" I told her I was out delivering invitations, but I couldn't tell her because I would have ruined everything. She felt so bad that I had been grounded the whole week over the misunderstanding. In fact, she said that I had earned a get-out-of-trouble-free card. She said the next time I get grounded, and there's something I really want to do, I can give her the card and not be grounded for the night. Even though I had to be grounded this past week, it was soooo worth it!

1. Circle the date written for this journal entry.

2. Summarize the main events and ideas told in this journal entry.

_____

_____

_____

_____

3. Underline several words and phrases that show how journal entries are informal and personal.

Name_____

Vocabulary

Directions Choose the word from the box that best matches each definition. Write the word on the line.

_____ 1. strikingly odd in appearance or style

_____ 2. the words printed in heavy type at the top of a newspaper article telling what it is about

_____ 3. very important

_____ 4. thrilling; exciting

_____ 5. to sit as birds do on a support; settle for the night

_____ 6. a high tone or sound

Directions Choose the word from the box that best completes each sentence. Write the word on the line to the left.

_____ 7. The baby's _____ squeal could be heard three rooms away.

_____ 8. It is _____ that you get plenty of rest when you are sick.

_____ 9. The morning's newspaper _____ was about the fire at McGill's Warehouse.

_____ 10. Andre's costume was so _____ that no one knew exactly what it was supposed to be.

Write a Journal Entry

On a separate sheet of paper, write about a bat or bird you have seen outdoors or in a book. Use as many vocabulary words as you can.

Home Activity Your child identified and used vocabulary words from *The Truth About Austin's Amazing Bats.* With your child, write a story about an interesting animal native to your area. Use as many vocabulary words as you can.

© Pearson Education, Inc., 5

Modifiers

Adjectives, adverbs, and prepositional phrases are **modifiers**, words or groups of words that tell more about, or modify, other words in a sentence. Adjectives modify nouns and pronouns. Adverbs modify verbs, adjectives, or other adverbs. Prepositional phrases can act as adjectives or adverbs.

As Adjective   The bats <u>over the river</u> are amazing.
As Adverb   They swirl <u>above the bridge</u>.

To avoid confusion, place modifiers close to the words they modify. Adjective phrases usually come right after the word they modify. Adverb phrases may appear right after a verb or at the beginning of a sentence.

The meaning of a sentence can be unclear if the modifier is misplaced.

No: The bats flew by the girls <u>with sharply curved wings</u>.
Yes: The bats <u>with sharply curved wings</u> flew by the girls.

The position of *only* in a sentence can affect the sentence's entire meaning. Place *only* directly before the word or words it modifies.

Example: <u>Only</u> he watches the bats. (Nobody else watches them.)
He <u>only</u> watches the bats. (He doesn't do anything except watch.)
He watches <u>only</u> the bats. (He doesn't watch anything else.)

Directions Write *adverb, adjective,* or *prepositional phrase* to identify each underlined modifier. Write *adjective* or *adverb* to identify how a prepositional phrase is used.

1. Austin's bats roost <u>under a bridge</u>. _____

2. The bats are attracted to <u>dark</u> crevices. _____

3. At sunset, the bats appear <u>gradually</u> in the sky. _____

Directions Each sentence has a misplaced modifier. Rewrite the sentence and put the phrase where it belongs.

4. A bat caught the boy's eye with fluttering wings.

_____

_____

5. He watched the bats as they multiplied with a smile.

_____

_____

 Home Activity Your child learned about modifiers. With your child, read a newspaper article. Ask your child to identify several modifiers, including adjectives, adverbs, and prepositional phrases.

© Pearson Education, Inc., 5

Suffixes -ous, -sion, -ion, -ation

Spelling Words				
famous	invention	election	furious	imagination
education	nervous	explanation	various	decision
relaxation	conversation	tension	humorous	exhibition
attraction	invasion	creation	occupation	destination

Synonyms Write the list word that has the same or almost the same meaning as the underlined word or phrase.

1. We will reach our <u>journey's end</u> after four days of traveling.   1. _____

2. People who are <u>well known</u> are often stopped by fans on the street.   2. _____

3. Sometimes it's very hard to make a <u>choice</u>.   3. _____

4. I had a very long <u>talk</u> on the phone with my cousin.   4. _____

5. The 5th graders had a special <u>art show</u> in the auditorium.   5. _____

6. I felt <u>worried</u> and had butterflies in my stomach.   6. _____

7. The army ants launched an <u>attack</u> at our picnic.   7. _____

8. It takes a lot of <u>creative thoughts</u> to write a story.   8. _____

9. What was your <u>excuse</u> for being late?   9. _____

10. Who won that close <u>vote</u> last month?   10. _____

Definitions Write the list word that fits each definition.

11. stretching or a strain   11. _____

12. a thing that delights   12. _____

13. something that is created   13. _____

14. funny and amusing   14. _____

15. knowledge and skills learned   15. _____

16. differing from one another   16. _____

17. condition of being relaxed   17. _____

18. something made for the first time   18. _____

19. what someone does to earn a living   19. _____

20. full of wild, fierce anger   20. _____

Home Activity Your child wrote words that have suffixes. Have your child underline the suffix in each word.

Story Sequence C

Title _____

> **Characters**

> **Setting**

> **Problem**

Events

_____
_____
_____
_____
_____
_____
_____
_____
_____
_____

> **Solution**

Name_____

Vocabulary · Unknown Words

- If you cannot figure out the meaning of an unknown word through context clues or word structure, look up the word in a **dictionary** or **glossary.**
- Glossaries and dictionaries contain definitions of entry words. The entry words are arranged alphabetically. Use guide words at the top of each page to locate the word quickly.

Directions Read the following passage about a day at the beach. Then use your glossary or a dictionary to answer the questions below.

Keiko lamented that she had never been to the beach. Deciding to give her a treat, her parents drove several hours with her to the shore. For the first time, she played in huge waves. She saw creatures of the sea, including jellyfish and sea urchins. She marveled at the green algae coating the rocks and the smooth driftwood at the shoreline. Her best surprise, though, was a tiny crab she found concealed under a shell. Keiko didn't want her day at the beach to end.

1. What is the definition of *lamented*? Use it in a sentence of your own.

_____

_____

2. What kind of creature is a sea urchin? Which of these pairs of guide words—*scuttle* and *seal,* or *season* and *second*—is a likely place to find the entry word *sea urchin*?

_____

_____

3. What is the definition of *marveled*?

_____

4. What is the definition and part of speech of the word *driftwood*?

_____

_____

5. What does *concealed* mean in the passage? Put the definition in your own words.

_____

_____

Home Activity Your child used a dictionary or glossary to find the meanings of unfamiliar words. Work with him or her to identify unfamiliar words in an article. Then ask your child to look up each new word in a dictionary or glossary. Confirm the meaning in the sentence together.

Follow and Clarify Directions

- Directions are instructions that are given in order, usually in numbered steps.
- Read through all the directions before you begin. Then **follow directions** by doing what is instructed, one step at a time.
- Try to visualize the end result of the directions. If you need to **clarify directions,** reread them, review them, or ask questions.

Directions Use the following directions to answer the questions below.

Rhythmic Breathing

The following directions will help you learn rhythmic breathing for swimming.

1. Stand in water that is about chest deep.

2. Lean forward, and turn your face to one side so that your ear is underwater but your face is just above the water line.

3. Breathe in and hold your breath.

4. Turn your head so your face is down, and exhale slowly through your mouth.

5. Rotate your head back to the start position and inhale again.

6. Try performing this action to the right and to the left to see which is more comfortable.

7. Then repeat steps 3 through 5 over and over in a regular rhythm.

8. Practice until you can do steps 3 through 5 smoothly.

---

1. What is the purpose of these directions?

_____

2. What is the first step in the directions? What is the last step?

_____

_____

3. To do rhythmic breathing, which steps must be repeated? Why?

_____

_____

4. Why must these steps be done in order?

_____

_____

5. Explain how you were able to visualize the directions. How were you able to clarify directions you didn't understand?

_____

_____

Directions Use the following directions to answer the questions below.

Coral Reef Word Puzzle

Follow these directions to complete the coral reef word puzzle.

1. Write down the letters of the word *seal,* the sea mammal that has four flippers, lives in cold water, and eats fish.

2. Next to these four letters, write down the first letter of a word that means the opposite of *push.*

3. Now add the four letters of a word that rhymes with *wrong* and means "the opposite of *short.*"

4. Cross out the letters *a, l,* and *l.*

5. Finally, unscramble the remaining six letters to find the name of something you might find at a coral reef.

6. What is the purpose of these directions? What did you do to follow step 1?

_____

_____

7. What is the word you wrote down to complete step 2? What letters do you have after completing step 2?

_____

_____

8. What is the word you wrote down to complete step 3? What letters do you have after completing step 3?

_____

_____

9. What answer do you find for the puzzle after completing steps 4 and 5?

_____

10. Why would it be impossible to solve this word puzzle without following the directions in order?

_____

_____

_____

Home Activity Your child learned about following directions step by step. Talk about a simple recipe for one of your child's favorite foods. Work together to follow the directions for making the recipe step by step.

Name _____

Suffixes -ous, -sion, -ion, -ation

Proofread an Essay Circle five spelling errors in the essay. Write the words correctly. Find a sentence with a capitalization error and write the sentence correctly.

Laughing Helps

When I feel nervos or edgy, I call my friend. Having a friendly conversasion really helps. My friend is truly funny and tells humorus stories. I told my friend that she would be famus one day. She laughed and said, "well, I don't want to be a performer. I have to finish my educasion first." Still, I think being a comedian seems like a great occupation for her.

1. _____ 2. _____

3. _____ 4. _____

5. _____

6. _____

Proofread Words Circle the word that is spelled correctly. Write the word.

7. varius	varous	various	7.	_____
8. invension	invention	invensiun	8.	_____
9. tention	tensiun	tension	9.	_____
10. furious	furyous	furius	10.	_____
11. attration	attraction	attracshun	11.	_____
12. destinashun	destinasion	destination	12.	_____
13. relacsation	relaxation	relaxasion	13.	_____
14. exsibition	exabition	exhibition	14.	_____
15. election	elektion	elecsion	15.	_____
16. invation	invasion	invashion	16.	_____

Spelling Words

famous
invention
election
furious
imagination
education
nervous
explanation
various
decision

relaxation
conversation
tension
humorous
exhibition
attraction
invasion
creation
occupation
destination

Frequently Misspelled Words

didn't
said
don't

© Pearson Education, Inc., 5

Home Activity Your child identified misspelled list words. Say a suffix and have your child tell you a list word ending in that suffix. Then have your child spell the word.

394 Spelling Suffixes -ous, -sion, -ion, -ation

Name _____

Modifiers

Directions Read the passage. Then read each question. Circle the letter of the correct answer.

Creatures of the Night

(1) The night is dark and quiet, and most animals lie down to sleep. (2) Still, many animals are busy after dark. (3) These nocturnal animals include some venomous snakes, agile monkeys, and tiny bats. (4) The kinkajou is a yellowish-brown animal that hops freely <u>along the treetops</u> at night. (5) Great horned owls are fearsome nighttime hunters, soaring <u>from the trees</u> to snatch its prey. (6) A bat uses high-pitched sounds to help tell what lies in its path. (7) The jaguar, <u>with its eight-foot body</u>, is a huge and ferocious predator.

1 What two adjectives are found in sentence 1?

 A dark/most

 B night/dark

 C dark/quiet

 D most/down

2 How many adjectives are found in sentence 3?

 A 4

 B 3

 C 2

 D 1

3 Which best describes the underlined phrase in sentence 4?

 A Adjective phrase

 B Adverb phrase

 C Prepositional phrase

 D None of the above

4 The underlined phrase in sentence 5 describes which word?

 A hunters

 B soaring

 C snatch

 D fearsome

5 Which best describes the underlined modifier in sentence 7?

 A Adjective phrase

 B Adverb phrase

 C Prepositional phrase

 D None of the above

© Pearson Education, Inc., 5

Home Activity Your child practiced for taking tests on modifiers. Copy a paragraph from one of your child's favorite stories, leaving blanks where modifiers go. Ask your child to suggest possible modifiers for the blanks. Compare with the original.

Main Idea and Details

- The **topic** is the overall subject of a piece of writing. The **main idea** of a selection is the most important idea about the topic of that selection. **Details** are small pieces of information that tell more about the main idea.

- Sometimes the author states the main idea in a single sentence. When the author does not state the main idea, the reader must figure it out.

Directions Read the following passage. Then complete the diagram below.

Plants, just like animals, can become endangered as a result of the actions of human beings. Some plants are threatened after the insects that pollinate the plant die off. For example, one type of milkweed has nearly disappeared because chemicals killed off the butterfly that pollinates the milkweed. In addition, a plant can become endangered when buildings and roads take over the open lands where it grows. Other human activities such as farming and logging can threaten plants too. Finally, human pollution of land and water threatens many types of natural life, including plants. People are often unaware of it, but human activities can have harmful effects on plants and other parts of the natural world.

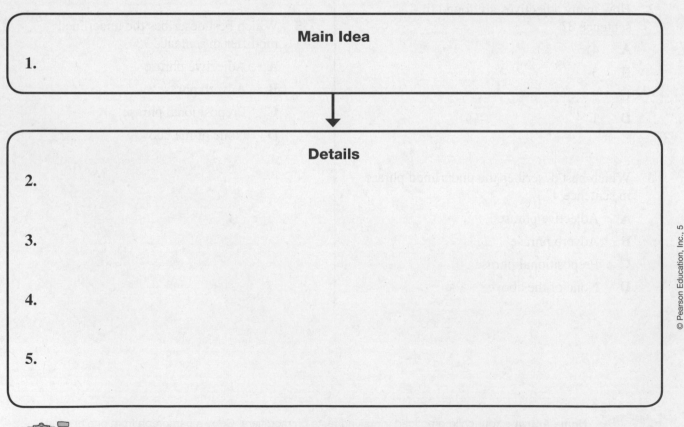

Main Idea

1.

Details

2.

3.

4.

5.

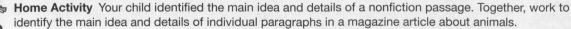

Home Activity Your child identified the main idea and details of a nonfiction passage. Together, work to identify the main idea and details of individual paragraphs in a magazine article about animals.

© Pearson Education, Inc., 5

Writing • Mystery

Key Features of a Mystery

- presents a problem or mystery early in the story with a clearly defined focus
- has a specific, believable setting described with sensory detail
- has a clearly defined plot with facts, details, and examples to help solve the mystery
- explains or resolves the mystery by the end of the story

It's in the Cards

I was asleep when the telephone jangled me awake. It was my grandma. She was frantic. "You must come over right away," she pleaded. "It's my secret fudge recipe. I was going to make a batch for your birthday, but the recipe has vanished!"

I was at her house in five minutes. "Where did you keep the recipe?" I asked.

"With my other recipe cards," she answered, pulling a shoebox from her pantry. It was full of index cards, all with recipes written on them. "See," she said, pointing to a table of contents, "here it is, Number 112. Fudge. I had the card two weeks ago. But when I looked for it tonight, it was gone."

"Who has been here in the last two weeks who might have had access to your cards?" I asked. Grandma said she had three visitors recently: a plumber, a visiting nurse, and a lady from the senior citizen center.

I found the plumber fixing a water fountain at the Boy's Club. "I need to ask you about a missing card that belongs to my grandma," I said. "Have you seen a missing card?"

"Card, you say," the plumber said calmly. "What kind of cards does she play?"

I asked the nurse the same question I had asked the plumber. Taking a deep breath, she said, "Why would your grandma keep her recipes on cards? Just about everybody uses a computer these days," she said, looking away quickly.

I repeated the same question to the lady at the senior citizen center. "No, I don't think so," she said thoughtfully, "and I think I would have noticed. I always send out greeting cards for every holiday."

"I know who took your fudge recipe card," I told my grandma.

"You solved the case already? Who was it?" she asked in a puzzled tone.

"It was the nurse. I asked all three suspects the same question. I never mentioned what kind of a card I was talking about. The nurse is the only one who knew I was talking about a recipe card, and the only way she would know it was missing is if she took it."

Grandma sighed. "Although she shouldn't have taken the card without asking, I'll tell her that I would be happy to let her make a copy of the recipe if she brings back my original card."

"Sounds like a sweet ending to me," I said.

1. Paraphrase the problem or mystery in the story.

_____

2. What clue tells us who took the recipe card? Underline the clue.

Vocabulary

Directions Choose the word from the box that best matches each definition. Write the word on the line.

_____ 1. a vast, treeless plain in arctic regions

_____ 2. living things that live on or in
                              others, from which they get food

_____ 3. having little flesh; lean; thin

_____ 4. whitened by exposure to sunlight
                              or the use of chemicals

_____ 5. beliefs; feelings; thoughts

Directions Choose the word from the box that best matches each clue.
Write the word on the line.

_____ 6. This ground is frozen even in summer.

_____ 7. Lice and tapeworms are examples of these.

_____ 8. This is an extreme form of hunger.

_____ 9. These are dead bodies of animals.

_____ 10. This is the process of rotting.

Write a Memo

Imagine that you are a zookeeper reporting on illnesses among animals at a zoo. On a separate sheet of paper, write a memo to the zoo's director about what you have observed. Use as many vocabulary words as you can.

Home Activity Your child identified and used vocabulary words from *The Mystery of Saint Matthew Island*. Together, read a story or nonfiction article. Have him or her point out unfamiliar words. Work together to figure out the meaning of each word by using other words that appear near it.

Name _____

Conjunctions

A conjunction is a word such as *and, but,* or *or* that joins words, phrases, and sentences.

- Use *and* to join related ideas: The snowy owl <u>and</u> snow bunting are arctic birds.
- Use *but* to join contrasting ideas: I like the snow <u>but</u> not the cold.
- Use *or* to suggest a choice: Is that a ringed seal <u>or</u> a hooded seal?

You can use conjunctions to make compound subjects, compound predicates, and compound sentences. Place a comma before the conjunction in a compound sentence.

Compound Subject   Frigid cold <u>and</u> deep snow make arctic life difficult.
Compound Predicate   Arctic foxes do not hibernate <u>but</u> withstand the cold.
Compound Sentence   They feed on live prey, <u>or</u> they can eat remains of a polar bear's meal.

Directions Underline the conjunction(s) in each sentence.

1. The arctic fox makes a burrow in a hill or cliff, but it does not hibernate.

2. It is well adapted for the cold with its furry feet and small, rounded ears.

3. A polar bear is huge but surprisingly fast and can outrun a caribou.

Directions Underline the conjunction in ( ) that completes each sentence.

4. The tundra has very little moisture (or, and) a short growing season.

5. The climate is harsh, (or, but) more than 1,700 kinds of plants live in the Arctic.

Directions Use the conjunction *and, but,* or *or* to join each pair of sentences. Write the new sentences. Remember to add a comma.

6. The Arctic is frigid in winter. It is much warmer in summer.

_____

_____

7. Arctic plants must grow quickly. They won't have time to reproduce.

_____

_____

Home Activity Your child learned about conjunctions. Have your child write *and, but,* and *or* on index cards and then read a short article, making a tally mark on the appropriate card each time he or she sees that conjunction.

Final Syllable -*ant*, -*ent*, -*ance*, -*ence*

Spelling Words

important	experience	ignorant	entrance	difference
instance	absence	appearance	intelligent	evidence
pollutant	clearance	confidence	conference	insurance
ambulance	hesitant	consistent	excellence	persistent

Antonyms Write the list word that has the opposite or almost the opposite meaning of the underlined word or phrase.

1. I was <u>certain</u> to ask for help on my assignment.

   1. _____

2. We thought his <u>presence</u> was the cause of the loss.

   2. _____

3. We had trouble finding the <u>exit</u> to the building.

   3. _____

4. The facts in the case are <u>unimportant</u>.

   4. _____

5. Our students strive for <u>poor quality</u> in all they do.

   5. _____

6. That constant buzzing in the television is a(n) <u>occasional</u> annoyance.

   6. _____

7. A good employee is hard working and <u>inconsistent</u>.

   7. _____

8. It takes a while to develop self-assurance and <u>shyness</u>.

   8. _____

9. Car exhaust is an air <u>cleaner</u>.

   9. _____

10. By human standards, slugs and snails are not <u>stupid</u>.

    10. _____

Definitions Write the list word on the line that has the same meaning.

11. anything that shows what is true and what is not

    11. _____

12. a kind of sale

    12. _____

13. financial protection against harm, illness, or loss

    13. _____

14. vehicle that provides transportation to the hospital

    14. _____

15. a change

    15. _____

16. a person or thing serving as an example

    16. _____

17. knowing little or nothing

    17. _____

18. what is seen, done, or lived through

    18. _____

19. a meeting of interested persons to discuss a particular subject

    19. _____

20. the act of coming into sight

    20. _____

School + Home **Home Activity** Your child wrote words that have syllables ending in -*ant*, -*ent*, -*ance*, -*ence*. Have your child underline the final syllable in each word.

T-Chart

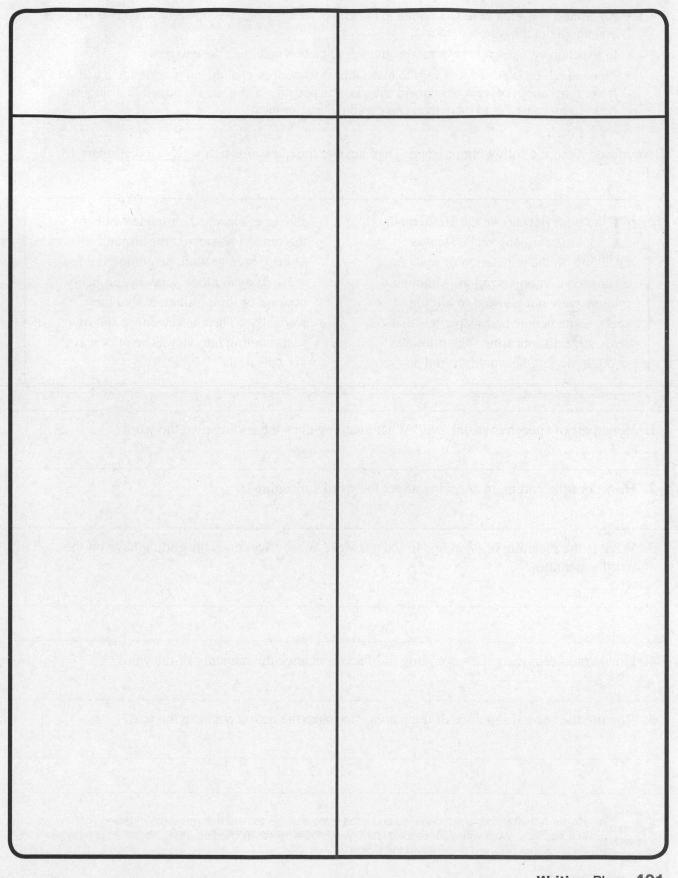

Vocabulary · Endings

- An **ending** is a letter or letters added to the end of a base word. Recognizing an ending will help you figure out the word's meaning.

- In a dictionary, listings for words with endings are found near their base words.

- The ending *-ed* is added to a verb to make it past tense. The ending *-ing* is added to a verb to make it tell about present or ongoing actions. The endings *-s* and *-es* are added to a singular noun to make it refer to more than one person, place, or thing.

Directions Read the following passage. Then answer the questions below. Use a dictionary to help you.

> The pilot flew above the arctic tundra, looking for baby seals. He was checking on the population of seals for a conservation organization. Although hunters were not allowed to kill the seals, some people had suspicions that seals were disappearing. The pilot was strongly hoping he wouldn't find any seal carcasses bleached, or made white, by the sun. As he steered the airplane closer to the frozen ground, he glimpsed a few seals. They did look scrawny, probably because of minor illnesses, but they were alive. Then he saw more and more seals coming into view. The pilot was very pleased.

1. What part of speech is *suspicions*? What meaning does the ending give the word?

_____

2. How does the ending in *checking* affect the word's meaning?

_____

3. What is the meaning of *bleached* in the passage? What effect does the ending have on the word's meaning?

_____

_____

4. How would removing the *-es* ending in *illnesses* change the meaning of the word?

_____

5. Rewrite the second sentence of the passage to make the action occur in the past.

_____

_____

Home Activity Your child identified and used word endings to help determine the meanings of new words in a passage. Work with your child to identify unfamiliar words in another article. Together, identify word endings that help you understand the words.

Time Line

- A **time line** is a chart that shows a sequence of events. Usually a time line uses a bar divided into periods of time to show the order of events. Some time lines are read left to right, and others are read top to bottom.
- You can use a time line to show the time order of events in a nonfiction text. A time line can also show the order of events in a work of fiction.
- A time line may cover any length of time, such as a day or thousands of years. Pay attention to the title and labels on a time line.

Directions Read the following time line. Then answer the questions below.

The Life of a Reindeer

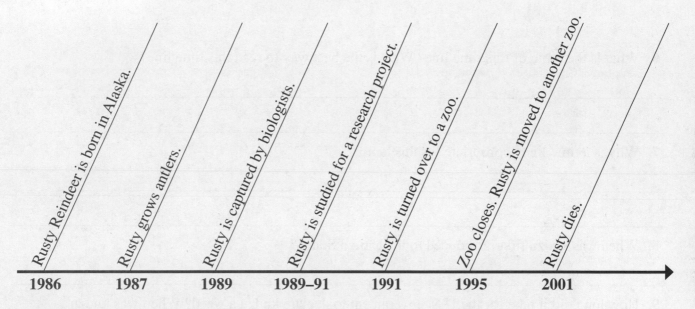

| 1986 | 1987 | 1989 | 1989–91 | 1991 | 1995 | 2001 |

1. How is this time line organized? What is the topic of this time line?

_____

_____

2. How many years passed between Rusty's birth and his capture?

_____

3. How long was Rusty in zoos?

_____

4. How old was Rusty when he died?

_____

5. The average age of a reindeer in the wild is ten to twelve years. How does the time line help you draw a conclusion about Rusty's life span? Explain.

_____

Name_____

Directions Read the following time line. Then answer the questions.

History of the Plant That Grew Too Well

1876	Kudzu, a vine from Japan, arrives in U.S.
1900s	Florida farmers begin to feed kudzu to animals.
1930s	U.S. Soil Conservation Service urges use of kudzu to prevent erosion.
1930s	U.S. Civilian Conservation Corps plants kudzu.
1940s	Government pays farmers to plant kudzu.
1940s	Georgia radio personality starts Kudzu Clubs.
1953	Government discourages use of kudzu.
1972	Government declares kudzu a weed.
2004	Kudzu covers 6 million acres in South; people work to eliminate it.

6. What is the topic of this time line? What is the best way to read this time line?

_____

_____

7. Why is a time line appropriate for this topic?

_____

_____

8. When was kudzu first introduced to the United States?

_____

9. How long did it take for the U.S. government to declare kudzu a weed? When was kudzu planted most heavily?

_____

_____

_____

10. What happened with kudzu most recently, according to the time line?

_____

_____

Home Activity Your child learned about using time lines as resources. Together, look at a time line in a history book. Ask your child to explain entries and to answer your questions about time order.

© Pearson Education, Inc., 5

Final Syllable -*ant*, -*ent*, -*ance*, -*ence*

Proofread an Article Circle and write six spelling errors. Circle one capitalization error and write the sentence correctly.

> ### Help Is on the Way
>
> With sirens wailing, the ambulence driver carefully winds through traffic. It takes a lot of confidents to do this importent job. In large cities, with persistant traffic, a driver must be extra careful. Still, the Driver must take the fastest route to the emergency room. Time makes all the differants when people need emergency care. All drivers try to get each won of their patients to the emergency room entrance as quickly as possible.

1. _____	2. _____
3. _____	4. _____
5. _____	6. _____
7. _____	
_____	

Spelling Words

important
experience
ignorant
entrance
difference
instance
absence
appearance
intelligent
evidence

pollutant
clearance
confidence
conference
insurance
ambulance
hesitant
consistent
excellence
persistent

Proofread Words Circle the correct spelling of the list word. Write the word.

8. absense	abcense	absence	8.	_____
9. intelligant	intelligent	intelagent	9.	_____
10. insurance	insurants	insurence	10.	_____
11. pollutent	pollutant	pollutint	11.	_____
12. ignorent	ignorint	ignorant	12.	_____
13. apperence	appearance	appearants	13.	_____
14. important	importent	inportant	14.	_____
15. hezitent	hesitent	hesitant	15.	_____

Frequently Misspelled Words

off
one
tired

Home Activity Your child identified misspelled list words. Ask your child to name the four words he or she has the most difficulty spelling and spell them for you.

© Pearson Education, Inc., 5

Name _____

Conjunctions

Directions Read the passage. Then read each question. Circle the letter of the correct answer.

The Living Arctic

(1) Although <u>you and I</u> might not like to live in the Arctic, many animals make their home in this cold _____ hostile land. (2) Reindeer are found across the northernmost parts of Canada and Asia. (3) Bitter cold but deep snow do not bother the Arctic Fox. (4) A year-round hunter, this fox can be snowy white or brown, depending on the season. (5) The climate here is harsh, _____ some plants do grow and provide food for the Arctic herbivores. (6) The muskox and Arctic hare are two animals that rely on plants and grasses for food. (7) Polar bears pose no threat to the hare, and wolves do prey the small Arctic animals.

1 Which best describes the underlined phrase in sentence 1?

   A   Compound sentence

   B   Compound predicate

   C   Compound subject

   D   None of the above

2 Which conjunction best completes sentence 1?

   A   however

   B   but

   C   or

   D   and

3 What change, if any, should be made in sentence 3?

   A   Change *do not bother* to **does not bother**

   B   Change *Bitter cold but deep snow* to **Bitter cold and deep snow**

   C   Change *Bitter cold but deep snow* to **Bitter cold, but deep snow**

   D   Make no change

4 Which conjunction best completes sentence 5?

   A   however

   B   but

   C   or

   D   and

5 What change, if any, should be made in sentence 7?

   A   Change *and wolves* to **but wolves**

   B   Change *and wolves* to **or wolves**

   C   Change *and wolves* to **because wolves**

   D   Make no change

© Pearson Education, Inc., 5

Home Activity Your child prepared for taking tests on conjunctions. Have your child find and circle *and, but,* and *or* in ads. Ask your child to explain why each word is used.

Compare and Contrast

- Writers sometimes use **comparison** and **contrast** to organize their writing. Clue words such as *same, also, before, although,* and *however* signal comparisons and contrasts.
- Good readers notice the author's comparisons and contrasts and make their own as they read.

Directions Read the following passage. Then complete the diagram below.

Hillary and her family wanted to move to New York City because it seemed exciting compared to their quiet hometown. They saved money for a year to afford the move. When it was time to move, their friends gave them a big send-off party.

After they moved to New York, they enjoyed the energy of the crowds as they bustled down the streets. They visited museums with amazing collections of art and artifacts. They experimented with new foods from all over the world.

They were unprepared, however, for how expensive everything was. And even though they were surrounded by people, they found it hard to make friends. They were surprised, but sometimes they longed for the peace and quiet of their home town. Over time, they understood that their new home was a mixture of advantages and disadvantages.

Advantages and Disadvantages of Moving to New York City	
Advantages	**Disadvantages**
1.	3.
2.	4.

5. What prior knowledge do you have about the advantages and disadvantages of living in a big city helps you makes comparisons and contrasts?

_____

_____

Home Activity Your child read a short passage and made comparisons and contrasts. After reading a historical article, work with your child to compare and contrast something at two different points in time.

Writing • Parody

Key Features of Parody

- imitates a familiar story's plot, style, and language
- changes details of the original story for comic effect
- may include action that rises to a climax

The Three Pigs

Frank was the oldest of the three pigs. He always had his own way of doing things. He thought he was smarter than everyone else, including his two little brothers. He also thought that you should work as little as possible.

The three pigs lived in a small brick house with their mother. Four pigs in one tiny house was too many! The pigs' mom decided it was time for the boys to move out.

"Build your own homes," she said. "Make them just right for you."

Frank decided he would think before working on his house. He would watch his brothers. He thought he would learn from their mistakes.

Frank's youngest brother built a house from straw. A wolf blew it down and ate Frank's brother. Frank's mom cried and cried. "You have to make your houses safe," she warned.

Frank's middle brother built a house from sticks. He tied them together tightly with rope.

Frank watched and waited. A week after his brother moved in, the wolf blew the sticks apart and ate Frank's middle brother. Frank's mom cried and cried. "Don't move out!" she said to Frank. "This brick house is safe. Stay here with me. You're all I have now."

Frank wiped his own eyes. He did miss his little brothers.

Soon, though, Frank smiled. Watching and waiting was so much better than working. He had decided he should build his own house from bricks. But bricks were heavy. Building with them was hard work. Yes, Frank decided, he was the smartest pig around.

As for the wolf, who also liked to watch and wait, he was sad.

1. Which character from the original "Three Little Pigs" story is most different in this parody? How is this character different?

_____

_____

2. What is the turning point? Circle the sentence that proves the tension is broken.

Vocabulary

Directions Choose the word from the box that best matches each definition below. Write the word on the line.

_____ 1. to add beauty to; put ornaments on

_____ 2. without life

_____ 3. as much as a spoon can hold

_____ 4. kingdom

_____ 5. to make clean

Check the Words You Know

___adorn
___cleanse
___lifeless
___precious
___realm
___spoonful

Directions Fill in the crossword puzzle using the clues below.

DOWN

6. to make pure
7. a king's empire
8. valuable

ACROSS

9. to decorate
10. without life

Write a Description

On a separate sheet of paper, write a short description of a king's castle. Use as many vocabulary words as you can.

Home Activity Your child identified and used vocabulary words from *King Midas and the Golden Touch*. Read a myth or fairy tale with your child. Ask your child to point out any of the vocabulary words he or she sees.

Commas

> **Commas** can clarify meaning and tell readers when to pause.
>
> - Put a comma after every item in a *series* but the last.
>   Poets pay attention to the sounds, meanings, and emotions of words.
>   The audience applauded, cheered, and stood up.
>
> - When you speak or write to someone, you may use the person's name or title. This noun of *direct address* is set off with a comma, or two commas if it is in the middle of a sentence.
>   Will you read some more, Mr. Berry?
>   I'd love to, children, if you aren't tired of sitting.
>
> - *Appositives* are noun phrases that describe another noun. They are set off by commas.
>   Ted Kooser, a wonderful poet, lives in Nebraska.
>
> - Put a comma after an *introductory word or phrase*, such as *yes, no, well, of course,* or *in fact*.
>   No, I haven't read the new book. As usual, I'm too busy.

Directions Add commas to each sentence where they are needed.

1. Harry enjoys writing stories poems and articles.

2. Voni do you prefer reading fairy tales tall tales or myths?

3. *King Midas* a myth about values features a greedy king.

4. Were you surprised Kaela when the glowing young man appeared?

5. No I expect magical things to happen in tales.

6. King Midas's gift is deadly because he cannot eat drink or touch people.

Directions Rewrite each sentence. Add commas where they are needed.

7. By the way King Midas what did you learn about gold?

_____

_____

8. I learned that gold is cold hard and meaningless by itself.

_____

_____

Home Activity Your child learned about commas. Record a short conversation with your child about his or her favorite foods or activities. Ask your child to write the conversation adding commas where they are needed.

© Pearson Education, Inc., 5

Latin Roots

Spelling Words				
portable	audience	decade	territory	auditorium
dictionary	terrace	reporter	December	contradict
export	decimal	audit	transport	audition
prediction	import	jurisdiction	decathlon	terrain

Words in Context Write the list words that complete each sentence.

She sang for her **(1)** _____ in the large **(2)** _____.

1. _____   2. _____

Most of the **(3)** _____ was hilly but we found a nice flat **(4)** _____ for a short rest.

3. _____   4. _____

We **(5)** _____ grain to China and **(6)** _____ Chinese toys and clothes.

5. _____   6. _____

The **(7)** _____ took her notes using a **(8)** _____ recorder.

7. _____   8. _____

He was bold enough to insist his definition was right and **(9)** _____ the **(10)** _____.

9. _____   10. _____

Word Definitions Write the list word that has the same meaning.

11. move something   11. _____

12. a statement made about the future   12. _____

13. a number written using base ten   13. _____

14. those who view or listen to a performance 14. _____

15. land or region   15. _____

16. a ten-year period   16. _____

17. examine carefully for accuracy   17. _____

18. legal power   18. _____

19. a competition having ten events   19. _____

20. twelfth month of the year   20. _____

Home Activity Your child wrote words that have Latin roots. Have your child tell you five list words and identify the Latin root in each word. Have your child spell each word.

Name _____

Story Sequence A

Title _____

Beginning

Middle

End

Vocabulary · Suffixes

- A **suffix** is added to the end of a base word to change its meaning or the way it is used in a sentence.
- The Old English suffix *-ful* can mean "full of _____," as in *careful,* or "an amount that fills something," as in *spoonful.* The suffix *-less* means "without," as in *harmless.*
- A dictionary is a book that helps us find the meanings of words we do not know.

Directions Read the following passage. Then answer the questions below. Use a dictionary to help you.

A wealthy king had all he could ask for except the one thing he needed most. His precious daughter was sick and lifeless. He sent out a message to all in his realm that he would give his fortune to anyone who could cure his daughter. In response, a penniless beggar came to the king's castle with a special potion. "If she takes a spoonful, she will improve," he said. Sure enough, with a spoonful she woke up, and with a cupful she was dancing around. As you might guess, the homeless beggar was well rewarded by the joyful king.

1. What is the base word in *lifeless*? How does the suffix help you understand its meaning?

_____

_____

2. What is the base word in *penniless*? How does the suffix help you understand its meaning?

_____

3. What is the base word in *homeless*? How does the suffix help you understand its meaning?

_____

_____

4. Change the word *powerful* so that it has the opposite meaning. Find the meanings of both words in a dictionary.

_____

_____

5. How does the suffix in the word *joyful* help you understand its meaning?

_____

Home Activity Your child identified and used suffixes to understand new words of a passage. Work with your child to identify unfamiliar words in an article. Ask your child if any suffixes can help him or her understand the new words. Confirm the meanings using a dictionary.

Name_____

Order Form/Application

Order forms and **applications** are charts with columns and spaces in which you can write or type. An order form is the means by which a person can purchase merchandise. An application is a form by which a person can apply for a job.

Directions Use this order form from an online catalog to answer the questions below.

GLITTER GOLD ORDER FORM

Click *SUBMIT* when you have completed this form.

Item Number	Item	Quantity	Price
13715	Big Bracelet		$
20166	Big Ring		$

+ $5 shipping and handling

TOTAL PRICE $

Billing Address

* Name
* Street Address
* City
* State   * ZIP
* Country
  Phone
* E-mail address

Shipping Address
☐ Check this box if same as billing address

* Name
* Street Address
* City
* State   * ZIP
* Country
  Phone

PAYMENT METHOD
* Type of Credit Card _____
* Account Number _____
* Expiration Date _____

Your comments and messages here.

* REQUIRED FIELD

Submit

---

1. When would you fill out only one of the two address fields shown?

2. If you are buying an item, what information do you need to specify on the order form?

3. If you wish to submit an online order at Glitter Gold, what payment options do you have?

4. How could you send comments to Glitter Gold?

5. If you are ordering from this Web page, what information is optional?

Directions Use this online job application form to answer the questions below.

MIDAS MINING CO. EMPLOYMENT APPLICATION
Click *SUBMIT* when you have completed this form.

PERSONAL INFORMATION

Last Name	First Name	Middle Initial
Address	City	State/ZIP
Phone Number	E-mail Address	Social Security No.
Position Applied For	Full-Time/Part-Time	Date Available to Start

EDUCATION

High School	Address	Graduated
College	Address	Graduated

WORK EXPERIENCE

Current Employer	Address	Duties	Start/End Dates
Employer Name	Address	Duties	Start/End Dates

OTHER SKILLS

REFERENCES

Name	Address	Phone	Relationship

SUBMIT

---

6. What is the purpose of this form?

_____

7. What is the first piece of information you need to provide on this form?

_____

8. In what section would you say when you could start working?

_____

9. What are three of the five main sections of the application?

_____

10. What directions are given on this form?

_____

Home Activity Your child learned about filling out order forms and applications. Look at an order form or application together. Discuss how to fill it out.

Name _____

Latin Roots

Proofread an Article Circle six spelling errors in the article. Write the words correctly. Find a punctuation error and write the sentence correctly.

Hard Work

Only a superb athlete can prevail in a decathalon The competition includes five events on each of two days. There is an enthusiastic audience for most events, especially those held in an auditorum. Races may be won by less than a thousandth of a second. However, the jumps, shot put, and javelin events may be won by as much as a decimeter. Reportors find it difficult to make a predikshion regarding a winner because winners are determined by a system which awards decemal values based on performance. Today, only male athletes may enter in too a decathlon. Women athletes compete in a heptathlon, a competition with seven events.

1. _____ 2. _____
3. _____ 4. _____
5. _____ 6. _____
7. _____

Spelling Words

portable
audience
decade
territory
auditorium
dictionary
terrace
reporter
December
contradict

export
decimal
audit
transport
audition
prediction
import
jurisdiction
decathlon
terrain

Frequently Misspelled Words

into
upon

Proofread Words Circle the correct spelling of each word.

8. esport axport export
9. terace terrace terrece
10. emport amport import
11. decade decad deckade
12. aduit audit audet
13. dictionary dictoinary dictionery
14. portabel portable portible
15. jursdiction juresdiction jurisdiction
16. territory terratory terretory
17. Dicimber December Dacember
18. trenspart trenspert transport
19. contradict contredict controdict
20. audition aduition audetin

Home Activity Your child identified misspelled list words. Ask your child to say five list words, tell the Latin root for each, and then spell and define each word.

© Pearson Education, Inc., 5

Commas

Directions Read the passage. Then read each question. Circle the letter of the correct answer.

Tales of Old

(1) Tales about medieval times usually share very similar elements. (2) Often, these tales involve royalty, such as a king a queen a prince or a lovely princess. (3) The story may tell of <u>a damsel in distress, a terrible plague, or a knight in shining armor.</u> (4) The kingdom's wizard, sometimes called Merlin, concocts potions and breaks witches' spells. (5) The bravest knight rides a white horse across the drawbridge while the wicked army plans its attack. (6) The proud king lives in a tall castle, while the poor serfs dwell in cold, leaky cottages. (7) Yes these tales are often quite similar, but they are always entertaining.

1 What change, if any, should be made in sentence 2?

   A   Insert commas after the words *king, queen,* and *prince*

   B   Insert commas after the words *king* and *queen*

   C   Change *royalty,* to **royalty**

   D   Make no change

2 In sentence 3, the underlined portion is an example of which?

   A   Direct address

   B   Appositive

   C   Series

   D   Introductory phrase

3 What change, if any, should be made in sentence 7?

   A   Insert comma after *tales are* and *often*

   B   Insert a comma after *Yes*

   C   Remove comma after *similar*

   D   Make no change

4 Which sentence in this passage includes an appositive?

   A   Sentence 1

   B   Sentence 3

   C   Sentence 4

   D   Sentence 5

5 Which sentence shows incorrect use of a comma?

   A   Ivy, do you like reading about kings and queens?

   B   Yes but I prefer more modern stories.

   C   My brother, a fan of fairy tales, has read all these books.

   D   I have read the first, second, and third books in the series.

© Pearson Education, Inc., 5

Home Activity Your child prepared for taking tests on commas. Ask your child to give example sentences to teach you about the four uses of commas he or she learned.

Fact and Opinion

- **Statements of fact** are objective, not personal. They can be proved true or false. **Statements of opinion** are personal judgments or beliefs. They cannot be proved true or false.
- Statements of opinion can be valid or faulty. **Valid** statements can be supported by facts and common sense. **Faulty** statements cannot.
- Examine statements of opinion by using your prior knowledge. Based on what you have seen or read or what you know, ask, *Is the statement valid or faulty?*

Directions Read the following passage. Then complete the chart below.

During the 1930s, ocean liners were a way of traveling in luxury. I'm sure that only the finest craftsmen were allowed to contribute to the most luxurious of these floating palaces. Immigrants as well as the wealthy traveled aboard these ocean liners. The ships were the most beautiful vessels on the water. The era of the transatlantic ocean liner continued from the 1920s until the 1960s. Each of us should learn more about the splendor of these ships.

Statement of Opinion	Support	Valid or Faulty?
I'm sure that only the finest craftsmen were allowed to contribute to the most luxurious of these floating palaces.	1.	2.
3.	4.	5.

Home Activity Your child identified statements of fact and opinion in a nonfiction passage. Work with your child to identify the statements of fact and opinion in a short magazine article. Challenge him or her to ask questions to check whether statements of opinion are supported by facts.

Writing · Book Review

Babe Ruth Was No Baby

I knew Babe Ruth was a famous baseball player before I read the book *Babe Ruth: One of Baseball's Greatest* by Guernsey Van Riper. But I did not know what a hard life Babe Ruth had as a boy. This book is a biography about Babe Ruth. I liked how this author gave a lot of detail about Babe's childhood. It tells how Babe was a tough boy and then turned his power into being a tough baseball player.

It is funny that his first name was George, but his nickname was Babe, like a small child. Babe was always big and strong even when he was a little boy. *Babe Ruth* explains that Babe got into trouble many times because his parents did not watch him. They ran a restaurant with rough customers. For example, in the book a neighbor named Mrs. Callahan says, "And the things that go on in that restaurant! The men seem to do nothing but fight and talk loudly." She felt, "It's certainly the wrong place for a headstrong boy like that George Ruth. One of these days, I've a mind to call to the police." Babe was only seven years old when she said that.

When Babe grew older, he kept getting into trouble. Finally, a teacher thought Babe would be good at baseball. He was right! Babe stopped being difficult when he used his strength to hit homeruns.

This biography is entertaining and shows an important lesson about how to use what you have to do well in life. The author shows through Babe's life how someone can take a problem and turn it into a success.

I think everyone will enjoy this book. Learning how someone famous started out poor and always in trouble and then worked to make something of himself is an inspiration.

1. What book is being reviewed? Who is the author?

_____

2. Which paragraph gives details about Babe Ruth's childhood? Circle two details.

_____

_____

_____

3. Why does the reviewer think people will want to read this book?

_____

_____

Vocabulary

Directions Choose the word from the box that best matches each definition. Write the word on the line.

_____ 1. finding fault with; disapproving of; blaming

_____ 2. act of bursting with a loud noise; a blowing up

_____ 3. wetting thoroughly; soaking

_____ 4. a period of time or history

_____ 5. traveled at the speed at which the vehicle operates best

Check the Words You Know

___criticizing
___cruised
___drenching
___era
___explosion
___hydrogen

Directions Choose the word from the box that best matches each clue. Write the word on the line.

_____ 6. This is said of extremely heavy rain.

_____ 7. An example of this is the colonial period or the Middle Ages.

_____ 8. A bomb could make this happen.

_____ 9. This element combines with oxygen to make water.

_____ 10. This describes how a ship might have moved along the water.

Write an E-mail Message

On a separate sheet of paper, write an e-mail message you might send from a ship after witnessing the eruption of a volcano. Use as many vocabulary words as you can.

© Pearson Education, Inc., 5

Home Activity Your child identified and used vocabulary words from *The Hindenburg*. Read a story or nonfiction article with your child. Have him or her point out unfamiliar words. Work together to try to figure out the meaning of each word by using other words that appear near it.

Quotations and Quotation Marks

A **direct quotation** gives a person's exact words and is enclosed in **quotation marks** (" "). Direct quotations begin with capital letters and end with proper punctuation. End punctuation is inside the closing quotation marks. Words that tell who is speaking are set off from the quotation by punctuation.

- When the quotation comes last in a sentence, set it off with a comma.
  Jamie asked, "What was the *Hindenburg?*"
- When the quotation comes first in a sentence, a comma, question mark, or exclamation mark sets off the quotation.
  "It was a dirigible," replied May. "It was enormous!" she added.
- When the quotation is interrupted by words that tell who is speaking, use two sets of quotation marks. Notice that words telling who is speaking are followed by punctuation. Use a comma if the second part of the quotation does not begin a new sentence.
  "Dirigibles were lighter than air," he added, "because they were filled with hydrogen."
- Use end punctuation and a capital letter if the second part of the quotation does begin a new sentence.
  "Isn't hydrogen flammable?" asked Jamie. "What kept it from exploding?"

Directions Rewrite each sentence. Add quotation marks where they are needed.

1. Are the blimps dirigibles? asked Max.

_____

2. No, they aren't, explained Vi, because they aren't rigid.

_____

Directions Write each sentence correctly. Add capital letters, quotation marks, and other punctuation as needed.

3. Vi said the framework is like a skeleton

_____

4. fabric covers it she added like skin

_____

Home Activity Your child learned about quotations and quotation marks. With your child, find quotations in a newspaper or magazine article. Have your child highlight the quotation marks and other punctuation and explain why they are used.

Related Words

Spelling Words				
clean	cleanse	inspire	inspiration	legal
legality	define	definition	please	pleasant
combine	combination	human	humanity	organ
organist	crime	criminal	recognize	recognition

Words in Context Write the list words that complete the sentence.

I use the **(1)** _____ of other artists to **(2)** _____ me. (inspiration, inspire)

1. _____   2. _____

The **(3)** _____ looked tiny as she stood in front of the **(4)** _____. (organ, organist)

3. _____   4. _____

(5) _____ the eggs and sugar; add the flour and spices to the **(6)** _____. (combine, combination)

5. _____   6. _____

She said, "Jake, **(7)** _____ be **(8)** _____ to your Aunt Martha." (please, pleasant)

7. _____   8. _____

"I'm not a **(9)** _____," he said. "I didn't commit the **(10)** _____." (crime, criminal)

9. _____   10. _____

Definitions Write the list word that has the same meaning as the word or phrase.

11. dirt free _____   12. wash _____

13. word's meaning _____   14. person _____

15. identify something _____   16. specify meaning _____

17. lawfulness _____   18. allowed by law _____

19. appreciation, fame _____   20. quality of being human _____

Home Activity Your child wrote related words that are spelled similarly but pronounced differently. Say list words and have your child say and spell the list word that is related.

Scoring Rubric: Critical Review

	4	3	2	1
Focus/Ideas	Summarizes the main idea, includes a thesis supported by facts and details from the book	Mostly summarizes the main idea and a thesis mostly by facts and details from the book	Somewhat summarizes main idea, may have a thesis with some facts and details from the book	Lacks a summary or main idea; no thesis; no facts and details from the book
Organization	Includes a strong introduction, body and conclusion	Includes basic introduction, body, and conclusion	Includes weak introduction, body, and conclusion	No introduction, body, and/or conclusion
Voice	Involved throughout	Involved most of the time	Tries to be involved	No involvement
Word Choice	Language matches purpose closely	Language matches purpose well	Language only partly matches purpose	Language does not match purpose
Sentences	Clear and complete	Mostly clear and complete	Somewhat clear and complete	Neither clear nor complete
Conventions	Few to no errors in use of quotations and quotation marks and in spelling of related words	Moderate errors in use of quotations and quotation marks and in spelling of related words	Several errors in use of quotations and quotation marks and in spelling of related words	Consistently incorrect use of quotations and quotation marks and spelling of related words

Vocabulary · Unfamiliar Words

- When you see an **unfamiliar word** while reading, use context clues, or words around the unfamiliar word, to figure out its meaning.
- Context clues include definitions, explanations, and synonyms (words that have the same or nearly the same meaning as other words).

Directions Read the following passage. Then answer the questions below.

In the early 1900s, many people were criticizing the Wright brothers for trying to make a flying machine. These people accused the Wright brothers of trying to do something humans were not meant to do. However, the brothers kept working on their invention, even in drenching, soaking rain. In 1903, they finally created an airplane with a propeller and a gas engine. They controlled the speed of the aircraft by increasing or decreasing the spark in the engine. This caused an explosion, or bursting, of fuel that drove the propeller. When they finally got a propeller-driven machine into the air, they cruised at a very slow speed, traveling at only about one mile an hour. Still, the Wright brothers' plane opened up a whole new era of transportation, the age of the airplane.

1. What does *criticizing* mean? What clues help you to determine its meaning?

_____

_____

2. What does *drenching* mean? What clue helps you determine the meaning?

_____

_____

3. What clue helps you to determine the meaning of *explosion*? What does this word mean?

_____

_____

4. What context clue helps you determine the meaning of *cruised*?

_____

_____

5. What does *era* mean? How can you use context clues to determine the meaning?

_____

_____

Home Activity Your child identified and used context clues to understand new words in a nonfiction passage. Work with your child to identify unfamiliar words in another article. Then have him or her find context clues to help with understanding the new words. Confirm the meanings with the glossary in the back of your book or a dictionary.

© Pearson Education, Inc., 5

Map/Globe/Atlas

- A **map** is a drawing of a place that shows where something is or where something happened. You may see different kinds of maps. These include picture maps, road maps, political maps, physical maps, and special-purpose maps. Look carefully at a map's **legend,** or key. It explains any symbols used in the map. It also shows directions as well as a scale of distance.

- An **atlas** is a book of maps.

- A **globe** is a sphere with a map of the world on it. Because the Earth is round, globes give a more accurate picture of the size and shape of the Earth than flat maps do.

Directions Study the following map. Then use the map to answer the questions below.

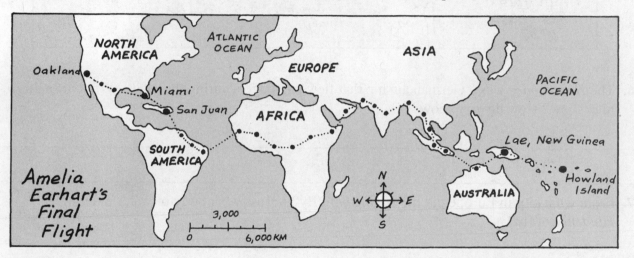

1. On May 20, 1937, Amelia Earhart took off on an airplane flight that she hoped would make her the first person to fly around the world. She began in Oakland, California. What was her last stop in the United States?

_____

2. Where did she land next?

_____

3. About how far was her flight across the United States? How do you know?

_____

_____

4. On which continents did she land along the way to Lae, New Guinea?

_____

5. On July 1, 1937, Amelia Earhart left Lae, New Guinea. What was her next intended stop? How far is this place from New Guinea?

_____

_____

Name_____

Directions Study the following map. Then use the map to answer the questions below.

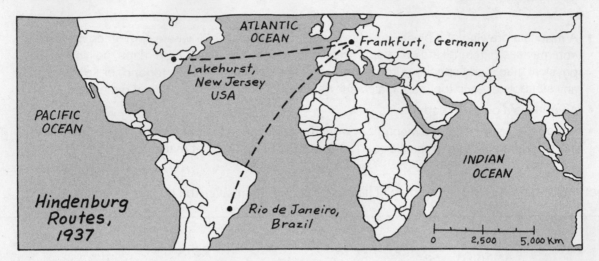

6. The *Hindenburg* was a German airship that flew passengers during the 1930s. What does this map show? How do you know?

_____

_____

7. From what city in Europe did the *Hindenburg* fly? Across what body of water did the *Hindenburg* fly?

_____

_____

8. According to the map, what were the *Hindenburg*'s two destinations in 1937?

_____

_____

9. What was the approximate distance of the route to each of these destinations?

_____

_____

10. Is this map similar to a globe? Which term would you use to describe this map—a road map, a political map that shows the borders of countries, or a physical map that shows elevations and other details of the land?

_____

_____

© Pearson Education, Inc., 5

Home Activity Your child learned about using maps as resources. Look at a road map together. Ask your child to determine distances and plot out routes to destinations you specify.

Name_____

Related Words

Proofread an Article Circle six spelling errors and one sentence containing punctuation errors. Write the corrections on the lines.

clean
cleanse
inspire
inspiration
legal
legality
define
definition
please
pleasant

combine
combination
human
humanity
organ
organist
crime
criminal
recognize
recognition

Courts

The United States Supreme Court is the highest court in the land. Often it is asked to determine the legalaty of a law. The Supreme Court has the right to either reconize or deny any appeal submitted to it. Some times it difines conditions under which an existing law may be leagle or illegal. The Constitution and laws of each state establish the state courts. These state courts handle criminul cases. States also usually have courts that handle specific legal matters. These include juvenile court; family court; and others.

1. _____   2. _____

3. _____   4. _____

5. _____   6. _____

7. _____

_____

Proofread Words Circle the correct spelling of the word.

8. crim   crieme   crime

9. recognition   raconition   reconition

10. plese   please   pleeze

11. orgunist   organist   orgenist

12. humen   homan   human

13. enspire   inspire   inspir

14. orgun   argon   organ

15. humanity   humenety   humenity

16. combination comination   cumination

sometimes
everything
maybe
a lot

School + Home

Home Activity Your child identified misspelled words. Write the first four letters of a list word and have your child write the two related words.

© Pearson Education, Inc., 5

Quotations and Quotation Marks

Directions Read the passage. Then read each question. Circle the letter of the correct answer.

Up In the Air

(1) "I'm going on a hot-air balloon ride," said Sherry. (2) "Wow!" That's so cool!" exclaimed Phillip. (3) "He added earnestly, "Do you think I could come along?" (4) That afternoon, Sherry asked her father if Phillip could go with them in the balloon. (5) "Sure answered her father, "as long as he isn't afraid of heights!" (6) Phillip had never been in a balloon or an airplane, and he was very excited. (7) "Thank you so much," he said. "For letting me go along for the ride!"

1 What change, if any, should be made in sentence 1?

  A Change *"I'm going* to **I'm going**

  B Change *ride,"* to **ride"**

  C Change *ride,"* to **ride."**

  D Make no change

2 What change, if any, should be made in sentence 2?

  A Change **"Wow!"** to **"Wow,"**

  B Change *That's* to **"That's**

  C Change **"Wow!"** to **"Wow!**

  D Make no change

3 What change, if any, should be made in sentence 3?

  A Remove quotation marks from the beginning of the sentence

  B Remove all quotation marks from the sentence

  C Change *"He added earnestly,* to **He added earnestly**

  D Make no change

4 Which is the correct form of sentence 5?

  A "Sure" answered her father, "as long as he isn't afraid of heights!"

  B "Sure, answered her father, as long as he isn't afraid of heights!"

  C "Sure" answered her father "as long as he isn't afraid of heights!"

  D "Sure," answered her father, "as long as he isn't afraid of heights!"

5 What is the correct form of sentence 7?

  A "Thank you so much," he said. "For letting me go along for the ride!"

  B "Thank you so much," he said, "for letting me go along for the ride!"

  C "Thank you so much he said for letting me go along for the ride!"

  D "Thank you so much, he said, for letting me go along for the ride!"

Home Activity Your child prepared for taking tests on quotations and quotation marks. Have your child interview you about your day and write your reply as a quotation, beginning with *He/She said* and using quotation marks correctly.

Sequence

- **Sequence** is the order of events in a selection. Dates and times of day or clue words such as *first, next,* and *then* can help you follow the sequence of events.
- Clue words such as *meanwhile* and *during* signal events happening at the same time.

Directions Read the following passage. Then complete the diagram.

> Will was nervous about playing the clarinet at a school performance for the first time. For five months, he had been taking lessons and learning to make notes come alive. But once the performance started, he got nervous. What if he played at the wrong time or forgot the notes? When the time came for his number, he forgot about all the people watching and just felt good about the music. Then when he heard the applause, he felt even better.

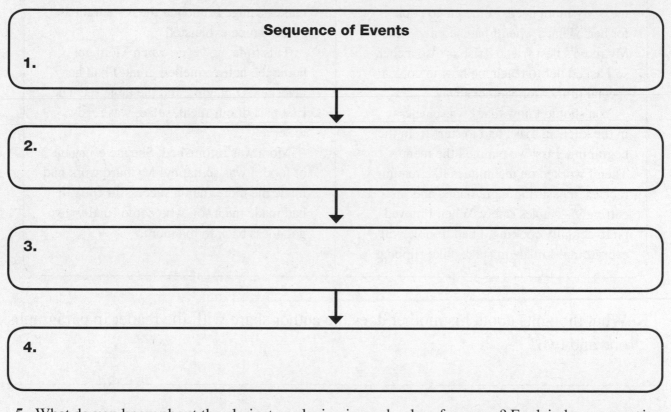

Sequence of Events

1.

2.

3.

4.

5. What do you know about the clarinet or playing in a school performance? Explain how your prior knowledge helps you to understand the story.

_____

_____

Home Activity Your child identified the sequence of a story and the prior knowledge he or she had of the subject matter. Work with your child to identify the sequence of the events in a short story. Encourage your child to describe the prior knowledge he or she has of the story's subject matter.

Writing · Personal Narrative

Key Features of a Personal Narrative

- tells a real story about a personal experience
- includes details that help readers understand the experience
- uses first-person point of view (I, me)
- reveals author's voice through thoughts and feelings

A Surprise for Mom

My mom works really hard at a job she loves. She's a chef, and her food is delicious! On her days off, she cooks me fancy pizzas or anything else I want.

A couple of months ago, a thought hit me: "My mom needs someone to cook for her." That's when I hatched my plan. My mom's best friend Trish is also a chef, so I asked her to teach me how to cook a special dinner for Mother's Day.

You should know that I was clueless in the kitchen. Trish had to start from the beginning. First we planned the menu. Then I worked on techniques like reading recipes, measuring ingredients, and cutting vegetables safely. When I moved on to actually cooking, I had trouble with everything! I made mistakes like flipping food out of the pan and burning sauces. However, Trish was really patient with me, and slowly I mastered each dish.

When Mother's Day arrived, I got busy as soon as Mom left for work. She always makes a huge brunch at the restaurant and comes home exhausted.

This time, however, when Mom got home the house smelled great. I had her favorite CD playing and the table set. The first part of our meal, salad, was ready to serve.

Mom was astonished. She ate every bit of food. I was so happy! My hard work had made me more than a successful cook. It had made me a son who could finally give goodness back to his mom.

1. What thoughts about his mother does the author share with the reader in paragraphs one and two?

_____

_____

2. What details in paragraph five help you feel like you are a part of this experience? Underline sentences that appeal to your senses.

Vocabulary

Directions Choose the word from the box that best matches each definition below. Write the word on the line.

_____ 1. not new; used already by someone else

_____ 2. made music with other musicians without having practiced

_____ 3. restless; uneasy

_____ 4. the largest, lowest sounding stringed instrument in an orchestra or band

_____ 5. apt to forget; having a poor memory

Directions Choose the word from the box that best completes each sentence below. Write the word on the line shown to the left.

_____ 6. The trio of jazz musicians _____, or played music together.

_____ 7. They met during the _____ after working all day.

_____ 8. One musician played both a trumpet and a stringed _____.

_____ 9. Another musician played the _____, a favorite woodwind.

_____ 10. The third musician's instrument was a used, or _____, saxophone.

Write a Review

On a separate sheet of paper, write a review you might compose after you go to a music concert or performance. Use as many vocabulary words as you can.

Home Activity Your child identified and used vocabulary words from *Sweet Music in Harlem*. Read a story or nonfiction article with your child. Have him or her point out unfamiliar words. Work together to try to figure out the meaning of each word by using other words that appear near it.

© Pearson Education, Inc., 5

Punctuation

You have already learned about punctuation such as commas, quotation marks, and end marks. Here are some other kinds of punctuation.

- A **colon (:)** is used to introduce a list of items. It is also used to separate hours and minutes in expressions of time. In addition, it is used after the salutation in a business letter.
  Use these ingredients: two eggs, one cup of flour, and a stick of butter.
  10:30 A.M.   9:15 P.M.   Dear Ms. Glover: Sir:

- A **hyphen (-)** is used in some compound words. Two common uses are numbers from twenty-one to ninety-nine and compound words that are thought of as one word.
  old-time music   best-known book   forty-nine   five-year-old boy

- A **semicolon (;)** can be used to join two independent clauses instead of a comma and a conjunction.
  Jazz is a mixture of different types of music; New Orleans was its birthplace.

- **Italics** or **underlining** is used for titles of books, newspapers, magazines, and works of art. Because you cannot write italics, underline titles in your writing.
  the *Chicago Tribune* (newspaper)   *Time for Kids* (magazine)
  or   the Chicago Tribune   Time for Kids

- A **dash (—)** sets off information or a comment that interrupts the flow of a sentence.
  Jazz had developed many styles—bebop and Dixieland, for example—by the 1940s.

Directions Rewrite each sentence on the lines. Add punctuation where it is needed.

1. Jinny is writing a how to book titled You Can Do Most Anything.

_____

_____

2. The first show is at 800 P.M. the second is at 1030 P.M.

_____

_____

3. Cuthbert we call him Chip is my best friend.

_____

_____

4. Mae made a last minute effort to learn twenty two songs.

_____

_____

Home Activity Your child learned about punctuation. Have your child explain and model a use for colons and semicolons.

© Pearson Education, Inc., 5

Name _____

Easily Confused Words

Spelling Words				
quiet	quite	finely	finally	except
accept	than	then	since	sense
affect	effect	from	form	later
latter	adapt	adopt	medal	metal

Definitions Write the list word that means the same as each word or phrase.

1. silent

2. at last

3. receive

4. shape

5. a type of award

1. _____

2. _____

3. _____

4. _____

5. _____

Words in Context Write a list word to finish each sentence.

6. How will this score ___ my grade?

7. I'll see you ___.

8. They plan to ___ a child soon.

9. By ___ we should know the results of the race.

10. My aunt has a good ___ of humor.

11. I think this project is not ___ finished yet.

12. This piano has been very ___ tuned.

13. Everyone was there ___ me.

14. I would rather go to a movie ___ do my homework.

15. I haven't seen her ___ last year.

16. What ___ will this poor test score have on my overall grade?

17. I like to walk home ___ school.

18. I prefer the former choice to the ___.

19. It is important to be able to ___ to new situations.

20. The magnet picked up the ___ pieces.

6. _____

7. _____

8. _____

9. _____

10. _____

11. _____

12. _____

13. _____

14. _____

15. _____

16. _____

17. _____

18. _____

19. _____

20. _____

Home Activity Your child matched words with definitions and finished sentences. Ask your child to define the word *adapt*.

Spelling Easily Confused Words **433**

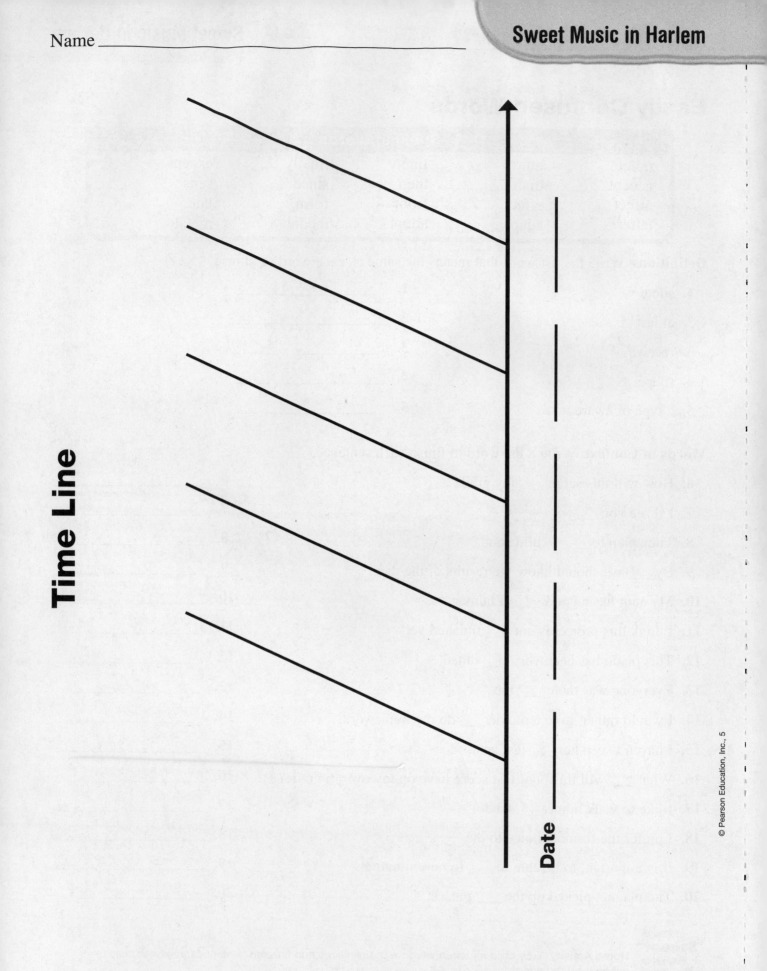

Time Line

Date

Name_____

Vocabulary · Homographs

- When you are reading, you might see a **homograph**. Homographs are words that are spelled the same but have different meanings and sometimes different pronunciations. For example, *object* can mean both "to protest" and "a thing."
- Use context clues, or words around the unfamiliar word, to figure out its meaning. Context clues include definitions, explanations, and synonyms.
- A dictionary is a book to help you find words you do not know.

Directions Read the following passage about jazz music. Then answer the questions below.

> Jeb played bass, a low-sounding stringed instrument, in a jazz quartet. Along with his bass, the group also had a clarinet, a trombone, and a piano. Every night when the group jammed, or made music without practicing, they would attract interest. Soon a crowd would gather. Usually they'd get so deeply involved in the music that they'd get forgetful of the time. Before they realized it, instead of nighttime it would be close to daytime.

1. *Bass* can refer to a musical instrument or a fish. What clues help you to determine the meaning in this passage?

_____

_____

2. In this context, is *jam* a noun referring to a fruit spread or a verb referring to playing music without practicing? What clues help you to determine the meaning?

_____

_____

3. Use one of the homographs in the passage twice in a sentence, showing both its meanings.

_____

4. Which meaning of the homograph *close* is used in the last sentence: "shut" or "near to"?

_____

5. *Interest* can mean "a feeling of concern or curiosity" or "money paid for the use of money." How do context clues indicate its meaning in the passage?

_____

_____

Home Activity Your child identified and used context clues to understand homographs in a passage. Work with your child to identify homographs in an article. Then your child can find context clues to help with the understanding of the new words. Confirm the meanings with your child.

Poster/Announcement

- **Posters** and **announcements** announce events. The events may be one time only, or they may be continuing, as with club and organization meetings.
- Usually, posters and announcements answer these questions: Who? What? When? Where? Why?
- To emphasize information, posters and announcements may use color and large type size.
- When you write a poster or announcement, include only important information.

Directions Use this poster to answer the questions.

Who is performing at this event? Who is sponsoring the event?	1.
What is the event? What is the cost?	2.
When is the event?	3.
Where is the event?	4.
Why is the event being held?	5.

Name_____

Directions Use this announcement to answer the questions.

JOIN TODAY!

Armstrong School
Junior
Jazz Club

This organization is dedicated to
the appreciation of jazz music.
Guest speakers, refreshments, and lots
of music are all part of the fun!

Come and bring your instrument!

Room 201
3:30 P.M. Every Tuesday

---

6. What is the purpose of this announcement?

_____

7. What is the event? Why do you think the event takes place?

_____

_____

8. When and where does the event take place?

_____

9. What does this announcement emphasize? How and why is this emphasis made?

_____

_____

10. On a separate sheet of paper, write an announcement for a school event.

Home Activity Your child learned about reading posters. Point out a poster to your child, and ask him or her how the poster answers these questions about the event it announces: Who? What? When? Where? Why? Talk about how to compose a poster for a school or community event.

© Pearson Education, Inc., 5

Easily Confused Words

Proofread a Dialogue Circle six spelling mistakes in the article below. Write them correctly. Find a sentence with a misplaced comma. Write the sentence correctly.

> My Brother the Hero
>
> When my brother finely got back form serving overseas, my family was happy and proud. We attended a ceremony where we watched him except a metal. When he stood up to receive his award, we were very quite. Latter we went out to dinner to celebrate his return.

Spelling Words

quiet
quite
finely
finally
except
accept
than
then
since
sense

affect
effect
from
form
later
latter
adapt
adopt
medal
metal

1. _____   2. _____

3. _____   4. _____

5. _____   6. _____

7. _____

_____

Proofread Words Circle the word that is spelled correctly. Write it on the line.

8. axcept	accept	8. _____
9. adupt	adapt	9. _____
10. adoped	adopt	10. _____
11. affect	afect	11. _____
12. except	exsept	12. _____
13. finaly	finally	13. _____
14. sense	sence	14. _____
15. then	thun	15. _____

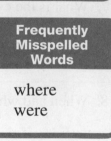

Frequently Misspelled Words

where
were

© Pearson Education, Inc., 5

Home Activity Your child identified misspelled words. Ask your child to pick a list word and use it in a sentence.

Punctuation

Directions Read the passage. Then read each question. Circle the letter of the correct answer.

Jazzing It Up

(1) Jazz was created as a blend of several musical genres; New Orleans was where it began. (2) African Americans migrated to northern cities New York and Chicago, most importantly and brought jazz with them. (3) During the Great Depression—from 1929 to the early 1940s—jazz gained popularity and began to change. (4) A new form of jazz emerged at this time () big band. (5) Big band music—also called "swing"—helped people forget about the problems caused by the Depression. (6) Best-known for this type of jazz were Bennie Goodman and Count Basie. (7) *Magazines* like Down Beat helped launch the careers of: many great musicians.

1 What change, if any, should be made in sentence 2?

   A Insert (—) before *New York* and after *importantly*

   B Insert (—) before *New York* and after *Chicago*

   C Insert (;) before *New York* and after *importantly*

   D Make no change

2 In sentence 3, what is the function of the phrase *from 1929 to the early 1940s*?

   A The phrase tells more about *jazz gained popularity*

   B The phrase tells more about *the Great Depression*

   C The phrase tells what happened during the Great Depression

   D The phrase has no function

3 What form of punctuation should replace the parentheses in sentence 4?

   A Semicolon (;)

   B Colon (:)

   C Hyphen (-)

   D Dash (—)

4 What change, if any, should be made in sentence 6?

   A Change *Best-known* to **Best known**

   B Change *Best-known* to **Bestknown**

   C Change *were* to **were:**

   D Make no change

5 What is the correct form of sentence 7?

   A *Magazines* like Down Beat helped launch the careers of: many great musicians.

   B *Magazines* like *Down Beat* helped launch the careers of: many great musicians.

   C Magazines like *Down Beat* helped launch the careers of many great musicians.

   D Magazines; like Down Beat—helped launch the careers of many great musicians.

 Home Activity Your child prepared for taking tests on punctuation. Have your child make index cards for the colon, semicolon, dash, hyphen, and italics and then search books and magazines for examples of the use of each mark.

© Pearson Education, Inc., 5

Suffixes -*ous*, -*sion*, -*ion*, -*ation*

Spelling Words

famous	imagination	various	tension	invasion
invention	education	decision	humorous	creation
election	nervous	relaxation	exhibition	occupation
furious	explanation	conversation	attraction	destination

Antonyms Write the list word that has the opposite or nearly the opposite meaning.

1. serious _____

2. relaxed _____

3. repulsion _____

4. unknown _____

5. destruction _____

6. calm _____

7. uncertainty _____

8. alike _____

Words in Context Complete each sentence with a list word.

9. Reading, writing, and math are important parts of your _____.

10. The lightbulb was a marvelous _____.

11. Nursing is a helpful _____.

12. In a good _____, everyone has a chance to speak.

13. We saw a(n) _____ of modern art at the museum.

14. Some people play card games for _____.

15. The beach is a popular summer _____.

16. Our picnic was ruined by a(n) _____ of ants.

17. You must use your _____ to write a compelling poem.

18. It is important for citizens to vote in each _____.

19. Stretching a rubber band increases its _____.

20. You must have a good _____ for missing soccer practice.

School + Home **Home Activity** Your child has been learning to spell words with suffixes. Call out some of the list words and ask your child to give a synonym or antonym for each word.

Modifiers

Directions Underline the adjectives, adverbs, and prepositional phrases in each sentence. (Do not underline the articles *a* and *the*.)

1. Little bats migrate from central Mexico.

2. Free-tails are medium-sized bats that live in colonies.

3. They roost annually under the Congress Avenue Bridge.

4. The helpful Free-tails eat moths and other harmful pests.

5. Concerned people in Austin want to save the shrinking bat population.

Directions Write *adverb, adjective,* or *prepositional phrase* to identify each underlined modifier. Write *adjective* or *adverb* to identify how a prepositional phrase is used.

6. Our science class studied <u>different</u> species.   _____

7. Insects live <u>everywhere</u>.   _____

8. Some insects blend <u>perfectly</u> with their environments. _____

9. Some insects are harmful because they feed <u>on our crops</u>. _____

10. The bat is a very <u>useful</u> creature.   _____

11. Many harmful insects are eaten <u>by bats</u>.   _____

12. The ladybug, <u>with its cheerful colors</u>, is my favorite insect. _____

Directions Underline the misplaced modifier in each sentence. Rewrite the sentence, and put the modifier where it belongs.

13. Farmers fight harmful insects in airplanes called crop dusters.

_____

_____

14. They only want to kill harmful insects and not useful ones.

_____

_____

15. Crops are poisonous to bats sprayed with pesticides.

_____

_____

Final Syllable -*ant*, -*ent*, -*ance*, -*ence*

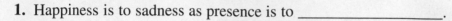

Spelling Words

important	difference	intelligent	confidence	hesitant
experience	instance	evidence	conference	consistent
ignorant	absence	pollutant	insurance	excellence
entrance	appearance	clearance	ambulance	persistent

Analogies Write the word that completes each comparison.

1. Happiness is to sadness as presence is to _____.

2. Sweet is to sour as educated is to _____.

3. Rose is to flower as smoke is to _____.

4. Trip is to journey as example is to _____.

5. Night is to day as exit is to _____.

6. Pretty is to lovely as smart is to _____.

7. Doctor is to hospital as paramedic is to _____.

8. Heat is to cold as sameness is to _____.

9. Game is to sport as meeting is to _____.

10. Difficult is to easy as insignificant is to _____.

Words in Context Complete each sentence with a list word.

11. The car repairs were paid for by the _____ company.

12. The jury considered the _____ against the man on trial.

13. Bright autumn colors gave the trees a lovely _____.

14. The soccer players liked the referee because his calls were _____.

15. Confronting a bear must be a frightening _____.

16. Because he was shy, Will was _____ to meet people.

17. There was a(n) _____ sale of snow boots at the end of the winter.

18. That baseball player has much _____ in his ability.

19. At the spring assembly, the best students were rewarded for _____.

20. To succeed in your goal, you must be _____.

School + Home **Home Activity** Your child learned to spell words with the final syllables -*ant*, -*ent*, -*ance*, and -*ence*. Ask your child to find an example of a word with each ending in a magazine and then spell each word without looking at the magazine.

© Pearson Education, Inc., 5

Conjunctions

Directions Underline the conjunction in each sentence.

1. Scientists look for facts and solve problems.

2. All problems are different, but each problem takes time to solve.

3. Scientists search for answers in an orderly and exact way.

4. They use scientific method, or a systematic approach to problem solving.

5. Eventually, they form a hypothesis, but this is not the end.

6. They must analyze the data and draw a conclusion.

Directions Underline the conjunction in ( ) that completes each sentence.

7. Is a scientific truth a theory (and, or) a law?

8. A theory may be logical, (or, but) a law is widely accepted.

9. Newton's ideas about motion are called laws, (and, but) Einstein's idea about relativity is called a theory.

10. Both Newton (and, or) Einstein used scientific method.

Directions Use the conjunction *and, but,* or *or* to join each pair of sentences. Write the new sentences. Remember to add a comma.

11. The reindeer population grew large. Then most of the reindeer died suddenly.

_____

_____

12. Were the reindeer diseased? Did they starve?

_____

_____

13. The animals had lost weight. Their bone marrow contained no fat.

_____

_____

14. The reindeer had eaten all the island's food. Then disaster struck.

_____

_____

Latin Roots

Spelling Words

portable	audience	decade	territory	auditorium
dictionary	terrace	reporter	December	contradict
export	decimal	audit	transport	audition
prediction	import	jurisdiction	decathlon	terrain

Classifying Write the list word that belongs in each group.

1. state, country, region, _____

2. patio, deck, balcony, _____

3. September, October, November, _____

4. week, month, year, _____

5. races, hurdle, shot put, _____

6. aquarium, solarium, gymnasium, _____

7. writer, investigator, researcher, _____

8. integer, fraction, whole number, _____

9. thesaurus, encyclopedia, handbook, _____

10. court, claims, civil, _____

Synonyms Write the list word that has the same or nearly the same meaning.

11. tryout _____

12. forecast _____

13. ground _____

14. onlookers _____

15. move _____

16. check _____

17. send _____

18. dispute _____

19. moveable _____

20. bring in _____

Home Activity Your child has learned to spell words with Latin roots. Take turns brainstorming a word that has one of the list word roots. Look up each word in the dictionary to confirm that it comes from a Latin word.

Name _____

Commas

Directions Add commas to each sentence where they are needed.

1. Rafael has joined the Fleet Feet a traveling soccer team.

2. He will have to buy shoes a uniform and a ball.

3. Dad how can I earn money?

4. Well son you could do more chores around the house.

5. Rafael washed the car walked the dog and watered the garden.

6. He also received money as gifts from his aunt grandparents and parents.

Directions Rewrite each sentence. Add commas where they are needed.

7. "Anna are you a good money manager?"

   _____

   _____

8. In general people are better at spending than saving.

   _____

   _____

9. Most people need a budget a plan for keeping track of their income and expenses.

   _____

   _____

10. I spend my money on lunches books and supplies.

    _____

    _____

11. George a friend who does not have a budget is always short of money.

    _____

    _____

12. "By the way George you owe me fifty cents."

    _____

    _____

Related Words

Spelling Words				
clean	inspire	legal	define	please
cleanse	inspiration	legality	definition	pleasant
combine	human	organ	crime	recognize
combination	humanity	organist	criminal	recognition

Analogies Write the word that completes each sentence.

1. Pepper is to salt as dirty is to _____.

2. Beast is to animal as person is to _____.

3. Stop is to go as separate is to _____.

4. Violin is to violinist as organ is to _____.

5. Good-bye is to hello as thank you is to _____.

6. Exhilaration is to excitement as encouragement is to _____.

7. Individual is to single as mixture is to _____.

8. Tool is to hammer as instrument is to _____.

9. Earth is to world as mankind is to _____.

10. Unwind is to relax as unlawful is to _____.

Synonyms Write the list word that has the same or nearly the same meaning.

11. wash _____

12. lawful _____

13. meaning _____

14. agreeable _____

15. acknowledgement _____

Antonyms Write the list word that has the opposite or nearly the opposite meaning.

16. not notice _____

17. discourage _____

18. confuse _____

19. unlawfulness _____

20. legal _____

School + Home **Home Activity** Your child has learned to spell related words. Read several pairs of words from the list. Ask your child to explain how knowing the spelling of one word in the pair can help in spelling the other word.

Quotations and Quotation Marks

Directions Write *C* if the sentence uses quotation marks and other punctuation correctly. Write *NC* if it is not correct.

1. "Are you going to take a vacation," asked Aaron? _____

2. "I usually fly to my grandparents' home in Michigan," said Pat. _____

3. "Do you like to fly," asked Aaron, "or would you rather take a train?" _____

4. "Pat replied, I like different things about both." _____

5. "A train lets you see more things," she explained. "However, an airplane is quicker." _____

Directions Write each sentence correctly. Add capital letters, quotation marks, and other punctuation as needed.

6. when does our flight take off asked Nina

_____

7. it is scheduled to leave at 8:00 A.M. said Mom

_____

8. she added that means we should be at the airport by 6:00 A.M.

_____

_____

9. no way cried Nina that's too early

_____

10. it is early agreed Mom however, we have to allow plenty of time

_____

_____

11. after we check our bags she suggested we can have breakfast

_____

_____

12. that sounds good said Nina can I buy a magazine to read

_____

_____

Easily Confused Words

Spelling Words				
quiet	except	since	from	adapt
quite	accept	sense	form	adopt
finely	than	affect	later	medal
finally	then	effect	latter	metal

Antonyms Write the list word that has the opposite or nearly the opposite meaning.

1. coarsely _____

2. reject _____

3. earlier _____

4. noisy _____

5. now _____

Synonyms Write the list word that has the same or nearly the same meaning.

6. result _____

7. reward _____

8. very _____

9. because _____

10. select _____

Analogies Write the word that completes each comparison.

11. First is to last as former is to _____.

12. Start is to begin as at last is to _____.

13. In is to out as to is to _____.

14. Milk is to drink as iron is to _____.

15. Buy is to purchase as influence is to _____.

16. North is to direction as sight is to _____.

17. Also is to too as but is to _____.

18. Gift is to present as shape is to _____.

19. Work is to labor as change is to _____.

20. Log is to dog as fan is to _____.

Home Activity Your child has learned to spell sound-alike words. Ask your child to name three pairs of list words, spell each word, and explain how they differ in meaning.

Punctuation

Directions Match the punctuation with a description of its use.

_____ 1. italics (underlining)   **A** join clauses without a conjunction

_____ 2. colons (:)   **B** introduce a list, express hours and minutes, and appear after the salutation in a business letter

_____ 3. dashes (—)   **C** join some compound words

_____ 4. semicolons (;)   **D** set off titles of books, magazines, and works of art

_____ 5. hyphens (-)   **E** set off words that interrupt the sentence

Directions Rewrite each sentence. Add the missing punctuation marks.

6. I'm always losing things I can usually find them in a few minutes.

_____

_____

7. I have lost several things this week six notebooks, twenty one pencils, and my America Sings book.

_____

_____

8. Now my jacket it's the one with the gold buttons is missing.

_____

_____

9. It could be in the car it might be in my locker.

_____

_____

10. There's one thing this ten year old will never forget. School ends at 345 P.M.!

_____

_____

KWL Chart

Directions Fill out this KWL chart to help you organize your ideas.

Topic _____

What I **K**now	What I **W**ant to Know	What I **L**earned

Controlling Question _____

Topic and Detail Sentences

Directions Decide how you will organize your paragraphs. Then write a topic sentence and supporting details for each paragraph.

Paragraph 1
Topic Sentence _____

_____

Detail Sentences _____

_____

_____

Paragraph 2
Topic Sentence _____

_____

Detail Sentences _____

_____

_____

Paragraph 3
Topic Sentence _____

_____

Detail Sentences _____

_____

_____

Paragraph 4
Topic Sentence _____

_____

Detail Sentences _____

_____

_____

Combining Sentences

Directions Use the word in parentheses to combine each pair of sentences. Remember to capitalize the first word of each new sentence and to add a comma when necessary.

1. (because) You can't see faults. They are far below the surface of the Earth.

_____

_____

2. (when) An earthquake occurs. Parts of the Earth's crust suddenly break and shift.

_____

_____

_____

3. (or) Are all earthquake waves the same? Are there different kinds of earthquake waves?

_____

_____

_____

4. (and) The Richter scale measures energy released. The Mercali scale measures the results of an earthquake.

_____

_____

_____

5. (but) Today geologists can neither predict nor prevent earthquakes. One day they hope to do both.

_____

_____

_____

© Pearson Education, Inc., 5

Peer and Teacher Conferencing Research Report

Directions Read your partner's essay. Refer to the Revising Checklist as you write your comments or questions. Offer compliments as well as revision suggestions. Then take turns talking about each other's draft. Give your partner your notes. After you and your teacher talk about your essay, add your teacher's comments to the notes.

Revising Checklist

Focus/Ideas
☐ Is the research report focused on one topic?
☐ Are there enough details?

Organization
☐ Does each paragraph have a topic sentence and supporting detail sentences?

Voice
☐ Is the report interesting to read?

Word Choice
☐ Has the writer paraphrased the material?

Sentences
☐ Have some short simple sentences been combined into compound or complex sentences to improve flow and clarity?

Things I Thought Were Good _____

_____

_____

Things I Thought Could Be Improved _____

_____

_____

Teacher's Comments _____

_____